T0340302

Chicago

Chicago went from nothing in 1830 to become the second-largest city in the nation in 1900, while the Midwest developed to become one of the world's foremost urbanized regions. This book is an economic history of the Chicago metropolitan area from the 1820s to the present. It examines the city in its Midwestern region and compares it to the other major cities of the North. This book uses theories of the economics of location and other economic models to explain much of Chicago's history.

Chicago maintained its status as the second-largest city through the first decades of the twentieth century, but rapid growth shifted to the Sunbelt following World War II. Since the 1950s the city's history can be divided into four distinct periods: growth with suburbanization (1950–1970); absence of growth, continued suburbanization, and central city crisis (1970–1990); rebound in the 1990s; and financial crisis and deep recession after 2000. Through it all Chicago has maintained its position as the economic capital of the Midwest. The book is a synthesis of available literature and public data, and stands as an example of using economics to understand much of the history of Chicago.

This book is intended for the college classroom, urban scholars, and for those interested in the history of one of the world's foremost urban areas.

John F. McDonald is Emeritus Professor of Economics, University of Illinois at Chicago, and Gerald W. Fogelson Distinguished Chair in Real Estate Emeritus, Roosevelt University, USA.

Routledge Advances in Regional Economics, Science and Policy

Chicago

An economic history

John F. McDonald

Routledge
Taylor & Francis Group

LONDON AND NEW YORK

First published 2016 by Routledge

2 Park Square, Milton Park, Abingdon, Oxfordshire OX14 4RN

52 Vanderbilt Avenue, New York, NY 10017

Routledge is an imprint of the Taylor & Francis Group, an informa business

First issued in paperback 2019

British Library Cataloguing in Publication Data
A catalogue record for this book is available from the British Library

Library of Congress Cataloging in Publication Data
McDonald, John F., 1943–
   Chicago : an economic history / John F. McDonald.—First Edition.
      pages cm
   Includes bibliographical references and index.
   1. Chicago (Ill.)—Economic conditions.   2. Chicago (Ill.)—Social conditions.
   3. Chicago (Ill.)—History.   I. Title.
   HC108.C4M33 2015
   330.9773'11—dc23   2015009253

ISBN: 978-1-138-91979-2 (hbk)
ISBN: 978-0-367-87366-0 (pbk)

Typeset in Times New Roman
by Keystroke, Station Road, Codsall, Wolverhampton

Contents

Figures and tables

viii   *Figures and tables*

Preface

In a sense I have been preparing to write this book for 40 years. I joined the economics faculty of the University of Illinois at Chicago (UIC) in 1971 after completing the Ph.D. at Yale, and began assisting the staff of the Mayor's Council of Manpower and Economic Advisors in 1974. This group of business and labor union people, public officials, and academics had been formed by Mayor Richard J. Daley to conduct studies of the Chicago economy and make recommendations for economic development policy. Donald Kane was the staff director of the Mayor's Council. I was appointed a member of the Council by Mayor Daley in 1975, and served until 1979, when the committee was disbanded by Mayor Jane Byrne. One of my first publications is an analysis of employment in the city of Chicago (McDonald, Giba, and Nealon, 1975). As chair of the Committee on Urban Economic Analysis and Reporting, I supervised the preparation of several economic reports.

My major research project during the 1970s was the preparation of my first book, *Economic Analysis of an Urban Housing Market* (1979), which is a study of the housing market in Chicago. This work is a direct outgrowth of Richard Muth's *Cities and Housing* (1969), which I had read as a graduate student. The empirical work in Muth's classic volume consists largely of studies of housing in Chicago. My book includes studies of land values in Chicago that were done jointly with H. Woods Bowman.

My work with the Mayor's Council led to the publication of my second book, *Employment Location and Industrial Land Use in Metropolitan Chicago* (1984a), and numerous articles in the 1980s. In 1989 I became the Research Director at NCI Research, a local economic development research organization affiliated with the Kellogg Graduate School of Management at Northwestern University. NCI was hired by the Chicago Economic Development Commission to produce periodic reports on the Chicago economy titled *Chicago Economic Update*, and I directed this work for two years. Work at NCI Research also included some policy evaluation, including a study of the Illinois Enterprise Zone program that operates in Chicago and its suburbs.

My regular teaching assignments at UIC included the undergraduate and graduate courses in urban economics, and I always included a great deal of material on the Chicago metropolitan area in those courses. Most UIC undergraduates are natives of the Chicago area, so the undergraduate course was popular. Students were assigned a textbook, but also read other material. The most popular extra reading for the undergraduates was William Cronon's *Nature's Metropolis: Chicago and the Great West* (1991), a great study of the Chicago economy in the nineteenth century. However, my interest in early Chicago was stimulated first by Homer Hoyt's *One Hundred Years of Land Values in Chicago* (1933) and *Chicago: Growth of a Metropolis* (1969) by Harold Mayer and Richard Wade.

During the late 1980s and early 1990s I teamed with UIC graduate students Edmond d'Ouville and L. N. Liu on a series of studies of traffic congestion. This work included empirical studies of traffic congestion on Chicago's Eisenhower Expressway based on data on traffic flow provided by the Illinois Department of Transportation at their expressway headquarters in the near-west suburb of Oak Park.

During the 1990s Daniel McMillen and I conducted a series of studies of land values and zoning in Chicago and its suburbs. We made use of data from the early 1920s as well as more recent data. We also did a series of studies on suburban employment centers in the Chicago metropolitan area. These studies documented the nature of suburban employment growth and examined the impacts of these employment centers on the surrounding territory. One study was done jointly with graduate student Paul Prather. More recent studies include an examination of whether Cook County suburbs introduced more restrictive zoning after World War II (for the most part they did not), and a look at concentrated poverty in Chicago over the decades.

The office market in Chicago is another continuing interest of mine. I was hired by the Building Owners and Managers Association of Chicago to assist with their downtown office market occupancy surveys, and during the late 1990s I conducted those studies at UIC with Jonathon Dombrow and several graduate student assistants.

RCF Economic and Financial Consulting, Inc. formed a unit called the Chicago Economic Observatory in 2006, and as a consultant to RCF I edited two reports titled *Databook Chicago* and wrote a series of four reports on the local economy for the Chicago Metropolitan Agency for Planning. Those reports dealt with export promotion, infrastructure, promotion of innovation, and a general discussion of the factors related to the growth of a metropolitan area.

Later, upon joining the real estate faculty at Roosevelt University in 2009, I teamed with Sofia Dermisi to conduct a series of studies of downtown Chicago office building values and capitalization rates. Other studies of industrial property values in Cook and DuPage Counties were done with graduate student Yulia Yurova. A very recent study is an examination of patterns of mortgage lending and foreclosures in Cook County during the financial crisis that began in 2007–2008.

I would also mention some of my family background. Both of my grandfathers were businessmen in Chicago. John V. McDonald came to Chicago with his family from Ireland in 1885 at age 12. He owned a restaurant on the south side of Chicago under the el tracks at 39th and Indiana Avenue. His father, also John McDonald, was a pianist who came to Chicago to work for the Kimball Piano and

Organ Company. The restaurant went out of business in the depression, and my grandfather passed away in 1937. His wife, Mary O'Hagan McDonald, came from Ireland as a young woman and reared five children. She died in 1947. My other grandfather, William A. Freeman, came to Chicago in the early 1900s from Dayton, Ohio. He served as president of a baking company, and was the inventor of the machine that put a date code on bread wrappers (that was not decipherable by consumers). This invention served as the basis for a Chicago business called Freeman Sales Service, which was operated by my two uncles on South Chicago Avenue into the 1970s. Mr. Freeman died on December 26, 1943, five months after I was born. His wife, Alice Hauswirth Freeman, was born in Wisconsin and came to Chicago with her family as a young girl. Her father, Augustus Hauswirth, was a Chicago policeman who was killed in the line of duty in 1893. My "gram," the only grandparent I knew, reared four children and died in 1952 in Decatur, Illinois. Both of my parents grew up in Woodlawn, a neighborhood just to the south of the University of Chicago. My father, also John V. McDonald, was born in 1915 and graduated from high school in 1933. He worked as a federal grain inspector in Decatur, Illinois, from 1941 until his retirement in 1971, and died in 1991. My mother, Jane Freeman McDonald, was born in 1920 and graduated from Hyde Park High School. She worked all her life as a physician's assistant (and volunteer Red Cross instructor) and in the payroll department of an auto parts manufacturer. My mother died in 1968. My parents and I traveled from Decatur to Chicago many, many times to visit my numerous great aunts, aunts, great uncles, uncles, first cousins, and cousins twice removed. It was only with my generation that some members of both families moved away from the Chicago area. I went to college and graduate school in Iowa, Texas, and Connecticut—but my first "real" job was in Chicago. Glena and I stayed 42 years until 2013, when we moved to Philadelphia to be near our daughter Elizabeth and her husband Charles.

Sometimes I have said with some justification that, while I am not a Chicago economist, I am Chicago's economist.

The people at Taylor & Francis have been most helpful and encouraging, especially my editor Robert Langham and editorial assistant Lisa Thomson. Four reviewers provided helpful comments and suggestions, so thanks to them as well. I want to express gratitude to all of the colleagues mentioned here for their friendship and help over the years. And heart-felt thanks to my wife Glena, who is the first reader of this book.

John F. McDonald
Philadelphia
February 25, 2015

Introduction

The Preface recounts my long and somewhat disjointed history of studying Chicago over a period of 40 years. My interest in the history of Chicago also is mentioned there. This book brings together my background in theoretical and empirical urban economics, interest in Chicago history, and my studies of Chicago.

This book is an economic history of the Chicago metropolitan area from the 1820s to the present. The book places Chicago in its Midwestern region and compares Chicago to the other major cities of the North. Theories of the economics of location and other economic models will be employed to explain much of Chicago's history.

The explicit use of economic models has become standard operating procedure in the field of economic history, and textbooks in American economic history teach both history and economics. Among these general texts, perhaps the one by Jeremy Atack and Peter Passell (1994) makes the greatest use of economic models to explore a wide array of topics in American economic history. The major contributions of this book on Chicago are; 1) coverage of the entire economic history of an important urban area, and 2) use of a large number of economic models to explain outcomes and basic trends for that urban area.

Chicago went from nothing in 1830 to become the second-largest city in the nation in 1900 as the Midwest developed rapidly. Chicago maintained that status through the first decades of the twentieth century, but rapid growth shifted to the Sunbelt—especially during and after World War II. The years since 1950 can be divided into four distinct periods: growth with suburbanization (1950–1970); absence of growth, continued suburbanization, and central city crisis (1970–1990); rebound in the 1990s; and financial crisis and deep recession after 2000. Through it all Chicago has maintained its position as the economic capital of the Midwest. The book is a synthesis of available literature and public data, rather than original historical research. Rather, the book stands as an example of using economics to understand much of the history of Chicago.

Chapter 1 provides short, non-technical explanations of the economic models that are used in the book to understand the development of the Chicago economy. Each of the remaining seven chapters covers a distinct time period. The second chapter recounts the history of Chicago from its beginnings in the 1820s to the end of the nineteenth century. Chicago had become the nation's railroad capital by the time of the Civil War, and this infrastructure was crucial to the development of the urban area. Chapter 3 covers the twentieth century up to the start of the Great Depression. During this time Chicago grew rapidly and became a modern industrial powerhouse. The era of depression and war follows in Chapter 4. As Chicago was an industrial city, the Great Depression was felt more strongly there than in much of the rest of the nation. But war production and the aftermath of the war brought Chicago industry back even stronger.

In Chapter 5 we take stock of what Chicago was in 1950 and take a brief look at what was ahead. The postwar period is divided into three periods. Chicago from 1950 to 1970 is presented in Chapter 6. This was a time of growth, suburbanization, and emerging urban problems. Those emerging problems became full-blown during the period of urban crisis for the city of Chicago, which can be dated roughly as 1970 to 1990 and is the topic of Chapter 7. I proposed a definition of urban crisis in a previous book (2008) based on seven economic and social indicators, which are:

- population loss,
- decline in median household income,
- increase in the percentage of the population in poverty,
- increase in the population living in areas of concentrated poverty,
- increase in the murder rate,
- increase in the percentage of single-parent families with children, and
- increase in the percentage of adults who dropped out of high school.

I submit that, if most of these indicators are moving in the wrong direction, the city is in urban crisis.

The final chapter in the book examines the prosperous decade of the 1990s, which was followed by the first decade of the new century with its financial crisis and deep recession. The 1990s were a decade of reversal of negative economic and social trends in the central city, but the new century brought negative outcomes. Which of these last two decades was an anomaly? Or were both anomalous? And where does Chicago stand in the end?

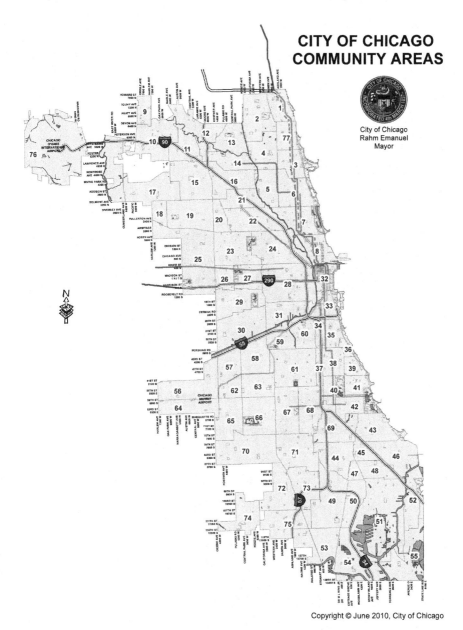

CITY OF CHICAGO
COMMUNITY AREAS

City of Chicago
Rahm Emanuel
Mayor

Figure I.1 City of Chicago community areas

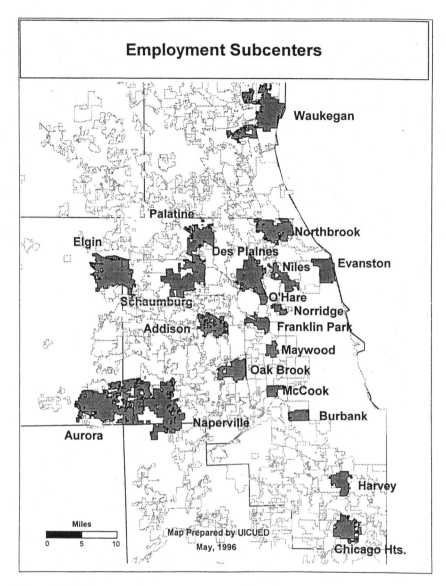

Figure I.2 Employment subcenters

1 Some useful economic models in prose

Introduction: Chicago as an economic phenomenon

This book is an economic history of Chicago. Cities have been formed for a variety of reasons—civic, defensive, cultural, economic, and so on. In my view Chicago can be considered to be primarily an economic phenomenon. The actors involved had economic motives. The recent death of the Nobel Prize economist Gary Becker reminds us of the economic approach to human behavior (1976), which consists of maximizing behavior, market equilibrium, and stable preferences. Maximizing behavior means that firms try to maximize profits (given the limits of technology and market opportunities) and consumers try to maximize their satisfaction given their money and time resources. Government actors are more complicated, but often act to provide public goods and services that provide economic benefit. Market equilibrium means that markets exist to coordinate the actions of the various participants. And stable preferences mean that economists do not explain economic changes by tautologically saying that tastes changed. For example, the long-run development of an economy is considered to be a function of the creation of new products and services and changes in production technology, and these innovations are often in response to perceived economic benefit.

This chapter is an introduction to the economic models pertaining to urban areas that are used in this book to explain the economic history of Chicago. Each model is a different version of the economic approach to human behavior as outlined above. The chapter also is an introduction to how economists think. I do not imagine that all readers will become conversant with all of the models in this chapter upon first reading. That is not a problem. Keep reading the book. The models will come up again, and you will recognize when they do. You may wish to refer back to this chapter now and then. All of the models are presented in prose form, but one model is supplemented by an equation (which can be skipped). The discussion of each model in this chapter includes an example of the model as applied to the economic history of Chicago.

The rest of the book (Chapters 2 through 8) divides the history of Chicago into discreet time periods. Each of these chapters makes use of some of the economic models presented in this chapter. The choices of the models utilized in a particular chapter are my judgment about the models that can help to explain best the most important economic outcomes in that time period. The models are not being subjected to formal empirical tests. Rather, evidence is provided to show that the economic outcomes for Chicago corresponded to implications of the model. Also, along the way, some historical events and facts about Chicago are included that are not necessarily important for an economic model.

Transportation costs

Throughout the book it is presumed that firms and households are motivated by transportation costs, which involve both time and money (and time is money, as they say). The period covered by the book includes all of the major changes in transportation technology that have occurred since the early 1800s. Chicago went from the horse and wagon era to the canal era to the railroad era to the internal combustion era to the airplane era. And it is not just these changes in the technology of moving people and freight that matter. The telegraph, telephone, radio, television, and internet are changes in the method for transmitting information that had great impact. These changes in transportation technology and costs shaped economic growth and economic geography. Transportation has always been at the heart of the Chicago economy and is the primary theme in Chapter 2 on nineteenth-century Chicago.

Consider the simplest model of where to locate production activity. Suppose that a firm uses one resource located at one location and provides its output to the market at another location. The firm has to pay the transportation cost for either shipping the input to the market (locating production at the market), or shipping the output to the market (locating production at the site of the resource), or locating somewhere in between. The model says that the choice of location is made to minimize transportation costs. If only one mode of transportation is needed so that either the input or the output can be shipped directly, then the answer is to locate at the market or at the site of the resource—not in between. Why? Either shipping input or output is cheaper per mile, so the firm chooses the cheaper option for the entire distance. Goods produced at the market are called "market oriented," and goods produced at the site of the resource are called "resource oriented."

Here is a simple example. Suppose your firm supplies firewood to people in the city by cutting down trees in the north woods. Do you ship the trees or the firewood? Shipping is done by truck. Where do you cut the trees into firewood? The answer is—cut the trees into firewood at the forest because shipping firewood is much easier, neater, and cheaper than shipping trees.

What if you cannot use the same mode of transportation to move your input or output? You are a firm that buys wheat from farmers in farm country to be consumed as flour in the city. But the transportation route requires moving freight over land (by railroad, let us say) and then over water (by ship). Where do you locate the plant that turns wheat into flour—in farm country, in the city, or at the point where the freight must be moved from train to ship? Each of these is a possibility depending on the transportation costs of shipping wheat and flour, and on any economies of scale in the production of flour. The place where freight is moved from train to ship is called a transshipment point. Chicago was and is a big transshipment point—one of the very biggest. One solution is to load wheat on trains as the train moves through farm country, and then build a large flour mill at the transshipment point (hello General Mills in Minneapolis). The initial solution in Chicago was to move wheat by train to Chicago and to transport the wheat by ship from Chicago's huge grain elevators—after the wheat had been sorted into quality grades.

What if your customers are located in a number of locations? Assume here that your input is found anywhere, so you are not resource oriented. Your job is to produce output somewhere and distribute it to your customers. As it happens, if at least 50.1 percent of your customers are located in one place, you produce at that location and ship the other 49.9 percent of your output from there. This is the Principle of Median Location. You locate next to your median customer. You find the median customer in terms of location, and locate production next to that customer. Consider any other location. If you move away from the median customer you can at best get closer to less than half of your customers and farther away from more than half of your customers. Here is a very simple example. Suppose you must schedule a face-to-face meeting for seven people, and four of them are located in one place. You choose to meet where these four are located to minimize transportation costs (assuming all have the same cost of transportation). If one of the people is the boss, and this person is not one of the four, then the meeting may have to be where the boss is located. You might say, ". . . but, but consider transportation costs." Maybe not.

Here is an important example that combines some of these location principles. Cronon (1991) provided data to show that half of the customers of the lumber companies in Chicago in the latter half of the nineteenth century were located in the Chicago urban area, and the other half were located around the Midwest. Raw lumber (not trees) was transported from the north woods to Chicago down Lake Michigan by ship, and then turned into usable lumber by the companies in Chicago. From there lumber was delivered to customers outside of Chicago by rail.

Now consider another more realistic example. Suppose that your customers are along three rail lines (north, west, and south) that all meet at a central point. You have a few customers at the central point, but the rest of the customers are along those three lines. You locate production at the central point because any other location along one of the three rail lines would mean higher transportation costs. Chicago is that central point, the major node in the transportation system. Economic historian Louis Cain (1985) has emphasized the importance of the creation of Chicago as the most prominent transportation node in the Midwest prior to the Civil War.

Here is a recent example. The largest mail sorting facility operated by the U.S. Postal Service is located in Chicago. Mail is transported in from a wide area around the Midwest, is sorted, and shipped out to the rest of the world. Likewise, mail from the rest of the world comes to Chicago, is sorted, and shipped out to destinations in that wide area around the Midwest.

As a final example, suppose that you must assemble several bulky inputs, and that they are shipped by different modes of transportation. Consider the basic steel industry, which must assemble iron ore, coal, and limestone. Iron ore comes from the Mesabi Range in Minnesota (discovered in 1866) and is moved by ship, while coal and limestone come by rail. The Chicago urban area (including Gary, Indiana) became the nation's largest producer of basic steel in the early twentieth century. The southern end of Lake Michigan was the point at which the three inputs could be assembled most cheaply—iron ore from Minnesota, anthracite coal from Pennsylvania (by rail), and limestone from Indiana and other more local sources (by rail). Indeed, Gary was founded in 1906 on an empty beach and a town was built expressly for the purpose of producing steel.

Economic base: Export and local goods

An urban area prospers by providing goods and services to people and firms located outside the urban area—export goods. I do not mean only goods exported to other countries, but all goods and services sent outside the urban area for which payment is received. Export goods provide employment (wages) and profits for the urban area, and the money earned is spent on goods and services produced locally and on goods and services imported from outside the urban area. A great deal of that money is spent on local goods such as housing, haircuts, medical care, restaurant meals, and so on. Other goods such as foodstuffs and many manufactured goods primarily are imported. An urban economy can pump itself up by expanding exports, or by replacing imports with goods and services produced locally. This is the urban version of the basic Keynesian model of the multiplier. Exports earn money, which turns into more income for the urban economy as local goods are produced and sold.

This simple idea is well understood by the general public—perhaps too well. You have all seen the TV reporter who is reporting on a plant closing down. The reporter goes across the street to ask the bar owner what will happen, and the bar owner says that business will drop. Of course. Plant closings are bad news for a local economy. Local merchants lose business, unemployment rises, property values fall, and so on. All of this is not really "news." The fact that Chicago was heavily dependent on manufacturing exports in the 1920s meant that the depression of the 1930s had an impact on Chicago that was larger than in many other local economies. On the other side of the coin, the positive multiplier effects of expanding exports often are exaggerated. Urban economies are called "open" economies because exports and imports are large in relation to total income. A big propensity to import from an increase in income limits the local multiplier effect. A basic rule of thumb is that an expansion of exports of $100 may produce about an additional $50 in local income. In other words, the local multiplier effect is about 1.5, not four or five.

Drivers of regional and urban growth: Then and now

Exports drive the regional and urban economy, but what determines the demand for exports? And what determines the ability to supply exports? Growth in the demand for exports from a particular urban area depends upon economic growth in the areas within the "economic reach" of that urban area, and upon the ability of the urban area to expand its economic reach. Chicago of the last half of the nineteenth century benefited greatly from both factors. The Midwest was growing rapidly, and Chicago's ability to supply goods to a wide area was created by its becoming the railroad capital.

On the supply side, the ability of an urban area (or any economy) to respond to the demand for exports depends upon:

- availability of critical natural resources,
- private capital,
- public capital (infrastructure),
- labor quantity and quality,
- technical change,
- entrepreneurship, and
- agglomeration economies.

Natural resources provide basic inputs into production. Chicago was blessed by being located adjacent to a large area of fertile farmland, and other basic resources such as iron ore, lumber, and coal were nearby. Private capital directly provides the buildings and equipment needed for the production of goods and services, and public capital (infrastructure) provides the facilities that make the urban area function. Some of the public capital is provided by government (public buildings, streets and highways, water and sewer systems, ports, and so on), while other portions of the public capital are provided by private firms under license from the government (telephone, rail lines, electricity, etc.). Labor has both the quantity and quality dimensions. In the late nineteenth and early twentieth centuries, a time in which the economy of Chicago was dominated by manufacturing industry, the quantity of the labor force was critical. Immigrants were drawn to Chicago by the prospect of jobs that did not require much formal education. However, as time passed the quality of the labor force in terms of formal education became more and more important. Indeed, numerous studies of the growth of urban areas in the U.S. after 1980 show that the one variable that consistently emerges as an important factor in growth over a decade is the percentage of the adult population with college degrees at the beginning of the decade.

Technical change in the economic sense means innovation—new products, changes in production methods that reduce costs, and changes in products that make them better for the user. New products and new methods make for Schumpeter's "wave of creative destruction." But assembling the capital and the labor force, and taking advantage of new products or methods, requires entrepreneurship. Chicago's entrepreneurs are legendary—McCormick, Ward, Armour, Pullman, and the many who came after. Chapter 8 includes a more detailed discussion of the modern model of innovation and economic growth as it pertains to metropolitan areas and metropolitan Chicago in particular.

The last factor on the list—agglomeration economies—requires some explanation. The general idea of agglomeration economies is that more economic activity in one location makes for higher productivity (lower costs). This can happen within an individual industry or group of related industries, an effect called localization economies. Alfred Marshall (1920, p. 225) famously wrote:

> When an industry has thus chosen a locality for itself, it is likely to stay there long: so great are the advantages which people following the same skilled trade get from near neighborhood to one another. The mysteries of the trade become no mysteries; but are as it were in the air, and children learn many of them unconsciously. Good work is rightly appreciated, inventions and improvements in machinery, in process and the general organization of the business, have their merits promptly discussed: if one man starts a new idea, it is taken up by others and combined with suggestions of their own; and thus it becomes the sources of further new ideas. And presently subsidiary trades grow up in the neighborhood, supplying it with implements and materials, organizing its traffic, and in many ways conducing to the economy of its material.

Agglomeration economies can also exist at the level of the entire urban area—urbanization economies. An urban area becomes the railroad capital, with many lines going in every possible direction. This system redounds to the benefit of every business in the urban area. An urban area contains a large and diverse population, which means that businesses can recruit workers from a large and deep labor market pool.

Urban economists have devoted a great deal of effort to document the existence of localization and urbanization economies. Industrial districts do generate benefits for individual firms. Innovation happens. The right workers can be found easily. Examples include: Silicon Valley in modern times, Detroit and the auto industry in the first decades of the twentieth century, and so on. Urban areas have tried to replicate these. But can the positive effects of industrial districts get reversed? Suppose an industrial district with some positive external features starts to decline. The demand for the particular products made there declines, foreign competition chips away at sales, technological change dictates a different location choice (one-story plants versus the old multi-story plants, for example), workers are required with different skills. Do the positive external effects of the industrial district start to decline, and does this accelerate the decline of the district itself? I think so, and we have seen this in the manufacturing sector in Chicago in roughly the last 40 years.

New technologies and shifts in the demand for goods and services have changed the list of important growth factors. In the nineteenth and early twentieth centuries it was the rail system, later it was the highway system, and now it includes the air transportation system and the internet backbone. Now it is not just quantity, but the quality of the labor force, and the education and training facilities. Now it is the ability to attract high-quality labor with an excellent "quality of life," i.e. opportunities for education, recreation, and entertainment. Before it was good water and sewer systems and public transit (and it still is), but now it is also good cable TV service, internet service, wireless telephone service, air travel service, medical care, and so on. But the same basic list of supply factors still applies. The trick for the actors in the local economy is to figure out how to enhance those factors.

Congestion, network, and other externalities

Agglomeration economies produce benefits to firms or households for which no direct payment is made. Andreu Mas-Colell, Michael Whinston, and Jerry Green (1995, p. 352) provide a very general definition: "An externality is present whenever the well being of a consumer or the production possibilities of a firm are directly affected by the actions of another agent in the economy." By directly they mean not mediated by prices. The existence of an externality has to do with the absence of a price. Two types of negative externalities are very important in urban areas: traffic congestion and pollution. Traffic that is heavy enough creates the situation in which each vehicle slows down the traffic by a small amount. The driver of the vehicle is aware of his or her own time and money cost, but ignores the fact that the other vehicles are negatively affected by his or her presence on the road at that particular time. In fact, every vehicle is slowing down every other vehicle present by a small amount, and the total effect can be quite large. Traffic congestion is not a new phenomenon; indeed it is not as bad as it once was. The photos of traffic in downtown Chicago at the turn of the twentieth century are startling. Similarly, air and water pollution involve the discharge of bad substances into the air or water that affect consumers and/or firms with no payment involved. In its early days Chicago faced very serious sanitation problems, and epidemics of cholera and other diseases were frequent. The infrastructure investments that were made to overcome these problems were enormous. Rapid urban growth and industrialization in the late nineteenth and early twentieth centuries produced a mixing of industrial, commercial, and residential land uses in Chicago and many other cities. The outcome was considered to be detrimental to the health and welfare of the public, and zoning ordinances were passed in the 1920s to control land use. Chicago adopted its first zoning ordinance in 1923.

An important positive externality for cities is called network externalities. The idea is that the more people who are in the network, the greater are the benefits for each member. Consider the telephone. At first Mr. Bell could call only Mr. Watson. That was fine, because he needed Mr. Watson to "come here." But the usefulness of having a telephone is greater the more people you can call. You do not have to communicate face-to-face all of the time. After the telephone system was established in Chicago the major firms (McCormick Reaper Works, Pullman Palace Car, and so on) moved their office staffs to downtown locations and away from the plant facilities. Downtown was the central point for the transit system, and provided immediate access to financial, legal, and other business services. It was no longer necessary to locate at the plant to manage the company.

The most important network to the history of Chicago has been the freight rail system. Chicago became, and still is, the most important point in that system. The creation of this network in the nineteenth century and its impact on the Chicago economy of that time are discussed in detail in Chapter 2.

Economics of migration

Economists model migration as an investment. People who migrate undertake costs in the near term in exchange for benefits in the longer run. Usually there are both "push" and "pull" factors involved. The purely monetary costs and benefits are based on better economic opportunity at the destination compared to the origin of the move. Monetary costs of moving play a role in the migration decision. However, there are many other motives for migration that can be included in the notion that migration is an investment. There is a psychic cost in moving away from friends and family. This cost can be offset partially by having friends and family who live at the destination. Migration tends to follow well-trod paths. The advantages of migrating often are related to social and political factors as well. African-Americans in the South were subject to unrelenting discrimination and segregation (and occasional lynching). They were prohibited from voting, and opportunities for education were sharply limited. A move to one of the cities in the North, such as Chicago, meant that job opportunities were better, children had the chance to attend better schools, and people could vote. Indeed, in many cities machine politicians actively sought the votes of minority residents. The African-American newspaper in Chicago, *The Chicago Defender*, was delivered by train to many areas in the South and touted the benefits of migration.

Prior to the migration of African-Americans out of the South, the primary sources of migration to the cities like Chicago were Europe and the rural areas of the U.S. European migrants came for economic opportunity, of course, but often also were escaping political instability and war, discrimination, and in some cases actual famine. It was no accident that most of the workers who built the Illinois and Michigan Canal in the 1840s to connect the Great Lakes to the Mississippi River watershed came from Ireland. And after 1830 or so people who were engaged in largely subsistence agriculture in the U.S. began to see that the growing cities offered much better opportunity. The economy began the transition away from agriculture to industry, and industry mainly was located in the cities.

Chicago is famous for the ethnic diversity of its population. Immigrants have arrived from all over the world, and Chicago had (and still has) discernable ethnic neighborhoods. The details of the ethnic diversity primarily are the province of the sociologists, so this study does not investigate this aspect of Chicago's history in detail. Some basic census data on the origins for the foreign-born population of Chicago are included in each chapter. For example, 50 percent of the city's population in 1860 was born outside the U.S. The largest sources of the foreign-born population at that time were Germany and Ireland. The percentage declined over time, but was still 36 percent in 1910, and then included large numbers of immigrants from Russia, Austria, Sweden, and Italy. (At that time the territory that is now the nation of Poland was divided between Germany, Russia, and Austria.) The percentage of foreign-born residents in the city fell 11 percent in 1970, but has since increased to 21 percent in 2010.

Migration has been studied by economists extensively and pretty exhaustively. People do indeed move to better economic opportunity. The cost of moving is associated with distance, and so migration is more likely for shorter distances. Migration is influenced by the familiarity that the migrant has with the destination. Younger people are more likely to migrate because they have more years to reap the benefits of moving. People with higher levels of education are more likely to move partly because they are better able to cope with the change. People move to destinations with larger populations because opportunities tend to be greater and more diverse. These days, people also move to locations with favored amenities, and are less likely to move to places that lack amenities. Good weather, low crime rates, good schools, and less pollution are among the factors that matter.

The urban hierarchy

Thus far the discussion has focused on location decisions for individual firms and households and on factors related to growth of an individual city. Now it is time to recognize the obvious fact that a modern economy contains a system of cities that form a hierarchy. The basic idea is pretty simple. First of all, farms are spread out over the landscape. There exists a large number of small towns that provide a limited range of goods and services to a relatively small area. Farmers earn money by producing crops, and come into town to buy a few basic items, go to church, and have a drink at the bar. One step up in the hierarchy come the larger towns that provide goods and services to a wider area that includes the small towns within its market area; maybe there is a doctor, a small bank, a couple of larger stores, etc. Farmers and the residents of small towns come into the larger town to patronize these businesses. The larger town also provides for itself the goods and services supplied by the small towns to their local populations. Then come the smaller cities, the large cities, and the top city. The top city provides all of the goods and services provided by the towns and cities lower in the hierarchy, but there are some goods and services that only it supplies. The model is based on the proposition that there exists a hierarchy of goods and services that vary in terms of economies of scale. The goods and services supplied by small towns have very limited economies of scale, and so many small towns exist. The doctor, the bank, and the larger store need a larger clientele than the small town can provide in order to survive, so they locate in the larger town. The goods and services in the model are entirely market oriented. The trade-off is between economies of scale in production and the cost of transporting the good or service to the consumers. (Indeed, if there were no economies of scale in the production of anything each household would produce everything it needs and there would be no need for towns or cities. More realistically, the feudal manor comes to mind.) The model fits together very neatly, and is a wonder to behold. All of the income and expenditures at each level are in balance. The model is known as urban hierarchy theory or central place theory.

All economic models leave something out; that is what makes them models. In this case central place theory leaves out goods that are input (or resource) oriented. Production of these goods is based on the locations of the inputs, not the locations of customers. Second, the model leaves out the features of real transportation systems such as transshipment points. And the model omits the forces of agglomeration economies. Firms in the same industry avoid each other in central place theory, but we can see that certain cities specialize in certain industries. For example, Rockford, Illinois, is a small city that is ranked routinely as one of the worst urban areas in the country in terms of quality of life, but it also is home to a highly productive machine tool industry. Then there is Detroit, Silicon Valley, Research Triangle Park in North Carolina, risk management services in Chicago, and so on. At a more mundane level, a shopping center contains stores that sell goods known as "shopping" goods. People devote time and effort to search for the best option, and suppliers wish to locate together to facilitate shopping. Retailers used to locate "downtown." Another example—car dealers locate in an automobile dealers' row along a major street.

Real urban areas larger than a small town are complex combinations of all of these forces. Chicago is a good example of a very complex case. Chicago began as the place where the Great Lakes and Mississippi River water transportation systems could be connected. Its location also helped make it into the center of the rail transportation system in the Midwest. Thus Chicago became the point for shipping agricultural products of the Midwest to points outside the region. These transportation facilities meant that Chicago could become the production center for goods that are market oriented and subject to large economies of scale in production. It could also become the transshipment point where the inputs for input oriented goods could be assembled. Some of both types of industries benefited from localization economies. Last, but not least, Chicago became the gateway city for people coming to the Midwest from Europe and other regions of the U.S. All of this, and more, made Chicago into the preeminent city of the Midwest. Its large size produced a variety of urbanization economies as well. But, as we shall see, Chicago produced its share of urbanization diseconomies— pollution of water, traffic congestion, slums, crime, and the rest.

The land market: The isolated state

So far there has been no mention of land, and the land market is at the heart of an urban economy. How is land allocated to its various uses? In 1826 Johann von Thünen (1966) invented a theory that provides a simple and powerful explanation for the determination of agricultural land allocations and values. He asked us to consider a large town in the center of an agricultural area. The town is isolated from the rest of the world, and the land is of uniform fertility. The crops are sold in the town at the market price (and the farmers buy what they need in the town).

The model runs from the fact that the crops must be transported to the town, and the farmers must pay the transportation cost.

First, suppose that there is only one crop. Each acre produces the same output, but the transportation cost increases with the distance to the town. The farmer rents land from the land owner. The farmer earns the revenue from the crop produced on one acre minus production cost, transportation cost, and land rent. Production cost includes a "normal" income level for the farmer. Revenue and production cost per acre are identical for all farmers, so greater transportation cost at greater distance to market translates directly into lower land rent. Competition among farmers ensures that land rents plus transportation costs equal a constant number. If land rent plus transportation cost per acre were less than this constant, some farmers would bid more to rent the land that is "under priced." Or, if land rent plus transportation cost exceeds the constant, the land owner would find that farmers are unwilling to rent the land. Other locations are better. In the end, no location is better than any other from the farmer's point of view. The land owner near the town, of course, receives a high rent. Oh, and at some distance land rent falls to zero because the entire revenue is used up in production and transportation costs. The land beyond this distance is vacant.

Now suppose that there is more than one crop. Assume that the output per acre is the same for both crop A and crop B. But suppose that crop A sells for a higher price per unit at the town market and is more expensive to transport per mile than crop B. In this case crop A is grown near the town and crop B is grown in a ring outside the area occupied by crop A. Why? The land rent generated by crop A is higher near the town because this crop commands the higher market price. But land rent on land devoted to crop A drops off sharply with distance because of the higher transportation costs. At some distance the land rents generated by the two crops are equal, and beyond that distance the land rent from crop B is the larger. Land is allocated to the crop that pays the higher rent. Crops are grown in neat von-Thünen rings around the town. As Martin Beckmann (1968, p. 62) put it:

> Thus, as distance from the city increases, the individual products or the yields or both must become lighter. Transportation costs are not just a function of weight but should include deterioration in transit as well. Thus emerges the typical sequence of truck gardening, milk production, cereals, grazing areas, and forests. Animals are raised in an outer ring, then shipped and fattened closer by.

This theory, von Thünen's theory of the isolated state, became the organizing model for Cronon's (1991) award-winning book on Chicago in the nineteenth century, *Nature's Metropolis*. Beckmann's statement comes very close to summarizing much of Cronon's book. More about this in Chapter 2.

The urban land market: Bid rent theory

William Alonso (1964) translated von Thünen's theory into a theory of the urban land market. He supposed that cities exist because of employment, and that there is great advantage to firms to be located in or near the center of the city, based on the ideas that "accessibility to customers will decrease with distance to the center" and "proximity of land devoted to an individual set of uses which are complementary in terms of both attracting customers and cutting costs" (1964, p. 44). As noted above, the latter point is now known as agglomeration economies. Workers commute to the jobs in and near downtown and are paid wages by the firms. The central concept in the model is "bid rent," the rent that firms or households are willing to pay for a unit of land. Bid rent is presumed to vary inversely with distance to the center of the city. In the case of firms, bid rent for central locations is very high and falls off sharply with distance to the center. Households' bids for land at the center are less than the bids of firms, but decline with distance less sharply—because the per-mile cost of commuting to downtown is not very much. In short, firms value the central location more than households do, and distance to the center is a greater disadvantage for firms compared to households. This is a pretty transparent version of von Thünen's model with two crops.

Alonso assumed that there is a free market for urban land uninhibited by public regulations. The actor with the highest bid occupies the site and pays bid rent. Suppose that the city is circular. In this case firms occupy a circular area out to the radius at which the bid rent of firms equals the bid rent of households. Beyond this distance households occupy the land. The city extends out to the distance at which farmers outbid households for the land, so households occupy a ring around the central business zone.

As in von Thünen's model, competition plays an important role. The bid rents for firms and households are negative functions of distance to the center, and bid rent for each location is set so that the firm or household is equally well off at every distance. For example, if one firm sets a bid rent that is lower than this amount, some other firm will bid more. The same mechanism exists in the household sector. So as a sector, firms and households have bid rent functions for a given level of well being (profits for firms and satisfaction for households). The final bid rent function for firms is the one that allows each firm to make what is called a "normal" profit—no more or no less. And the final bid rent function for households is the one that permits every household to have a level of satisfaction that is identical to the level that could be achieved by living somewhere else outside the city. Equilibrium rent as it depends upon distance to the center is a combination of the final bid rent functions of the two sectors: firms in the center, and households in their ring.

Note that Alonso's model determines land rent and the allocation of land to the two sectors, and therefore determines location patterns. It also implies that the density of firms and households declines with distance to the center. Because land rent declines with distance to the center, both firms and households have an incentive to use more land (and less of other goods and services) at greater distances. Consider the case of households. Households spend their wages on commuting, land, and other consumer goods. As distance increases commuting cost rises and land rent falls (and the price of other consumer goods does not change). The bundle of land and other consumer goods must maintain the household's level of satisfaction. At greater distance commuting cost takes a bigger bite out of the household's budget, but the household can maintain its level of satisfaction by renting more land and buying less of other goods. This means fewer households per square mile as distance to the center increases.

The previous paragraph is an adequate summary of the implications of Alonso's model, but a simple and powerful equation may be helpful. The equation is known as Muth's (1961, 1969) equation. Suppose that households have a cost of \$t per additional mile of travel to the central business district. At a particular distance (u) they rent L square feet of land at a rent of \$R per square foot, a total of \$RL. Now suppose that a household decides to move one mile farther from the center at the cost of \$t. If order for the household to maintain the same level of satisfaction (the equilibrium condition of the model), it must be that the household saves that same amount \$t on its land rental. Therefore, Muth's equation is:

$$t = - L \, \Delta R / \Delta u.$$

Here $\Delta R / \Delta u$ is the change in land rent as distance (u) increases by one mile, which must be a negative number because t and L are positive numbers.[1] The equation says that the change in the cost of transportation is just offset by the reduction in the amount of money spent on renting land. The equation can be rewritten as:

$$\Delta R / \Delta u = - t / L.$$

The slope of the land rent function is negative and equal to the per-mile transportation cost divided by the quantity of land rented by the household. This second version of Muth's equation says that, because households rent more land at a greater distance to the center (because land rent is lower at greater distance), the slope of the land rent function gets flatter as distance to the center increases. Population density is the inverse of land rented per household. If a household rents one square mile, density is one household per square mile; if households rent ½ square mile, the density is two per square mile, and so on. Therefore, population density declines with distance to the center as land rent falls and land rented per household increases.

Taken to its ultimate conclusion the model says that, in final equilibrium, one is equally well off no matter where you are, at least within the confines of your own nation. Some economists buy into this concept, and study how wages and housing costs vary from urban area to urban area. The idea is that, if a particular type of household is equally well off in all urban areas, then its wages should be lower and housing prices higher in urban areas with nice weather, less crime, less pollution, etc. Their studies do indeed find that there is something to this idea. Other economists are skeptical that such a full-blown equilibrium across urban areas is ever really reached. Maybe the idea of equilibrium is fine for an individual urban area because it is easy for people to move around in it in response to disequilibria, but not so fine for the entire nation. Non-economists might find this debate bizarre.

Alonso's model can be made more complex in numerous ways. Muth (1969) supposed that houses are built by combining land and capital, and that households demand housing. This model produces the same kind of land allocation and location patterns in the long run as the Alonso model. More than one business sector and/or household sector can be assumed. For example, businesses might be divided into legal/financial/business services, manufacturing, and retailing. Each sector has its own bid rent function. Legal/financial/business services bid the most for downtown locations. Manufacturing bids more for various locations outside the downtown area (based on access to transportation). The Union Stockyards and the steel industry are examples of early concentrations of manufacturing outside the downtown vicinity. Residential districts pop up around these employment concentrations. Retailing bids more for some downtown locations and some locations out in the residential districts. For various reasons high-income households bid more for suburban locations than do low-income households. The model and the resulting location patterns become quite complex—and more realistic, of course. The issue for an economist is to specify a model just of sufficient complexity to "explain" what needs to be explained, but no more complex than that.

Muth's extension of the Alonso model to the case of building actual residential structures is not innocuous. Suppose we have a given population and a given urban transportation system to move people to the jobs downtown. A city gets built, and the residential structures are very durable. Land rent and the density of population both decline with distance to downtown. The two variables are highly positively correlated; high land rent means a lot of housing units per acre and high population density, low land rent means not so many units of housing per acre and low population density. Now suppose that something changes.

Suppose the population increases—a lot, as in Chicago during the latter part of the nineteenth century and the early years of the twentieth century—and the transportation system does not improve. More houses are built at the edge of the existing city, and the density of population increases in the existing durable housing structures. Houses are cut up into small apartments, and the number of persons per room increases. Another house is built at the back of a lot. Eventually housing developers come in and tear down the old houses and build taller residential structures, and long-run equilibrium is restored with greater land rents, taller structures, and greater population densities. Rapid population growth in Chicago in the late nineteenth and early twentieth centuries, combined with a decent public transportation system, meant that the city grew outward much more than upward.

Now suppose that population is constant (more or less) and that the transportation system is vastly improved. We build efficient limited-access highways, and people buy cars in order to use them. The Alonso model without durable houses says that land rents will fall near downtown and increase at the edge of the city and beyond, so population density near downtown will fall and people will move (and pitch their tents) beyond the edge of the city. Land rent and population density are still highly positively correlated. But wait. Muth says that we have inherited a durable housing stock. What happens inside the confines of the old city? Population density declines for sure, but the process is not smooth. Vacancy rates in the existing housing structures go up and rents go down, and some landlords find that their structures are no longer economically viable. They no longer have enough tenants to cover expenses. Residential structures are abandoned, and the process is not pretty. Some neighborhoods start to get abandoned, and abandonment breeds more abandonment as the quality of the residential environment deteriorates. Some old neighborhoods start to look like the teeth of a hockey player, but others may remain largely intact. In other words, the process of reducing population density in an existing stock of residential structures creates a negative externality. Land rents fall, and if the negative externality is bad enough, land rents collapse. It is possible that land rents can fall to very low levels even as population density remains fairly high (but declining) because some people have not yet moved out. The high positive correlation between land rent and population density is broken, and this pattern can last for some years until the neighborhood is redeveloped with new residential structures at lower density. Land values are the capitalization of future land rents, so a future of declining land rents translates into an immediate drop in land values. This story is a reasonably simple explanation for what happened in the city of Chicago after World War II, as laid out in McDonald (1979). This point is related to the concept of filtering in the housing market, which is discussed in the next section.

What needs to be explained depends on what matters to people. Do we care about job opportunities for low-income people? Our model would emphasize the reasons for changes in the location patterns of jobs that low-income people can fill, and would worry about the cost of commuting to the jobs. An important early study in urban economics titled *The Urban Transportation Problem* (1965) by John Meyer, John Kain, and Martin Wohl found that jobs were moving to the suburbs, and that public transit systems that are used by low-income people are not designed to transport people to suburban jobs. Thus job opportunities for low-income people were declining. This book documented what has become known as the "jobs-housing spatial mismatch." The locations where jobs are growing are not accessible to people who most need those jobs. What can be done about this problem? This study made extensive use of data from Chicago.

The filtering model of the urban housing market

Urban areas are built up over a long period of time—decades, even centuries. They start small, and expand upward and (mainly) outward. As the population grows, new housing is built at the edge of the city and those who can afford new housing move in. The older housing inside the city eventually becomes obsolete, is demolished, and replaced by new housing. All of this is good. But now suppose for some reason that more new housing is built at the edge of the city than is needed to accommodate the population increase. This can happen because, for example, some people wish to escape the problems of the old city—crowded conditions, crime—and seek the more open space of the "suburbs." Now what happens?

The excess supply of new housing on the edge draws households out, and their old housing units become available for other households. Since the households that moved out generally have the money to afford new housing, they vacate relatively good housing in the city. That means other households can move into these better housing units in the city, leaving other units vacant. These units are occupied by another group of households, who vacate units—and so on. In the end some households move up to somewhat better housing and leave the worst housing vacant. Vacancies are not distributed randomly around the city. Rather, demand for some residential areas in the city collapses, leaving abandoned buildings and urban blight. This process is called filtering, in which households filter up the spectrum of housing unit quality, and housing units filter down the spectrum of household wealth.

The filtering process is not likely to produce abandoned neighborhoods if the population of the urban area is growing rapidly, but the process can work with a vengeance if population growth is slow and households seek the greener pastures of the suburbs. The filtering process did indeed work with a vengeance in Chicago (and many other northern cities), especially during the 1970s and 1980s. As discussed in detail in Chapter 7, some inner-city neighborhoods lost 50 percent of their population.

Tiebout's "vote with the feet" model

The public sector has been left out of the discussion until now. Conventional economists divide into two schools when it comes to modeling the public sector. Economists on the more liberal side think that the public sector tries to serve the public by providing public goods and services, and does the job tolerably well. Good government is good politics. Economists on the conservative side tend to think that, all too often, good intentions do not lead to good outcomes. Government is not subject to the same forces of competition that make private firms efficient. Both groups think that government regulation sometimes is "captured" by special interests. And both groups think that government programs should be subject to cost-benefit analysis, and that government officials should face real incentives (not just nostrums) that foster efficiency. Public finance economists of both types have a model of the local public sector that they think overcomes these problems. The reader is warned that this section is longer than the other sections of this chapter—because government is complicated even as depicted in simple models.

Local governments mainly are in the business of supplying several public goods and services, including:

- public education,
- hospitals and health care,
- transportation (streets, highways, public transportation),
- public safety (police, fire protection, public health, courts),
- parks and recreation,
- community development and planning,

- water, sewerage, and solid waste management (garbage), and
- other local infrastructure.

Public education is, by far, the largest portion of local public goods. With one exception, it is clear that these indeed are public goods. That one item is public education. It is true that the main beneficiary of public education is the individual student. How much "spillover" to other people could there be? However, it is clear that we as a society regard public education as a public good. First of all, students up to grade 12 are children, and are not held responsible for making major decisions. The *states* have decided that school attendance in some approved form is compulsory up to age 16 in order to protect children from irresponsible adults or their own immature decisions. In addition, there are spillover benefits to the rest of society. The current and future families of the students benefit from their enhanced ability to earn a living and handle family matters. People with better education have a better understanding of public issues, are less likely to become delinquent or engage in crime, and are less likely to be unemployed or need public assistance. Educated people have greater demands for information in the form of books, newspapers, informational internet sites, etc., and information has a public good component. So much for what local governments do. How do they decide how much to do?

Paul Samuelson has been described as the most prominent academic economist of the twentieth century, and one of his most important contributions is the theory of pure public goods (1954). This model actually is pretty unsettling. Pure public goods have two features: the good or service is jointly consumed by everyone, and no one can be excluded from consuming it. National defense is the iconic example. Consider a decision at the margin. Should we have another aircraft carrier? Suppose we all know about the benefits of having another carrier, and we know the price tag. How do we know whether we are willing to pay that cost? We could do a survey and ask a random sample of people how much their household is willing to pay to have another carrier, and then send bills out to everyone based on the responses. But there is a big problem with this approach. Why should anyone tell the truth? An individual survey respondent might well think, "My contribution means little, and besides I will benefit from another aircraft carrier regardless." People have an incentive to be free riders. Instead the decision is made by our elected representatives, who have complex bundles of motivations. An efficient outcome is far from assured. Markets allocate resources to private goods by charging prices, people decide how much to buy based on the prices, and under reasonably competitive conditions an efficient allocation of resources is the result. The market mechanism is absent for pure public goods.

Charles Tiebout (1956) took note of Samuelson's result, but thought that things might be different at the level of local government. He wondered whether there might be a mechanism that would force households to reveal their true willingness to pay, would supply the public goods and services, and levy a tax that equals the value of benefits received. He devised a simple model that is known as the "vote with the feet" model. He had us consider the class of public goods that are local in nature. The benefits of these goods extend only to the residents of a local jurisdiction. There are no spillovers to other jurisdictions. Households can move freely from one jurisdiction to another to find the one that best matches their preferences for public goods and willingness to pay. Households are not constrained by other location factors such as the location of jobs, and are fully informed about the available choices—which are numerous, with a wide range of options. Suppose that each jurisdiction operates at the minimum average cost per unit of its public good, and levies an equal "head" tax on each household residing inside its borders. That tax equals the total cost of the quantity of the public good divided by the number of households. Under these conditions, which Tiebout admitted are unrealistic, the local public sector acts like an efficient market. Each household locates in the jurisdiction that matches its preferences, and pays a local tax for a marginal unit of the public good that just equals its willingness to pay (i.e. marginal benefit). All households in a jurisdiction have the same willingness to pay at the margin because they all pay the same amount of tax. Decisions about resource allocations are unanimous within each jurisdiction. Do we and our fellow residents want more of the public good? We know that each of us will pay an equal share of the cost for another unit of the good. Are we willing to pay this amount? We all either say "yes" or "no." There is no argument. For example, should we hire another teacher for the public school? The salary is $50,000, and the jurisdiction has 500 households. Each household must pay $100 a year to hire the teacher. Are we willing to pay this amount?

Tiebout himself recognized that several of the assumptions of the model are not realistic. Indeed, while all economic models are to some degree unrealistic by design, the Tiebout model has more features of unreality than most. Here is a partial list:

- The Tiebout model includes a head tax, but in reality households and firms pay a property tax and other taxes and fees.
- Jurisdictions contain businesses as well as households, and businesses are not direct consumers of many of the local public goods, including public education. The people who work at the businesses demand public education, of course, but do so where they live. Businesses and households have different motivations.
- Local governments get revenue from the state government (and a much smaller amount from the federal government).
- The central city and some larger suburbs contain households with very different income levels and demands for public goods.

How are these shortcomings of the model handled? The property tax is a problem in that, since the tax a household pays is based on the value of the house, there is an incentive for households to enter a jurisdiction with good public services and build a cheap house. In reality jurisdictions address this problem with building codes, housing codes, and zoning codes in an effort to ensure at least a minimum property tax payment. But all of this does not work perfectly. The term "fiscal zoning" is applied to this phenomenon. What about businesses? Businesses must locate somewhere, and most places are dominated by the resident voters. Businesses argue for tax breaks and try to find jurisdictions with lower taxes. However, they all cannot succeed in avoiding property taxes. Businesses tend to contribute more to the local fisc than they receive in benefits of local public services. They do benefit from police and fire protection, streets and highways, sanitation systems, and local planning work, of course. Some jurisdictions win at the game of attracting businesses and, as a result, get to spend more of local public services. The "tax price" for another public school teacher for each household is lower if a larger part of the cost is paid by businesses. As an extreme example, shopping centers generate a lot of sales tax revenue, some of which comes to the local government. Schaumburg, Illinois—where the giant Woodfield Shopping Mall is located—did not find it necessary to impose a property tax at all.

Support for local governments that is provided by the state and federal governments comes in a variety of forms with different incentives. The interaction among levels of government is a field of study in itself. The largest form of state aid to local government is in the form of state funding for local public schools that exists to address partly the unequal spending per pupil that results from Tiebout sorting of households into poor and rich school districts.

What about the large central city with its diverse population? Here the Tiebout model does not provide a good theory of how resource allocation decisions are made. Instead models of voting behavior are used. Remember the Principle of Median Location? One simple voting model is called the Median Voter Model. Imagine that those diverse households have very different demands for public services. Suppose that the demand for local public expenditures varies from a low amount to a high amount. And suppose that an election is held with two candidates, each with a platform that specifies an amount to be spent. Who wins? It is the candidate whose platform matches the preferences of the median voter (whoever that is). The other candidate, not located at the median voter, gets less than half of the votes. This sort of model is tested by supposing that the median voter is in the household with the median income for the jurisdiction. Local public expenditures per household are a positive function of median income. Jurisdictions with higher median incomes spend more. This is not a very startling result, but it works.

Where do all of these caveats regarding the Tiebout model leave us? It is fair to say that the model is relevant for the suburbs of large metropolitan areas such as Chicago. People really do shop around for suburban jurisdictions, mainly by looking at the quality of the local schools and the property tax rate. However, the real suburbs are far more complex than the model. Suburbs do impose building, housing, and zoning codes—fiscal zoning. Suburbs do vary substantially in the amount of business property they can tax. States do have programs to provide aid for local school districts based on the ability of the local district to raise revenue. People care about other location factors such as where jobs are located. Still, the Tiebout model does provide insight. However, the model does not now really apply to a large central city such as Chicago with its diverse population.

The Tiebout model does seem to provide a perspective on the early history of suburban growth around Chicago. Ann Durkin Keating (2002) shows that early suburbs in the nineteenth century were created to provide the services demanded by the people who lived there. Some suburbs provided an extensive set of services (water and sewer systems, police and fire protection, and so on), while other suburbs provided very few, if any, services. Instead, this second group provided cheap land and no taxes. However, most of these early suburbs were annexed by the City of Chicago in 1889, and six more were added by 1893. Those annexed in 1889 were mainly large townships with diverse populations. The suburbs that were providing the more extensive set of services thought that joining the City of Chicago would reduce costs and/or improve services as the population increased. And, by that time, people who demanded municipal services had moved into the suburbs with few services. Joining the City was the more expedient solution, and a majority of the voters voted for annexation. At the same time, several other suburbs were already happy with the basket of services provided and did not wish to join the City. These suburbs were smaller units with pretty homogeneous populations. Very little annexation by the City of Chicago took place after 1893 because at that point the City was mostly surrounded by these smaller suburbs such as Oak Park, Evanston, and Cicero.

Economics of discrimination

Gary Becker, the economist mentioned at the beginning of the chapter, began his career by inventing the field of the economics of discrimination (1957). Becker's basic idea for one form of discrimination is pretty simple: some people are willing to pay to avoid other types of people. Discrimination is translated into money terms as a willingness to pay. For example, Becker supposed that white households are willing to pay more (other things equal) for houses in locations with no African-American people, or that are not near the areas in which African-Americans live. This is the passive form of discrimination. The other form is active discrimination—some types of people are made to pay more than others people for the same good or service (or are denied the good or service).

In this theory, discrimination exists in employment because either the business owner or the white workers (or both) do not wish to be associated with African-American workers in the workplace. Employers pay a price for this preference because they do not hire African-Americans who are skilled workers, but instead hire white workers some of whom are less skilled. Employment segregation and lack of job opportunity for African-Americans result. Other employers may hire all African-American workers because white workers do not wish to work for employers who hire African-Americans, and because they get to hire very good workers who have limited job opportunities. Becker (1957) found a high level of segregation among industries in the South in the 1940s and 1950s. African-American workers were confined to a small list of industries. In Chicago George Pullman was famous for hiring all African-American Pullman Porters. These gentlemen are legendary for the quality of service they provided.

In the urban housing market the propensity of whites to avoid African-Americans resulted in the high degree of racial segregation that still exists. Active discrimination was at work as well. Landlords and sellers refused to rent or sell housing to African-Americans outside designated zones. Intrusions into all-white neighborhoods were met with active resistance and, in some cases, with violence. As the African-American population grew rapidly during the Great Migration from the South, there was great tension on the racial borders as neighborhoods were converted from white to African-American occupancy. Nowhere was this phenomenon greater than in Chicago, and housing discrimination (both in passive and active forms) and segregation are a critical parts of Chicago's economic history.

Effects of concentrated poverty

As Jesus said in Mathew 26:11, "For ye have the poor always with you, but me ye have not always." Nevertheless, we are instructed to help the poor, and as a society we do (and we do as individuals, as well). But it turns out that, according to leading sociologists such as William Wilson (1987), the problems faced by the poor are much worse if the poor are segregated away from the general population. Given a particular number of poor people, it is better for them not to be living in areas of concentrated poverty. While this idea is primarily a sociological proposition, it has important economic elements. Wilson defined the urban underclass as follows (1987, p. 8):

> Today's ghetto neighborhoods are populated almost exclusively by the most disadvantaged segments of the black urban community, that heterogeneous grouping of families and individuals who are outside the mainstream of the American occupational system. Included in this group are individuals who lack training and skills and either experience long-term unemployment or are not members of the labor force, individuals who are engaged in street crime and other forms of aberrant behavior, and families that experience long-term spells of poverty and/or welfare dependency. These are the populations to which I refer when I speak of the *underclass*. (Emphasis is in the original.)

Wilson thinks that the underclass is the result of social isolation—lack of connection to mainstream society. Places dominated by the underclass are characterized by a "tangle of pathology in the inner city," crime, drug addiction, out-of-wedlock births, female-headed families, and welfare dependency. Children who grow up in this kind of environment have little chance of success in mainstream society. Wilson (1987) was a member of the faculty of the University of Chicago at the time, and was writing about Chicago. Wilson's work has been debated and challenged over the years, but he has not changed his mind (2009). Economists are among the researchers who continue to study concentrated poverty and its effects. The matter of concentrated poverty in Chicago is examined in detail in Chapters 7 and 8.

Myrdal's vicious and virtuous circles

We return to economics and to Gunnar Myrdal, whose massive report on the African-American population of the U.S. in the 1940s has influenced American society for 70 years and was cited as the main reason he received the Nobel Prize in Economics in 1974. The book is titled *An American Dilemma* (1944), and in that study he introduced the concepts of the vicious circle and virtuous circle. (It is circle in Myrdal's version, by the way, not cycle.) In my view these concepts are highly useful for explaining the history of a major American urban area.

Let Myrdal (1944, p. 75–76) say what he meant:

> Throughout this inquiry, we shall assume a general interdependence between all factors in the Negro problem. White prejudice and discrimination keep the Negro low in standards of living, health, education, manners, and morals. This, in its turn, gives support to white prejudice. White prejudice and Negro standards thus mutually "cause" each other. If things remain about as they are and have been this means that the two happen to balance each other. Such a static "accommodation" is, however, entirely accidental. If either of the factors changes, this will cause a change in the other factor, too, and start a process of interaction where the change in one factor will continuously be supported by the reaction of the other factor. The whole system will be moving in the direction of the primary change, but much further. This is what we mean by cumulative causation.

The African-Americans of the South had reached a very low standard when Myrdal wrote this, but he hypothesized that a reduction in white prejudice could bring forth a virtuous circle of improvements in the lives of African-Americans and reductions in white prejudice. And he thought that this basic idea has wide application to the study of society.

It is clear that William Wilson has been influenced by Myrdal's ideas. The underclass in the inner city resulted from a cumulative process that included loss of jobs in the city, movement of middle-class households away from the inner city, decline in city schools, increases in crime, and so on. The vicious and virtuous circles in Chicago are examined in Chapters 7 and 8.

Conclusion

This chapter has presented a brief survey of the economic models that will be used to provide the backdrop for the economic history of Chicago. In my view, this portfolio of models explains a lot. But they are models of reality. They do not and are not intended to explain everything. Lots of historical details are included, but lots are left out as well. This study may gloss over things that the reader thinks are very important. Sorry, but this book is intended to be a history of manageable length.

An economy in which individuals and firms maximize and markets exist can be efficient or inefficient, and can produce an outcome that society considers to be inequitable. This chapter has pointed out examples of efficiency and inefficiency. Clearly the building of a railroad network with Chicago as its focal point made the economy more efficient. But the creation of a major city in the nineteenth century brought with it terrible negative external effects—pollution of the water that produced epidemics and hasty construction that was a huge fire hazard are just two examples. An important part of the story of Chicago is how the metropolitan area has attempted to mitigate some of the negative externalities and inequities while capturing the beneficial effects of growth and change.

Once the urban area had reached some minimal size (beyond being a small military outpost with a few fur traders and other villagers scattered about), it can be argued that all of the models discussed in this chapter apply in all time periods. Transportation costs always matter, the same determinants of long-run growth always operate, exports are always important, externalities are always present, probably poverty is always concentrated to some extent, virtuous and vicious circles operate, and so on. The recitation of how each of the models can be applied in each time period would be tedious. The particular models selected for emphasis in each chapter are my judgment as to which models best explain the most important outcomes in that time period. Such is the heart of the problem, of course. Read on to learn my answers, which are here in print, but not carved in stone.

Note

1 This equation ignores the fact that the household will rent more land at the greater distance. If the equation is put in differential calculus form by having the change in distance approach zero, this effect approaches zero, so $t = -L \, dR/du$.

2 Chicago and the development of the Old Northwest

Introduction

Cities exist for a variety of reasons, but the existence and development of Chicago are attributable almost entirely to economic factors. Two major forces were at work in the nineteenth century—the development of the region known as the Old Northwest, and changes in transportation technologies and costs. The purposes of this chapter are to describe these two forces and to show how they played out to make Chicago the preeminent city of the Midwest. The story of Chicago in the nineteenth century has been told many times by a sizable group that includes Alfred Andreas (1884–1886), Milo Quaife (1913), Homer Hoyt (1933), Bessie Louise Pierce (1937–1957), and more recently William Cronon (1991) and Donald Miller (1996). This chapter adds to these admirable studies by placing Chicago squarely in the context of the development of its region, by drawing on some additional scholarship, and by explicitly using several aspects of location theory.

The story of Chicago begins with the expedition of Marquette and Joliet in 1673. These explorers made their way by canoe down Lake Michigan from Sault Ste. Marie to Green Bay, and then through Wisconsin to the Mississippi River. They then proceeded downstream to someplace along the river in Arkansas. On the return trip an Indian guide directed them to paddle up the Illinois River and thence to what became known as the Chicago Portage. This portage connected the Mississippi River system to the Great Lakes via the short Chicago River. During the rainier seasons the portage became Mud Lake, which could be navigated by canoe. Thus did Marquette and Joliet actually arrive at what became Chicago not from Lake Michigan, but via the back door. Louis Joliet immediately grasped the importance of this location, and proposed that a canal should be constructed to make the needed connection between the two great watersheds. It took just 175 years to complete this project. Table 2.1 is a timeline up to 1900 for Chicago that provides details of the Illinois and Michigan Canal project, completed in 1848.

The French controlled the region up until 1763, and development occurred in southern Illinois and across the river in Missouri. The Illinois country became the breadbasket of New Orleans, which was founded in 1718. The British took over the region at the conclusion of the French and Indian War, and in 1763 drew a line

Table 2.1 Chicago timeline to 1900

From earliest days, Chicago Portage and Mud Lake	

1673	Marquette and Joliet explore the region. Joliet proposes a canal.
1785	Federal Land Ordinance, DuSable erects trading post.
1787	Northwest Ordinance prohibits slavery north of Ohio River.
1803	Fort Dearborn built.
1808	Secretary of Treasury includes Illinois-Michigan Canal in plans.
1812	Fort Dearborn massacre.
1816	Fort Dearborn rebuilt. Federal government purchases land for canal from Indians.
1818	Illinois admitted as state with population of about 36,000—the smallest population for any state when admitted. Northern boundary moved to the North from southern point of Lake Michigan to include canal. Governor Shadrach Bond includes canal in first message to legislature.
1825	Erie Canal opens.
1826	State gets land grant from federal government of alternate sections for five miles. State of Illinois given 20 years to complete canal.
1829	State appoints three canal commissioners; 90-mile route selected; sell land @ $1.25 per acre.
1830	First lots in Chicago platted. Population 50.
1831	Cook County organized with Chicago as county seat.
1832	Blackhawk War. Treaty relocates Indians west of Mississippi River.
1833	Chicago incorporated as a town, cholera epidemic, land boom begins.
1835	U.S. dredges, Chicago River made a harbor. Indians assemble for final payment, and engage in final defiant dance. Northern Illinois is opened for settlement by whites.
1836	Work on canal begins.
1837	Chicago incorporated as a city with population of 4170. Early land boom crashes. William B. Ogden is first mayor.
1837–1842	Depression.
1838	First grain elevator built.
1841	Canal work suspended.
1845	Canal work resumes.
1847	McCormick reaper factory opens on north side of Chicago River.
1848	Illinois and Michigan Canal opens. Galena and Chicago Union Railroad built to DesPlaines River. Chicago Board of Trade founded. Telegraph line reaches Chicago.
1852	Michigan Central Railroad connects city to the East.
1854	Cholera epidemic claimed 1,124 lives.
1855	City begins to raise level of streets up to 12 feet.
1859	First horse drawn railway operates.
1860	Abraham Lincoln nominated for President in Chicago.
1865	Union Stockyards established.
1867	Sanitary water system installed.
1869	Calumet Harbor improvements begin.
1871	Great Chicago Fire on October 8–10.
1872	Ordinance outlaws wooden buildings in downtown area. Montgomery Ward Company founded.
1877	Great railway strike.

(Continued)

Table 2.1 (Continued)

From earliest days, Chicago Portage and Mud Lake

1880–1884	George Pullman builds factory and town of Pullman.
1882	Cable car system starts. Belt Railway of Chicago begins operations.
1885	Home Insurance Building, progenitor of the skyscraper, built.
1886	Haymarket Riot.
1889	Annexations increase area of city from 36 to 168 square miles.
1890	Central Manufacturing District, the first organized industrial district.
1892	University of Chicago founded.
1893	World's Columbian Exposition.
1894	Pullman strike.
1897	Chicago Loop elevated line completed.
1900	Chicago Sanitary and Ship Canal opened, replacing the Illinois and Michigan Canal and effectively reversing the flow of the Chicago River.

that prohibited migration of Europeans into the Great Northwest. St. Louis was founded in 1764 by French residents of Illinois who moved across the river and out of British territory. DuSable, the first permanent resident of Chicago, arrived in 1779— near the end of the Revolutionary War. The treaty that ended the war was signed in 1783, and Congress promptly passed the Land Ordinance of 1785 and the Northwest Ordinance of 1787. These acts, passed under the Articles of Confederation, are still on the books, and set out the system of legal description for land based on rectangular survey, and prohibited slavery north of the Ohio River. Veterans of the Revolutionary War were granted plots of land in the Ohio country, and development of the Old Northwest began in earnest. Cincinnati emerged as the first real city in the region. Wars were waged against the resident Indian populations, and army outposts were established, including Fort Dearborn at the mouth of the Chicago River in 1803 (to protect the Chicago Portage). The Fort Dearborn garrison was massacred in 1812 as it attempted to escape as ordered during the War of 1812. The fort was rebuilt in 1816, and a few people were drawn to the site to trade in furs. Illinois was granted statehood in 1818 based on its population in southern Illinois. Illinois had to fudge its 1818 population figures to reach the required 40,000 (reduced from 60,000) by counting people who were just passing through—sometimes more than once. Congress needed to admit a northern state at that time to match the admission of Alabama, and Illinois was the likely candidate. Population growth in northern Illinois followed after the opening of the Erie Canal in 1825.

The transformation of Chicago from a trading post to a small city is all about building a critical link in the national transportation system. Basic principles of transportation costs were at work. Chicago became a transshipment point in the system, where goods are transferred from one means of shipment to another—in both directions. Farm products could be brought to Chicago by canal boat for shipment to the East by lake ship, and goods from the East could be distributed from Chicago. The Illinois and Michigan Canal to link the Great Lakes to the

Mississippi River system and to provide access to the Illinois interior was born when the Secretary of the Treasury mentioned it in 1808. Land for the project was purchased by the federal government from the Indians in 1816, and the northern boundary of this purchase is still on the map as Indian Boundary Road. The immediate impetus for the canal project was the opening of the Erie Canal in 1825, which enhanced trade on the Great Lakes all the way to Chicago. The federal government made a land grant to Illinois for the canal in 1826, and gave the state 20 years to complete the project. Three Canal Commissioners were appointed in 1829, a route was selected, and a plat map for the town was drawn. These steps stimulated migration to Chicago, and a land boom commenced. See Table 2.2 for details of the land boom, taken from Hoyt (1933). Chicago was incorporated as a town in 1833 with a population of 350, and then incorporated as a city in 1837 with 4,170 souls. Hoyt (1933, p. 22) noted that in 1837 Chicago had become a central place with dry-goods stores, hardware stores, grocery and provision stores, taverns, a branch bank, the federal land office for the region, and lawyers' offices to serve a trading area within a radius of 200 miles. Farmers brought their produce in by wagon and camped around town. Chicago was also a refitting point for immigrants and, as the county seat, the legal center for a large area of northeastern Illinois. The newly dredged Chicago River served as the harbor by ships plying the Great Lakes, including those with cargo from the Erie

Table 2.2 Canal land boom

Land values, 1830–1842	
1830	$1.25 per acre; 80'x100' lot $100 highest price. Small increases from 1830 to 1832.
1832	Boom begins; lot sold for $42 in 1830 sells for $800 in November 1833.
1833	Prices increase daily. Lot that sold for $100 in 1832 sells for $3,500, and later for $67,000. "Dazzling fortunes quickly made."
1836	Peak in land values; total value of land in current boundaries of city of Chicago go from $168,000 in 1830 to $10.5 million in 1836. Construction starts, based on $500,000 loan from state and $1.6 million in land sales. School section sold for $38,000 in 1833, $1.2 million in 1836, 1000% increase since 1830. Spatial pattern; land along Chicago River sells for eight to ten times land ½ mile back and 25 times land 1 mile back from river. State starts railroad project of 1,300 miles, state bonds of $10 million to be issued. State Bank of Illinois buys bonds with increase in capital.
1839	Banks suspend specie payment. Fort Dearborn land sold for $100,000; would have been sold for $900,000 in 1836. Land values have dropped by 75% to 90%.
1841–1842	Low ebb of land values and state finances. State Bank of Illinois fails. State owes $14 million, bond values drop to 18 cents on dollar. Internal improvements plan abandoned, including canal. Buyers of canal lots unable to pay on loans, state reduces price by 1/3, permits clear title to part of land that was paid for. Total value of land in Chicago fell from $10.5 million to $1.4 million.

Source: Compiled from Hoyt (1933).

Canal. But, as Hoyt (1933, p. 22) stated: "At this time the surrounding country was not even self-sufficing, and all the goods sold were imported from the East, the ships going back with sand as ballast."

Work on the canal began in 1836, but was halted in 1841 when Illinois defaulted on its bonds. The economic depression stopped progress until 1845, when work started again. As noted above, the Illinois and Michigan Canal opened in 1848. By then the population of Chicago had reached about 20,000. Perhaps it is worth noting that the opening of the canal was within living memory when my father was born in Chicago in 1915.

Chicago was founded because the site, with its short river, provided a potential port and the most convenient link between the Great Lakes and Mississippi River water sheds. Water routes were the dominant form of long-distance transportation at the time. However, before pushing the Chicago story further, it is time to examine the development of the Old Northwest.

Population growth in the Old Northwest

The purpose of this section is to use population data to show that the Old Northwest no longer had a frontier in 1900. The region had reached mature status at that time, and therefore 1900 is a good end point for this discussion of Chicago and the development of the Old Northwest. Settlement of the Old Northwest was relatively rapid because, as demonstrated by the studies reviewed by Atack and Passell (1994), improvements in the transportation system that occurred over time meant that money could be made in producing farm products for market. And Chicago, with its highly fertile hinterland, became the central point in that market.

Kentucky was admitted to the union in 1792, followed by Tennessee in 1796 and Ohio in 1803. As one would expect, the settlement of the region proceeded from East and South to the West and North. Population figures of the relevant states from 1810 to 1900 (and beyond) are shown in Table 2.3.[1] The appendix to the chapter contains population figures for Chicago, Cook County, the urban area, and the foreign-born population in Chicago up through 1900. Table 2.3 shows that the population of Ohio grew continuously, but that its share of population of the Old Northwest declined as the other states became populated. Note that Ohio had a population of 231,000 in 1810, and that Missouri was home to only 20,000 (even with St. Louis). Indiana, Illinois, and Michigan had few people at that time. Population growth was rapid; by 1840 Ohio had 1.52 million, followed by Indiana with 686,000, Illinois with 476,000, and Missouri with 384,000. Ohio had 45.3 percent and Illinois had only 14.2 percent of the population of the region in 1840. On the eve of the Civil War in 1860 Ohio had 1.98 million and Illinois had achieved second place in the region with 1.71 million people.

The population of Illinois grew rapidly during the Civil War decade, and had pulled nearly even with Ohio by 1870. These top two were followed by Missouri, Indiana, Iowa, Michigan, Wisconsin, and Minnesota. The region had almost achieved its longer-run population shares. Those shares changed somewhat between 1870 and 1900. Minnesota continued to develop and reached a regional

Table 2.3 Population of the Old Northwest (1000s)

Year	Ohio 1803*	Indiana 1816	Illinois 1818	Mich. 1837	Wisc. 1848	Missouri 1820	Iowa 1846	Minn. 1858	Total
1810	231	25	12	5		20			
1820	581	147	55	9		65			
1830	938	343	157	32		140			
1840	1,519	686	476	212	31	384	43		3,351
	45.3%	20.5%	14.2%	6.3%	0.9%	11.5%	1.3%		
1850	1,980	988	851	398	305	682	192	6	5,402
1860	2,340	1,350	1,711	749	776	1,182	675	172	8,955
1870	2,665	1,681	2,540	1,194	1,055	1,721	1,194	440	12,480
	21.4%	13.5%	20.4%	9.6%	8.5%	13.8%	9.6%	3.5%	
1880	3,198	1,978	3,078	1,637	1,315	2,168	1,625	781	15,780
1890	3,672	2,192	3,826	2,094	1,693	2,679	1,912	1,310	19,378
1900	4,158	2,516	4,822	2,421	2,069	3,107	2,232	1,751	23,076
	18.0%	10.9%	20.9%	10.5%	9.0%	13.5%	9.7%	7.6%	
1930	6,647	3,239	7,631	4,842	3,952	3,629	2,471	2,538	33,936
	19.6%	9.5%	22.5%	14.3%	8.7%	10.7%	7.3%	7.5%	
1960	9,706	4,662	10,081	7,823	4,892	4,320	2,758	3,414	46,716
	20.8%	9.8%	21.6%	16.7%	8.5%	9.2%	5.9%	7.3%	

Source: U.S. Bureau of the Census.

Note
* Year state was admitted to the union.

population share of 7.6 percent in 1900 (up from 3.5 percent in 1870). This increase in share came at the expense of the older states in the region—Ohio and Indiana. The shares of the other five states changed very little during these three decades, during which the population of the region grew by 85 percent. One indicator that the region no longer includes a frontier is that the state of Minnesota no longer gained regional population share, and that Ohio stopped losing share. Data for 1930 show that Minnesota's share had stabilized and that Ohio had gained share after 1900. Indeed, the gains in shares after 1900 by Ohio, Illinois, and Michigan were the result of industrialization, and that the less heavily industrial states of Indiana, Missouri, and Iowa lost share. Ohio had gained share in 1910 and 1920 as well, and Minnesota had a small gain in share to 8 percent in 1910 and 1920—but its share moved down to 7.5 percent in 1930.

Illinois had the largest population among the states of the Old Northwest in 1890, and then the state added almost one million people in the 1890s. One big reason for this leadership in population is the emergence of Chicago as the preeminent city in the region. Illinois had (and still has) no other major city.

Development of the urban hierarchy of the Old Northwest

The notion of a hierarchy of urban areas was first posited formally by Walter Christaller (1933), and the topic has generated a large literature. A modern economy based on industry and trade contains a hierarchy of urban areas that includes one preeminent urban area that provides goods and services to the economy that no other city provides. In the case of Chicago, initially that unique service was transportation. Furthermore, there are a few cities of second rank, more cities of third rank, and so on. See Beckman (1968) and Edwin Mills (1971) for formal presentations of urban hierarchy theory. However, no economic theorist was needed to tell the people who were developing the Old Northwest that a system of cities would emerge, and that one of those cities would become dominant. Cronon (1991, pp. 279–295) points out that the creation of a hierarchy of cities would go hand-in-hand with the development of this rich agricultural region. Cronon argues that it is incorrect to think that cities develop "bottom-up" from villages to towns to cities. He states (1991, p. 282) that "the highest-ranking regional metropolis consolidated its role at a very early date, it promoted the communities in its hinterland as much as they promoted it." Let us examine the record.

Table 2.4 displays the population figures in order for the largest towns and cities for the Old Northwest from 1840 to 1900. In 1840, just before construction on the Illinois and Michigan Canal was halted, Cincinnati with 46,000 residents was the only city that was larger than a small town. St. Louis was in second place with a population of 16,000. Chicago had 4,470 residents, and stood in eighth place between Zanesville (Ohio) and New Albany (Indiana). In 1850, just after the opening of the Illinois and Michigan Canal, Chicago had moved up to third place with 30,000 people, but was well behind Cincinnati and St. Louis. Several other towns such as Detroit, Milwaukee, Columbus, and Cleveland were developing

Table 2.4 Urban hierarchy: 1840–1900 (population in 1000s)

1840	1850	1860	1870	1880	1890	1900
Cincy 46	Cincy 151	Cincy 161	St. L 311*	Chgo 503	Chgo 1100	Chgo 1699
St. L 16	St. L 78	St. L 161	Chgo 299	St. L 351	St. L 452	St. L 575
Detroit 9	Chgo 30	Chgo 112	Cincy 216	Cincy 255	M-SP 298	Cleve. 382
Cleve. 6	Detr. 21	Detr. 46	Cleve. 93	Cleve. 160	Cincy 297	M-SP 368
Dayton 6	Milw. 20	Milw. 45	Detr. 80	Detr. 116	Cleve. 261	Cincy 326
Colum. 6	Colum. 18	Cleve. 43	Milw. 71	Milw. 116	Detr. 206	Detr. 286
Zanesv. 5	Cleve. 17	Dayt. 20	Indy 48	M-SP 88	Milw. 204	Milw. 285
Chgo 4.5	Dayton 11	Colum. 19	KC 32	Indy 75	KC 133	Indy 169
New Alb. 4	New Alb. 8	Indy 19	Tol. 32	KC 56	Indy 104	KC 164
	Indy 8	Peor. 14	Colum. 31	Colum. 52	Colum. 88	Tol. 132
		Quin. 14	Dayt. 30	Tol. 50	Tol. 81	Colum. 126
		Dubq. 13	Quin. 24	Dayt. 39	Dayt. 61	St. J 103
		E'ville 11	Peoria 23	GRpd 32	GRpd 60	GRpd 88
		St. P 10	E'ville 22	St. J 32	St. J 52	Dayt. 85
			St. P 20	Peoria 29		
			Dav. 20	E'ville 29		
			St. J 20			

Source: U.S. Bureau of the Census.

Note
* Population figure widely regarded as fraudulently too large.

rapidly. On the eve of the Civil War in 1860 St. Louis had pulled even with Cincinnati at 161,000 and Chicago had almost quadrupled to 112,000. Fifty percent of the population of Chicago had been born outside the U.S. in 1860; the largest immigrant groups were from Germany and Ireland. Detroit, Milwaukee, and Cleveland had emerged as the leading cities at the next level with populations of over 40,000. The next lower group, with populations of about 20,000, consisted of Dayton, Columbus, and Indianapolis. St. Paul, Minnesota, appeared on the list for the first time, just two years after admission of the state to the union.

The Civil War decade brought growth to the Chicago population of 167 percent that outstripped Cincinnati and St. Louis. St. Louis is listed as the top city in the region with a population of 311,000, ahead of Chicago with 299,000 and Cincinnati with 216,000. However, many population experts believe that the St. Louis figure is fraudulent. One piece of evidence of the fraud is what some experts regard as the implausibly small population growth figure for 1870 to 1880 of 13 percent. The people of St. Louis and Chicago saw themselves as in competition to be the top city in the region, a story that is well told by Wyatt Belcher (1947). St. Louis was relying on a transportation system dominated by rivers (Mississippi, Missouri, and Illinois), while Chicago had adopted the railroad (to be described in detail later). Indeed, Chicago was in a much better geographic location to become the railroad capital. St. Louis fought a losing legal battle to prevent rail lines from crossing the Mississippi River. The Chicago and Rock Island Railroad crossed the river in 1856.[2] The (allegedly) fraudulent population figure was one aspect of the competition. In 1870 the group of cities at the next level was, as in 1860, Cleveland, Detroit, and Milwaukee. Indianapolis emerged as the next-largest city, followed by a group consisting of Columbus, Dayton, Toledo, and Kansas City. As the state population data show, the population figures for the cities indicate that the region had not reached maturity.

We now come to the decades in which Chicago became a leading city not only in the nation, but in the world as well. Reasons for this growth are discussed later. Downtown Chicago and much of the north side of the city burned to the ground in 1871, but recovery was swift and the population reached 503,000 in 1880—growth of 68 percent in ten years. The Great Chicago Fire, in effect, gave the city the opportunity to rebuild in a manner that accommodated more growth in population and industry. And wooden buildings were banned in and near the downtown area. Chicago was by far the leading city in the Old Northwest. The land area included within the city limits had not kept up with the population. According to Hoyt (1933, p. 483), in 1880 some 51,000 people were living in areas that later became part of the city. St. Louis remained in second place and Cincinnati held its third position, but Cleveland had grown to the fourth-place position well ahead of Detroit and Milwaukee. Minneapolis-St. Paul had jumped up in the rankings with a combined population of 88,000, and Indianapolis held down the next position, followed by a group consisting of Kansas City, Toledo, and Columbus. The sudden emergence of the Twin Cities signaled that the frontier was closing and the region was heading toward a mature state.

Rapid growth, combined with annexations, brought the Chicago population to 1.1 million in 1890. The largest annexations occurred in 1889, and some smaller annexations during 1890–1893 brought the boundaries of the city almost to their final positions. According to Mayer and Wade (1969, p. 176), the population of the "old" city as of 1880 grew from 503,000 to 792,000 in 1890 and annexed townships jumped from 40,000 to 308,000. In addition, in 1890 there were 13,000 people living in areas that would be annexed in the 1890s. An estimate of population growth for the City of Chicago from 1880 to 1890 therefore is 557,000 (289,000 in old boundaries plus 268,000 in annexed areas). The foreign-born population in the city in 1890 was 451,000, up from 205,000 in 1880. It is nearly always true that rapid population growth of the urban area translates into growth in the "old" central city and very rapid growth in the suburban areas. Spatial patterns within the city are discussed in detail later. Chicago had become the "second city," surpassing Philadelphia and second only to New York.

The population of Chicago in 1890 was more than double that of St. Louis (452,000). The rank-size rule for urban hierarchies is that rank times size equals a constant. That number is 1.1 million for Chicago and 904,000 for St. Louis. If one considers a separate urban hierarchy for the region, by that rule Chicago was too large, and/or St. Louis was too small. However, the rule is only an approximation, and by 1890 it probably is more correct to consider the urban hierarchy for the nation rather than for just one region. The cities next in the hierarchy with populations of 298,000 to 204,000 were, in order, Minneapolis-St. Paul, Cincinnati, Cleveland, Detroit, and Milwaukee. Note that the Twin Cities had just barely passed Cincinnati, and that Cleveland had separated itself from Detroit and Milwaukee and was closing in on Cincinnati. The next group down included Kansas City and Indianapolis, followed by Columbus and Toledo.

The population growth of Chicago in the 1880s of 557,000 looms large in the region. Population growth for the State of Illinois was 748,000 over the same decade, so growth in Chicago was 74.5 percent of the growth of the state. The eight-state region had added 3.598 million to the population during the 1880s, and the city of Chicago was 15.5 percent of that growth.

The 1890s, in spite of the depression that occurred in the middle of the decade, saw Chicago greatly widen its lead over the other cities of the region. The population of Chicago reached 1.699 million, and St. Louis at 575,000 was only 34 percent of its rival. Cleveland had surpassed its neighbor Cincinnati and Minneapolis-St. Paul to take over third place, and the Twin Cities trailed Cleveland by only 14,000. Detroit and Milwaukee continued to grow in tandem, and were gaining on Cincinnati. Indianapolis and Kansas City came next, followed by Toledo and Columbus. The movement from 1890 to 1900 of Cleveland in the ranking was the only change that was more than one position. The foreign-born population of Chicago was 588,000 (34.6 percent).

We now turn to the reasons for the emergence of Chicago as the preeminent city in the Old Northwest and the second city of the nation.

Railroad capital

It is said that the canal to link the Great Lakes and the Mississippi River system made Chicago. Belcher (1947) attributes to the canal the redirection of shipments of the agricultural products of the Illinois River valley from down river to St. Louis instead to Chicago. But canals were becoming outdated technology in 1848. While the Illinois and Michigan Canal did carry a great deal of freight up through the 1880s (one million tons in the peak year 1882) and competed with the railroads with low freight rates, it was the railroad that made Chicago into an economic capital. One question is, "Why did Chicago become the railroad capital?" This section describes the development of the rail network centered on Chicago, and then provides some answers to this question. The basic principle of network economics is that members of the network benefit when the network becomes larger. The addition of more people and places to a network is of benefit to these new members, but also confers an external benefit on the existing members of the network. The addition of a rail line to an existing railroad network confers direct economic benefits to those along the new line, but the people and places already in the network can now travel and ship goods to more places as well. A network needs points at which the lines of the network meet, and Chicago became the largest such point. However, as described below, the creation of a truly integrated network of rail lines was not a smooth process.

The Baltimore and Ohio was the first real railroad in the U.S. The company was chartered in 1828 and the first 13 miles of track were put into operation in 1830. According to George Taylor (1951, p. 79) there were 73 miles of railroad lines in

1830 (compared to 1,277 miles of canals). The decade of the 1830s saw the first boom in railroad construction that occurred almost entirely in states on the east coast. The total railroad mileage was 3,328 in 1840; Pennsylvania was the leader with 576 miles, followed by New York with 453 miles, Virginia with 341 miles, Maryland with 273 miles, and Massachusetts with 270 miles. Railroad mileage in the Old Northwest totaled 199 miles, of which 114 miles were located in Michigan. Illinois had just 26 miles of railroad in 1840. Canal mileage in 1840 was 3,326—equal to railroad mileage. Pennsylvania was the leader with 954 canal miles, Ohio had 744 miles, and New York had 640 miles. Illinois had no canal miles.

George Taylor and Irene Neu (1956) argued that the first real railroad lines were designed to provide a city with access to specific interior markets, and not to create a rail network. Boston was in competition with New York and Portland, and New York competed with Philadelphia, which competed with Baltimore. One aspect of the competition was the use of different track gauges to prevent integration of routes. The chief railroads that emerged were the Grand Trunk from Michigan to Portland via Canada, three railroads that originated in Boston, the New York Central, the Pennsylvania Railroad, the New York and Erie Railroad, and the Baltimore and Ohio.

Railroad mileage more than doubled in the 1840s to 8,879, while canal mileage increased only to 3,698 (including the 100-mile Illinois and Michigan Canal). Illinois had 118 miles of railroads in 1850. Because of its western location, Illinois came late both to canal and railroad building. The first railroad in Chicago, the Galena and Chicago Union, was built to connect Chicago to the lead mining town of Galena on the Mississippi River and to bring farm products to Chicago. William B. Ogden had announced the intention to build the railroad in 1847, but found no investors in Chicago or in the East. Instead he and his partner sold shares in the proposed railroad to the farmers and businessmen whose land would be served by the line. The first eight miles of track were completed in 1848, and shipments of wheat commenced immediately. Note that Ogden and his partner chose to build a railroad, not a canal. This tiny railroad ultimately was extended into Wisconsin, and became part of the Chicago and Northwestern system in 1864. The success of the Galena and Chicago Union helped stimulate the construction of the other railroads that connect Chicago to the South, North, and West. Ogden is considered to be the top business leader in early Chicago. He had arrived in 1835 to sell at a sizable profit land that his brother-in-law had purchased and served as the first mayor of Chicago in 1837. He ran a steamboat company, a brewery, and had a major investment in timber land in Wisconsin and a lumber company in Chicago. He became president of the Union Pacific Railroad and was a key figure in the completion of the first trans-continental railroad in 1869. He is considered to be the first great railroad man.

The Illinois Central was foremost among those additional railroads. The original plan in 1836 and 1837 was to build a line from Cairo at the southern tip of Illinois north to Galena, with no direct route to Chicago. Hoyt (1933, p. 54) noted that:

The railroads finally became an interlocking network of lines covering the entire United States, but in the beginning they were conceived of as merely connecting links between waterways, and hence a city with a large existing canal and lake commerce provided a magnet that was sure to draw them to it. Chicago did not play a prominent role, however, in the calculations of the first railway promoters, probably because its lake and canal commerce had not been sufficiently developed.

Fund raising and actual construction of the Illinois Central lagged until Senator Stephen A. Douglas, a Chicago resident, convinced the company to run a "branch line" to Chicago as well, and then secured the first federal land grant for railroad construction in 1850. The "branch line," which really became the main line, split from the line to Galena just 100 miles north of Cairo at Centralia (named after the railroad). These two lines played a major role in the development of rich agricultural lands of Illinois by providing rail access to the grain and livestock markets in Chicago, a history well described in the classic volume by Paul Gates (1934). Other rail lines to Chicago under construction at the same time in the early 1850s include the Chicago, Burlington, and Quincy; the Chicago and Rock Island; the St. Louis, Alton, and Chicago; and the Chicago and Northwestern. However, the original plan for the Rock Island was to run the line from the Illinois and Michigan Canal to the Mississippi River, but Hoyt (1933, p. 55) stated that, "The influence of astute eastern capitalists, however, who foresaw the possibilities of Chicago in 1851, compelled the Rock Island to make Chicago its terminus." Other railroads followed suit, and all of these railroads had arrived in Chicago by 1856. The Illinois Central line from the mouth of the Chicago River (east of the old Fort Dearborn property) to Cairo was completed on that date. The first leg of the route took the rail line on a long trestle in Lake Michigan that was located a quarter mile from the shore. Table 2.5 lists by direction the rail lines to Chicago as of 1900, along with the dates of their arrival. As the map from Taylor and Neu (1956) shows, Chicago was served by 11 rail lines in 1861.

Rail construction had boomed even more in the 1850s as total rail mileage reached 30,636. Ohio was the leader with 2,946 miles, but Illinois was a close second with 2,799 miles. New York had 2,682 miles, Pennsylvania was served by 2,598 miles, and Indiana was in fifth place with 2,163 miles. The Taylor-Neu map for 1861 shows a dense set of rail lines for northern Illinois and southern Wisconsin.

The boom in railroad construction in the 1850s included two lines that reached Chicago from the East. The Michigan Central and the Michigan Southern and North Indiana railroads reached Chicago on the same day in 1852, and provided service to Detroit and Toledo. The MS&NI line connected to the Cleveland and Toledo Railroad at Toledo, which provided service to Cleveland, from which a series of four short railroads provided service along Lake Erie to Buffalo and the New York Central. All of the rail lines that served Chicago were built to the standard track gauge of 4'8.5", but the series of short lines between Cleveland and Buffalo used a gauge of 4'10". Rolling stock designed for the standard gauge

Table 2.5 Railroad network of Chicago to 1900

North	Chicago & Northwestern	1855*
	Milwaukee Road	1872
Northwest	Wisconsin Central (Becomes part of Minneapolis, St. Paul & Sault St. Marie—The Soo Line.)	1886
	Chicago & North Western	1854
	Illinois Central (Route to Iowa grain district.)	1888
West	Galena & Chicago Union (Reaches Mississippi River in 1854, merges with Chicago & North Western in 1864.)	1848
	Chicago, Burlington & Quincy (Used G. & C.U. to enter Chicago until 1864, when its own entry line was built.)	1850
	Chicago & Rock Island (First railroad to cross Mississippi River, 1854.)	1852
	Milwaukee Road (Route to Milwaukee and St. Paul.)	1873
	Chicago Great Western	1887
Southwest	St. Louis, Chicago & Alton (Route to St. Louis completed in 1857.)	1854
	Norfolk & Western	1880
	Atchison, Topeka & Santa Fe	1884
	Wabash (Connection to main Wabash line from Toledo to KC at Decatur.)	1886
South	Illinois Central (Chicago-Cairo line complete, including lakefront link.)	1856
	Chicago, Danville & Vincennes (Becomes Chicago & Eastern Illinois RR, route to Evansville and St. Louis.)	1871
	Chicago, Indianapolis & Louisville (Main carrier of Indiana building stone and coal to Chicago.)	1882
Southeast	Cincinnati & Chicago (Connects to Chicago via the Pittsburgh, Ft. Wayne & Chicago. Track gauge was 4'10".)	1858
East	Michigan Central	1852
	Michigan Southern & N. Indiana (The two arrived one day apart. Link to New York with gauge change to 4'10" at Cleveland, became part of New York Central system.)	1852
	Pittsburgh, Ft. Wayne & Chicago (Becomes part of Pennsylvania RR. Track gauge was 4'10".)	1858
	Baltimore & Ohio	1874
	Grand Trunk	1880
	New York, Chicago & St. Louis (Known as The Nickel Plate, low-cost freight carrier along Great Lakes trunk line.)	1882
	Erie-Lackawanna	1883
Belt Line	Belt Railway of Chicago (Linked every major railroad and served industries in the South Chicago and Calumet districts.)	1882
	Elgin, Joliet & Eastern (Outer belt line served freight connections around city.)	1890

Sources: Compiled from Chicago Historical Society (2005), Taylor and Neu (1956), Cutler (1976, p. 118), and Miller (1996).

Notes: Railroad names as of 1861 from Taylor and Neu (1956). All track gauges 4'8.5" unless otherwise noted. Rolling stock built for standard gauge of 4'8.5" could run on 4'10" gauge track, but this was not really satisfactory.
* Date railroad entered Chicago.

could be used on the 4'10" gauge, but the results were not really completely satisfactory. This route from Chicago to New York had been established by 1856. The New York and Erie also provided service from a point on Lake Erie to New York, but it used a track gauge of 6', which meant that a "change of bulk" was required—i.e. freight had to be hauled from one railroad to the other. The "gauge wars" centered in Erie, Pennsylvania, are legendary in the annals of railroad history.

As Taylor and Neu (1956) showed, rail service from rich agricultural areas of the Old Northwest through Chicago to the east coast had been established before the outbreak of the Civil War. However, the railroads were far from an integrated system that provided efficient long-distance service. In addition to gauge differences, railroads refused to permit rolling stock owned by other railroads to travel on their lines, and local business interests favored having transshipment points in their localities because they create jobs. As Taylor and Neu (1956, p. 58) documented, as of 1861:

> The task of railroad management over the next twenty-five years was to build an integrated network. This called for action on two levels: first, the struggle with vested interests at transfer points, entailing a long-drawn-out battle between entrenched local businessmen and city fathers on the one hand and shippers and railroad interests on the other; and second, the solution of technological problems involved in the process of integration.

The Civil War years brought about some integration of the rail systems. Military necessity called for long-distance movement of troops and supplies. Rapid growth in the grain trade during these years also required more efficient long-distance service. By the end of the Civil War the grain production in the Old Northwest had outstripped the capacity of both the water and rail systems. And, after some debate, the decision was made to build the trans-continental railroad connected to the existing railroads at Omaha with the standard gauge of 4'8.5". Gradually nearly all of the railroads converted to the standard gauge. The exception was the narrow gauge (3'6") movement that took place during the 1870s and early 1880s. This exception is discussed below.

One of the innovations made during the years after the Civil War was the creation of fast freight lines. One form of this service was an administrative organization operated by the cooperating rail lines. Cars were owned by the individual rail lines, but they operated as a pool. Freight could be loaded on a car, and that car would be hauled to its final destination without interruption. The bill of lading covered the entire route. The first such service was the Red Line, which operated south of Lake Erie from Chicago to Buffalo, New York, and Boston starting in 1866. The second one was the Blue Line, which served the same cities starting in 1867—but on the northern route through Canada. The number of fast freight lines increased rapidly; Taylor and Neu (1956, p. 76) cited the existence of more than 20 fast freight lines serving Chicago in 1891. Fast freight lines had their critics. Each fast freight line had agents in the cities they served, and these men had considerable discretion over rates. Price competition was fierce—good for customers, but not so good for the railroads. Calls were made for the abandonment of fast freight lines in favor of a clearing house that would permit rail cars to operate on all railroads. This fierce competition resulted from overbuilding and led to the creation in 1887 of the Interstate Commerce Commission (ICC) to regulate railroad rates, although Taylor and Neu (1956) did not mention the formation of the ICC.

Railroad mileage in the U.S. increased from 30,636 miles in 1860 to almost 160,000 miles in 1890 as the railroad companies created a network that covered virtually the entire nation. The gauge had been standardized, many transshipment points had been eliminated, and fast freight lines provided efficient service—and Chicago was the primary central point in the system. The short book by Taylor and Neu (1956) is an impressive piece of economic history scholarship, but they overlooked one important point. Chicago remained a transshipment point. Indeed, it had become the one big transshipment point in the system. Railroads from the West stopped in Chicago, as did the railroads from the East. Freight going through Chicago had to be transferred from one railroad to another. A set of massive rail yards was built and an internal rail system with a special belt railroad was created to handle the business. Shipments of less than a carload had to be unloaded, moved by wagon (later by truck), and reloaded.

Christian Wolmar (2012, p. 70) asks the question, "Why did all railroads from both East and West stop in Chicago?" In his opinion, this is one of the great mysteries of the railway system. His answer (2012, p. 70) is as follows. "The reason they (the major trunk lines to the East) stopped there and did not progress westward was because, by the time of their arrival, the Granger railroads had already established themselves." The Granger rail lines, that served the farm country to the south, west, and northwest of Chicago, were weak and could not expand. And the trunk lines would not build lines into the territory of another railroad, partly on the grounds that they might lose the competition. Wolmar (2012, p. 70) thinks that the trunk lines probably could have won this competition, but did not try. One might add that the Illinois Central, not a weak railroad, was intent on establishing service to New Orleans—not to the East.

The story of the development of the network of railroads should sound familiar to the modern economist. The theory of network economics and the concept of network externalities were developed after Taylor and Neu (1956) published their major case study. Jeffrey Rohlfs (1974) was an early contribution to this literature; he pointed out that the utility a customer obtains from a communication service increases as others join the service. The best-known article is "Clio and the Economics of QWERTY" by Paul David (1985), and a major theoretical article by Michael Katz and Carl Shapiro (1985) appeared at the same time. A rail network provided much better service for customers than did the fragmented system, and the demands of customers eventually won the day over those vested interests that stood in the way of integrating the system. Douglas Puffert (1992, 2002) applied the theory to railway gauge standardization in the latter part of the nineteenth century. As David (1985) concluded with the typewriter keyboard,

Puffert concluded that the process was path-dependent. Specific events had long-run effects on the eventual outcome. Furthermore, it would seem that the development of Chicago as the very big transshipment point was a path-dependent outcome as well.

The story of the narrow gauge railroads provides a confirming example. Narrow-gauge advocates of the 1870s argued that these railroads were cheaper to build and maintain. Narrow-gauge equipment was lighter and cheaper to maintain as well. They pointed out that, by using longer trains, the same volume of freight could be transported. And it made sense to use the narrow gauge in mountainous areas where construction conditions were difficult and traffic was light. They had the statistics to demonstrate these propositions. However, the railroads had settled on the standard gauge by this time. Some narrow-gauge railroads were built, but soon it was discovered that travelers and shippers avoided routes with breaks in gauge. The narrow-gauge railroads had to provide standard-gauge service or lose business. As quoted by Taylor and Neu (1956, p. 65), *The Railroad Gazette*, no fan of the narrow gauge, stated (1883, p. 674) that, "the influence of this remarkable delusion has probably expended itself." David (1985) pointed out that more efficient typewriter keyboard configurations exist, but have not been adopted. So too was it with the narrow-gauge railroads.

The financial weakness of some of the Granger railroads and the hesitation of the trunk lines to build beyond Chicago suggest that some early railroads had been built ahead of demand. Indeed, the evidence provided by Robert Fogel (1960) suggests that the first trans-continental railroad falls into this category. However, Albert Fishlow (1965) found that Midwestern railroads of the 1850s were not built ahead of demand. The rapid development of the Midwest after the 1850s generated a shortage of transportation capacity. The rapid expansion of the rail system after the Civil War went hand-in-hand with the development of the economy, and eventually did produce excess capacity. During this time Chicago, the railroad capital, boomed. We turn now to the nature of that boom.

The economy of Chicago

As we have seen, by 1850 Chicago had become an important town with a canal and its first railroad. However it was still overshadowed by Cincinnati and St. Louis, and with a population of 30,000, was only a little larger than Detroit, Milwaukee, Columbus, and Cleveland. This section traces the development of the economy of Chicago from that point by focusing on the industries that were attracted to and thrived in Chicago.

Information about the industries located in Chicago in 1850 is found in the 1850 Social Statistics Census, summarized in Table 2.6. At that time most of the businesses were small shops run by artisans who made products for the local population and the farmers who brought their goods to market. For example, 41 firms made clothing, hats, gloves, etc. and 24 firms did woodwork and/or made furniture or cabinets. Shoemakers and blacksmiths were the next-most numerous businesses. Some of these businesses probably made products primarily for use

Table 2.6 Products of industry in Chicago, 1850 (number of producers)

Clothing, hats, millinery, gloves	41
Furniture, cabinets, woodwork	24
Shoes and boots	20
Blacksmith	17
Metal work	15
Wagons, carriages	11
Shingles	11
Cigars, food/confections, barrels, alcohol, agricultural implements*	5–10
Guns, stone products, watches, carpenters, foundry, candles, bricks, machines, soap, painter, harness maker, saddles	2–4
Glass, baskets, pianos, trunks, washboards, coffins, matches, bowls, rope, pottery, boilers, flour, stoves, lancers, vinegar, photos, bookbinder, upholstery	1

Source: 1850 Social Statistics Census for Cook County, IL.

Note
*Includes the McCormick Reaper Works

outside the city. In particular, the McCormick Reaper Works had moved from Cincinnati to Chicago in 1847 because the inventor and proprietor could foresee that wheat production would become a large crop in the Chicago area and beyond. This company became Chicago's first major manufacturer. Four other firms were making agricultural implements, including the plows that were needed to turn fields of prairie grass into farmland. Another 11 companies were making wagons and carriages, including one that listed itself as a wagon factory. Only seven firms were listed as producing food products, including confections, likely because people of that day cooked mainly from scratch. There was but one coffin maker (although some of the cabinet makers may have made coffins too). Table 2.6 provides a fascinating snapshot of the nature of an urban economy in 1850.

The outstanding study by Cronon (1991) concentrates on three major Chicago industries—the grain trade, lumber, and meat. These three were the primary products of the great hinterland of Chicago, so Cronon labels the city "nature's metropolis." All three of these industries relied, each in its own way, on the transportation system that had Chicago at its center. The next paragraphs will not repeat Cronon's detailed discussions of these three industries, but rather will concentrate on the importance for each one of location factors and the transportation system.

The grain trade, both actual and potential, was the basic reason for the construction of the canal and the first railroads. By the 1850s migration to central and northern Illinois, northern Indiana, southern Wisconsin, and eastern Iowa had accelerated and market-oriented farm output grew rapidly. Both the canal and the early railroads brought this growing output to Chicago. The primary crops were wheat and corn, although barley, oats, rye, and other crops also were cultivated. Some of the farm implements needed were being made in Chicago and shipped out to the farmers. Initially the grain crops were shipped in bags that tended to pile up at various locations in Chicago before being transported by lake boat or rail to the East. This "system" (or lack thereof) was soon overwhelmed by the volume of output, and the need for a more efficient method for handling the grain was obvious. The first steam-powered grain elevator was built in Buffalo in 1842, but the grain elevator was quickly adopted and refined in Chicago. The grain elevator was a crucial innovation that created an economy of scale in handling grain and permitted the use of the economies of scale available in the rail system, and so reduced transport costs. The first steam-powered grain elevator in Chicago was built in 1848, and by 1857 Chicago had a dozen elevators located along the banks of the Chicago River. Early photos of Chicago in 1857 show the Illinois Central terminal and rail yard along with two massive grain elevators at the mouth of the Chicago River. Grain elevators contained vertical silos, one for each type of grain that was handled. Steam power was used to raise the grain from the rail cars or canal boats to the top of the elevator. The lake boat or rail car that would be used to ship the grain to the East was then positioned at the bottom of the silo, and gravity loaded the cargo aboard.

The grain elevator turned grain into a standardized commodity. The Chicago Board of Trade was founded in 1848 as a voluntary organization of grain traders. Arguably their first really important action took place in 1856, when they first promulgated standard grades for wheat. Wheat was to be graded according to type and quality before being regarded as ready for shipment from Chicago. Grain of equal type and grade was stored in its own elevator silo, and the purchaser bought grain of that type and quality—not the grain from a particular farmer's sack. During the remaining years of the 1850s grading standards were refined and extended to corn, oats, barley, and rye. Then in 1859 the State of Illinois adopted a law that gave the right to the Board of Trade to hire inspectors whose judgments would have the force of law on the Board members, which now included virtually all of the traders in Chicago. Charges of corruption by inspectors and grain elevator operators led the State of Illinois to adopt the Warehouse Act of 1871, which moved the work of grain grading to a state agency and regulated the grain elevators. This law also included the requirement that a grain producer could require the railroad to deliver grain output to the elevator of the producer's choice, even if that required construction of additional links in the rail network. (The U.S. Department of Agriculture took over the mission of grading grain in the twentieth century, but the profession of grain inspector remains a quintessential Chicago occupation.)

As Cronon (1991, p. 120) noted, by 1859 Chicago had created the system for the grain trade that involved the grain elevator, the grading system, and the central market for grain trading governed by the Board of Trade. Of course, the fourth part of the system was the transportation network that had created the industry. Cain (1985) used data from the Chicago Board of Trade to show that shipments of grain from Chicago grew rapidly from 1854 to 1871; 9.1 percent per annum for corn, for example. Receipts of grains exceeded shipments because Chicago itself was a major consumer. But now transactions were carried out in a new manner. Sellers of grain were given receipts for their grain (of a particular type and quality), and these receipts were sold to buyers. However, very soon the receipts were being sold to traders on the Board of Trade who sold those receipts to other traders, and not to ultimate users of the grain. The market for grain had been turned into a market in which pieces of paper were bought and sold.

Then another remarkable transportation system arrived. The first telegraph lines reached the city in 1848, so orders for grain from New York and responses from Chicago could be transacted quickly. Those orders were often for future delivery, not "spot" sales. The telegraph office played a critical role in the operation of the Board of Trade in its new trading room in 1860. Purchasers of grain wished to ensure that supplies were going to be there when needed, and wished to avoid the problem of storage. Thus the futures markets in grain were born and emerged in the late 1860s. A buyer and seller wrote a contract for grain to be delivered on a date in the future at a certain price. These contracts were required to be for standardized quantities. The contract had a market value and could be bought and sold at will. Very soon traders realized that these contracts did not need to involve actual movement of grain at all; when the exercise date arrived, the difference between the contract price and the "spot" price would be exchanged. In 1844 Samuel F. B. Morse had sent his famous message "What hath God wrought" from Washington, DC to his assistant in Baltimore to demonstrate his invention. What indeed.

Chicago was home to the nation's largest lumber market. The rapidly developing farm country, with its system of towns and cities, needed lumber in massive quantities. Little lumber was available nearby, but nature had supplied a great supply of excellent lumber in the form of the white pine forests of northern Wisconsin and Michigan. Lake Michigan provided the route for transporting the rough lumber to Chicago, which provided the port for the lumber ships. And the canal and the rail system provided access to farm country. Cronon (1991, p. 155) noted that the opening of the Illinois and Michigan Canal in 1848 produced a doubling of lumber receipts in one year.

Here is how the system worked. Trees were felled in the winter months and positioned near the frozen rivers and streams. The felled trees moved down river to sawmills on the Wisconsin and Michigan coasts in the spring, and the rough lumber was transported to Chicago by lake ship. Upon arrival in Chicago the lumber merchants would purchase an entire shipload of rough lumber at the dock. The ability to sell an entire shipload easily was a critical feature of the Chicago lumber market for lumber producers, who needed to repay the loans taken out to produce the lumber. Indeed, Chicago was the central source of work crews (farm workers looking for winter employment) and the loans needed to operate the business. From the docks on the Chicago River, the rough lumber was moved to the lumber firms located on the south branch of the river. There rough lumber was sawed into the standard lumber sizes needed for the construction of houses, barns, fences, and so on. Lumber was sold to the lumber dealers out in the farm country, as well as lumber dealers in the Chicago area for local use. In fact, later in the nineteenth century Sears, Roebuck & Co. sold disassembled houses that would arrive on a flat car (with instructions). One could order a house from the Sears catalog, a very useful publication that also found its way into many outhouses of the day. Many of those Sears houses still stand.

Cronon (1991, p. 204) provided a chart that shows lumber receipts in Chicago from 1847 to 1900. Hoyt (1933, p. 48) stated that lumber receipts had jumped from 7.5 to 32 million board feet from 1843 to 1847, reached 457 million board feet in 1856, but fell to 279 million board feet in the depression of 1858. Cronon's chart shows that lumber receipts averaged about 1.1 billion board feet from 1868 to 1877. Then receipts almost doubled again to an average of around 2 billion board feet from 1881 to 1891. Receipts fell to 1.5 billion board feet during the remaining years of the 1890s, the result of the depression in the early part of the decade and the exhaustion of the supply. About one-half of the lumber received in Chicago was used locally, except during the building booms after the Great Chicago Fire of 1871 and during the late 1880s. By the 1890s the industry had moved on to the forests of western Wisconsin and Minnesota (remember the Paul Bunyon statue in Minnesota?), and the transportation routes used by the lumber industry moved to the North and West as Minneapolis-St. Paul became a rail center in its own right. The sandy soils of northern Wisconsin, Michigan, and Minnesota are not productive farmlands. This area that provided the lumber for building the Midwest and beyond became a problem known as the economically depressed "cutover region." Not all structures in the region were built of lumber, of course. Bricks can be made from local sources, as can sod houses. My father began his career as a grain inspector in Illinois in the early 1940s, and his first supervisor was a man who was born in Nebraska in about 1900 and grew up in a sod house.

The meat industry is the third part of Cronon's natural triad. The shipping of livestock and meat packing were part of the Chicago economy from the beginning because farmers could turn corn into a more valuable and less bulky commodity by feeding it to hogs and cattle. Several small stockyards were developed around the city, and each had only one or two rail connections by the mid-1850s. Chicagoans were used to having livestock being driven through the streets of the city as drovers moved animals to a stockyard and from stockyard to stockyard. The huge demand by the Union Army during the Civil War meant that this inefficient situation needed to change. The railroads stepped in to solve the problem and make Chicago into the greatest livestock market in the world. The nine largest railroads, along with the local pork packer's group, created the Union Stock Yards in 1865. The scattered stockyards were consolidated into one very big facility. Union Stock Yards (which closed for good in 1971) was located four miles south of downtown, and was furnished with connections to all of the railroads. The stockyards contained 2,300 pens, each assigned to one of four large shipping and receiving yards. A rail line surrounded the stockyards so that shippers could unload and load from every part of the facility. The stockyards as an enterprise initially made money by charging shippers for feed. The Stockyards Exchange Building was where suppliers met demanders and arranged for the sale and shipment of livestock or packed meat to the cities in the East. But note the critical active role that was played by the railroads in providing Chicago with a major industry, as well as enhancing their own businesses.

Cain (1985) used data from the Chicago Board of Trade to show that shipments of cured meat from Chicago grew rapidly from 1854 to 1871: 21.2 percent per annum. As noted above, receipts of grains exceeded shipments because Chicago itself was a major consumer. Receipts of lumber exceeded shipments because lumber was used to build much of Chicago. Cured meats and lard were the only food products tracked by the Board of Trade for which shipments far exceeded receipts in 1871—because Chicago was in the business of turning livestock into cured meat.

The creation of the Union Stockyards was only the first major step in the transformation of an industry and a large section of the nation as well. First consider cattle. As settlers moved beyond Iowa and Missouri, they found that the more arid land was not well suited to the grain products of the farm belt, but that cattle could be reared on the range. There were two obstacles to such an enterprise—the bison and the Native Americans who depended upon the bison. With the coming of the railroads bison hunters became numerous, but as Cronon (1991, p. 216) put it, in 1870 "all hell broke loose." Philadelphia tanners had invented a method for turning bison hides into leather that had many uses. Bison had become a commodity that could be shipped by rail. The slaughter began in earnest from the great plains of the North to Texas, and by 1883 the bison had all but disappeared. The Native Americans were the other victims of this slaughter. The Indian wars of the 1870s can be seen as the last, desperate attempts by a starving people to preserve their old way of life. Once again note the important role played by the railroads in these momentous events.

So during the 1870s and 1880s the way was cleared for the cattle business of the West. Initially cattle were driven on the hoof from the ranches to a town such as Abilene, Kansas. The western adventure story usually ends there, but why Abilene? Of course, Abilene was the end of the rail line that led to the feedlots in Iowa and Illinois, which led to the Union Stockyards. Cattle that had walked long distances needed to be fattened up, so the business of cattle feeding was a necessary intermediate step. The cattle business with its headquarters in Chicago expanded to include the area from West Texas to Montana. The livestock industry is a major reason why Cronon appealed to von Thünen's isolated state model, in which the intensity of land use and land rents decrease as distance from the city increases. In modern times this model has been used to understand the land use and land rent patterns inside a city.

Allan Pred (1966) proposed a model of cumulative causation to explain urban industrial growth in the U.S. up through 1914, and Chicago is one of his main examples. The basic idea is that industrial growth in a city begets more industrial growth through a virtuous circle similar to the one suggested by Myrdal (1944). The factors involved include economies of scale at the individual firm level, the development of a workforce accustomed to manufacturing work, the spillover of knowledge from one firm to another in a local industry, the growth of suppliers and business customers (backward and forward linkages of industries, including improvements in transportation), the development of knowledge of local industries among local bankers so that lending can be done efficiently, and technical change that Pred measured with data on patents granted to persons in a city. As an example of the linkages among industries, the development of steel production and continued improvements in steel enabled the railroads to become more efficient and expand, which expanded the market for Chicago steel. Pred (1966) found that Chicago was a leader in patents per manufacturing employee. The figures for patents per manufacturing employee in the leading cities are as follows:

	1860	1880	1900
New York	60	59	43
Chicago	73	62	50
Boston	65	71	53
Philadelphia	21	29	32
St. Louis	37	41	37

Other industries beyond Cronon's three quickly took advantage of locating in Chicago. Manufacturing employment in Chicago was just 5,450 in 1860, but the Civil War boom brought that total to 31,006 in 1870. The following decade added another 141 percent to the 1870 figure, bringing total manufacturing employment in 1880 to 74,799 and gross value of output to $250 million. The Census of Manufactures for 1880 shows that the leading Chicago industries in 1880 in terms of gross value of output are:

Meat packing	$85 million
Clothing	$19 million
Iron and steel	$10 million
Foundry and machine shop products	$9 million
Beer and liquor	$8 million
Printing	$6 million
Agricultural implements	$3 million

Then manufacturing employment in Chicago took off in earnest, reaching 170,000 in 1890 and 297,624 in 1900. The leading Chicago industries in 1900 in terms of approximate gross value of output from Dixon Fox (1920) are:

Food products	$327 million
Iron and steel	$115 million
Textiles	$40 million
Land vehicles and equipment	$40 million
Paper and printing	$40 million

Other industries in Chicago included Liquor and beverages; Leather and leather products; Glass, clay and stone products; Tobacco products; Chemicals; Lumber; and Metal (not iron). Note that Iron and steel had moved up to second place among Chicago industries. The gross value of output for Chicago exceeded the gross value of output for the entire state of Ohio—and every other state in the Midwest.

The food products industry was, by far, the leader in gross value of output. And the leader in the food products industry was Meat packing. The Stockyards provided the animals for Armour, Swift, and the other pioneers in the industry that mainly located their meat packing plants just to the West of the Stockyards. The meat packing industry initially was dominated by pork, which could be preserved by salting or smoking. But consumers preferred their beef fresh. The extensive use of the refrigerated rail car by Gustavus Swift in the late 1870s was a major breakthrough that changed the industry from one in which live cattle were shipped by rail to the East to an industry that shipped packed meat.

The iron industry was present in Chicago from the early 1840s, but steel manufacturing did not arrive until 1865 when steel rails began to be produced. The industry was dominated by pig iron producers until 1880, when the North Chicago Rolling Mill Company, the first producer of steel rails, opened a plant on the Calumet River in South Chicago. The federal government began to improve Calumet Harbor in 1869, its wharves were in operation by 1871, and this facility began to supplant the Chicago River as the major port of Chicago. This location had excellent transportation connections by water and by rail. Iron ore was shipped from the Mesabi Range in Minnesota, limestone was widely available, and anthracite coal was shipped from Appalachia via Ohio lake ports and rail lines. Steel is an input oriented, weight-losing industry. Production tends to be located at the points that minimize the cost of assembling the bulky inputs. The industry grew rapidly in the Calumet area, and concentrated initially on the production of steel rails for the rapidly expanding railroad network. So not only was the Calumet area an excellent place to assemble inputs, it also had the transportation network that could be used to ship the output to the customers. The Illinois Steel Company was formed in 1889 as a merger of North Chicago Rolling Mills and two other firms, and the company built the famous South Chicago Steel Works on 260 acres adjacent to Lake Michigan and the Calumet River. By 1893 Illinois Steel employed over 10,000 men on its coal lands and in its plants. This company became part of U.S. Steel in 1901. U.S. Steel began building the town of Gary, Indiana, in 1906.

The McCormick Reaper Works, which moved to Chicago in 1847, were revolutionary in more ways than one. The mechanical reaper was a major technological advance for farmers, but the product had to be marketed and shipped to the customers—and often credit had to be advanced. The business really grew with the construction of the railroads in the 1850s. The John S. Wright Company, producers of reapers and mowers, was founded in Chicago in 1853. Pred (1966) showed that the industry consisted of four establishments with 294 wage earners in 1860 and value added in current dollars of $103,000 per establishment. In the early days of the industry the reapers were sold primarily to farmers who could be reached by water transportation. By 1860 reapers were being sold widely in Illinois, Indiana, Iowa, and Wisconsin and shipped by rail. In order to market reapers McCormick began publishing detailed advertisements in the *Chicago Defender* and other newspapers, and hired a network of agents who were located out in the farm belt. In 1900 the industry included just six establishments, but had 10,245 employees and $2.33 million in value added per establishment (current dollars). Indeed, the rail network centered on Chicago changed the nature of wholesale and retail trade in the region. Wholesale firms congregated in Chicago because they could use the railroads to ship their wares, and retailers in the smaller cities and towns could travel often to Chicago to replenish their stocks of goods. Prior to the railroads retailers in the Old Northwest had to make one or at most two trips to large wholesale centers and purchase what they guessed would be the stocks needed for the season. Now they could operate with smaller amounts of capital and be more responsive to their customers.

Not everything went well for McCormick. His factory on the north bank of the Chicago River was destroyed by the Great Chicago Fire of 1871. He built a new factory on the southwest side of the city adjacent to the Chicago River. The rapid growth of industry and railroads had created a mass of urban industrial workers. Chicago workers played a major role in the labor movement in those days (and in later days as well). There was a fractured labor movement at that time, consisting of three types of labor organizations. As Joseph Rayback (1966) explained, the three types were socialists and anarchists on the left, the Knights of Labor (and similar organizations in favor of "one big union") in the middle, and individual trade unions on the right. A general strike had begun on May 1, 1886 as part of the campaign for the eight-hour day. McCormick's workers went on strike on May 3. Two workers were killed by the police in the ensuing demonstration, and anarchists called for a meeting in Haymarket Square for the following evening. Mayor Carter Harrison attended the meeting, and concluded that the crowd was orderly. He left and on his way home he ordered the riot squad to be assembled at a nearby police station to discharge its reserve force for the night. However, the captain ignored that order, sent the squad to the meeting, and ordered the crowd to disperse. An argument between the captain and the speaker began, and a bomb exploded in Haymarket Square, killing one policeman. The police opened fire, and the fire was returned. Rayback (1966, p. 167) stated that, "About ten people were killed and another fifty were wounded." This was the famous Haymarket incident. The story has been told many times. The bomb thrower was never identified, but eight anarchists were convicted because they had advocated violence. Seven men were sentenced to death and one man was sentenced to prison. Four men were hanged and one man committed suicide before the sentence could be carried out. The other two facing death had their sentences reduced to life in prison. The three surviving anarchists were pardoned by Governor Altgeld in 1893 in one of the most courageous acts by an American politician. The speaker who argued with the police captain was one of those pardoned. The general strike on May 1 and the Haymarket incident are the origin of May Day, a day that is celebrated mainly by socialists around the world (but not so much in Chicago).

George Pullman began to build his rail car plant and the town of Pullman in 1880, near the North Chicago Rolling Mill plant. Both the town and parts of the plant still exist on the far south side of the city, and have just been declared a National Historic Site. The Pullman company was very successful with its Pullman Palace Cars and the Pullman Porters who worked on them. The cars were leased to the railroads, and the Pullman Porters were Pullman employees. However, the Pullman saga is one of tragedy as well. Workers were required to live in the town of Pullman, and the company controlled wages, rents, taxes, utility bills, and the prices of consumer goods. During the depression of the 1890s Pullman in 1893 decided to cut wages by 22 percent, but not rents and prices. The strike and riots of 1894 were the result. A boycott of railroads that used Pullman cars was organized in sympathy with the Pullman workers by the American Railway Union (ARU), a new industrial union. President Cleveland sent federal troops. Injunctions against interference with the U.S. mail were issued on the notion that the boycott was a "conspiracy in restraint of trade." This was the first use of the Sherman Anti-trust Act of 1890, and it was against a labor union. The Pullman strike, along with other defeats in the early 1890s (including the famous Homestead strike near Pittsburgh against the Carnegie Steel Company in 1892), set industrial unionization back. Over the next few years the American Federation of Labor, founded by Samuel Gompers in 1886 and consisting of the more conservative craft unions, emerged as the leading labor organization.

Financing is required for economic development, but chaos perhaps is the best word to describe the state of banking in the U.S. from 1830 to 1863, when the National Banking System was established. As financial historian F. Cyril James (1938, p. 293) put it:

> In each state, the legislature had created banks of various kinds, and the Supreme Court of the United States had declared that those banks could issue circulating notes without, in any way, violating the federal Constitution. As a result, paper money in thousands of different forms had come into existence, each note varying from all the others in value even when they were nominally of the same denomination. Many of them had no acceptability outside the state in which they were issued. Congress, in fact, had so far abrogated its monetary powers that, recognizing the wretched quality of "heterogeneous rags," it refused to accept them. For the operations of the federal government, it established the Independent Treasury, which operated solely on the basis of metallic currency, but Congress did nothing at all to provide a sound currency for the nation as a whole.

In simple terms, in those days a borrower walked out the door of the lending bank with a pile of currency printed by the bank. In Illinois banks were chartered individually by act of the legislature, the first Bank of Illinois in 1818, and another followed in 1819. The first bank failed in 1823, and the second one had already failed in 1821. A few more banks were chartered in the 1820s and 1830s, but most banks in Chicago, including the Second State Bank, failed after the financial panic of 1837 because they suffered runs in which holders of their notes demanded more metallic currency than the banks had on hand or were able to acquire. The void was filled by uncharted "private" banks that could not issue currency, but would supply currency from banks in other states. One George Smith founded a private bank in Chicago in 1839 that circulated "certificates of deposit" from his insurance company in Wisconsin that were redeemable in specie (but illegal). James (1938, p. 203) noted that George Smith's money was very popular through the 1840s and into the 1850s because of Smith's wealth and reputation. At the end of the 1850s there were no incorporated banks in Illinois. The State of Illinois adopted a "free banking" law in 1851 that permitted the secretary of state to issue incorporation charters for banks (instead of requiring an act of the legislature for each bank). The opportunity to form banks in growing Chicago led to the creation of ten incorporated banks by the end of 1854. These banks could issue notes in the amount of U.S. bonds and bonds of other states deposited with the state auditor. James (1938, p. 220) reported that these banks had issued $728,000 in notes based on $890,000 in bonds deposited and had specie reserves of $196,000. As of 1854 Mr. Smith's illegal "money" had been retired. However, by 1856 only three of the incorporated banks had survived. Twenty-five "private" banks had stepped in, but there was another serious dearth of banking services in Chicago. Another financial panic occurred in 1857 which caused two of the three incorporated banks and many of the private banks to fail. The remaining incorporated bank, the Marine Bank, failed at the beginning of the Civil War because it was unable to repay funds that had been deposited. Chicago was reduced to relying on small private banks with no power to issue notes. James (1938, pp. 667–671) listed 87 private banks, note brokers, and real estate brokers. The Illinois experiment with free banking in the 1850s is considered to be a complete failure.

The National Banking Act of 1863 created a system of national banks supervised by the U.S. Comptroller of the Currency. National banks could issue national currency equal to 90 percent of the value of U.S. bonds deposited with the Comptroller. This currency was redeemable at the bank's place of business in "lawful" money, which at the time meant the Greenbacks issued by the U.S. Treasury to pay for the Civil War. Greenbacks were legal tender for all but import duties and interest on public debt, so they were the first paper currency with uniform value throughout the nation. National banks were required to hold reserves in Greenbacks. The notes issued by state banks were taxed out of existence. This act was a serious attempt to provide the nation with a reliable banking system, but the provision for a lender of last resort to handle bank failures was weak.[3]

Chicago, with its non-existent system of incorporated state banks and large number of private "banks," greeted the new system with enthusiasm. Thirteen national banks were chartered in Chicago between 1863 and 1865, and the number increased to 19 by 1871. The first of these national banks was the First National Bank of Chicago, the venerable Chicago bank that survived as an independent bank until it merged with another bank in 1998. Nineteen Chicago banks (the 13 national banks plus six others) created the Chicago Clearing House Association in 1865 to facilitate inter-bank transactions. By 1871 27 state banks were incorporated in Chicago as well, but these banks could not issue notes that served as currency. Instead checks written on deposits in these banks began to emerge as an important part of the supply of money. There was no law that prohibited these banks from engaging in deposit banking. These national and state banks, along with the private banks, provided Chicago with a system that was adequate to support the currency and credit needs of the rapidly growing region and metropolitan area.

The last decades of the nineteenth century saw Chicago emerge as the nation's second-leading center of banking (second to New York, of course). Deposits in

Chicago banks were made by banks in its banking hinterland, which by 1880 had extended from Cleveland to Denver. James (1938, p. 444) found that in 1881 the First National Bank of Chicago held deposits from 80 national banks in 15 states. As Cronon (1991, p. 305) stated, "Whatever the city's population, or transport linkages, or natural advantages, the bottom line was that Chicago controlled and had access to more capital. That more than anything else placed it atop the regional system of cities."

Research by Michael Conzen (1977) showed that the banking system developed a four-level hierarchy between 1880 and 1910 in which banks established correspondent links to banks at the next level higher up. With the exception of New York, Chicago had, by far, the largest number of links to other cities. Conzen (1977) placed Chicago at the top of the second level of the hierarchy. Indeed, Conzen (1977, p. 104) found that in 1910 Chicago had almost as many links to second-order banking cities as did New York (17 versus 20). Only New York, Chicago, and St. Louis were regarded by Conzen (1977, p. 104) as having central reserve status in 1910. One might argue that Chicago was the only second-order banking city, and that there really were five levels to the hierarchy. Conzen also argues that urban hierarchies are complex and that many nonhierarchical linkages exist as well.[4] Data compiled by Hoyt (1933, p. 489) show bank clearings in Chicago:

Year	Bank clearings ($ billions)
1870	0.81
1880	1.73
1890	4.09
1900	6.80

Financial services in Chicago also included a stock exchange and insurance companies. A stock exchange was formed in 1865, but did not last. The Chicago Stock Exchange that survives was founded in 1882. Chicago was home to fire and casualty insurance companies, most of which were wiped out in 1871 by the Great Chicago Fire. However, the industry came back strongly after Chicago imposed fire regulations.

What is close to the ultimate in responsiveness to customers was begun in Chicago in 1872, when A. Montgomery Ward invented the mail-order business. The railroads had, among many things, greatly improved the service of the U.S. mail. Ward began to print his catalog and mail it out. He bypassed the retailers and sold directly to the customers at lower prices because he bought in large quantities for cash. Ward had arrived in Chicago in 1865 to work for the innovative retail firm of Potter Palmer, Marshall Field, and Levi Leiter. As Cronon (1991, p. 336) recounts, Ward started his own mail-order business in 1872 with 163 items listed on a single sheet of paper. The response was "enthusiastic," and by the end of 1874 the catalog was a 72-page booklet. By the end of the 1880s the catalog was 540 pages and offered over 24,000 items, and in 1900 the catalog of 1,200 pages described some

70,000 items. In 1900 2,000 clerks handled orders from two million customers. Sears, Roebuck and Company was founded in 1890 in Minneapolis, and the company moved to Chicago in 1894. At that time the Sears-Roebuck catalog was 500 pages. Rural free delivery began in 1896; this service further stimulated the mail-order business. The catalog included various types of balloon frame houses, sold with all needed pieces (and instructions). Miller (1996, p. 250) noted that by 1900 Sears advertised that enough houses had been sold to house 25,000 people.[5] Wards and Sears-Roebuck had become vast department stores. The motto of Sears-Roebuck was, "We sell everything," (except fresh fruit, vegetables, and live animals). As the central point in the railroad network, products were shipped from the East and other locations to Chicago wholesalers, who moved the goods down the urban hierarchy to the customers. Thus did Chicago become the major center for wholesale trade in the Midwest (and beyond) that sold "everything."

The tremendous success of Wards and Sears-Roebuck created demand for manufactured products of every sort. Chicago became a center of light manufacturing of apparel, shoes, kitchen appliances, hardware, and many other products. Many of these firms were located on the south and west sides of Chicago. One of those manufacturers was the Kimball Piano and Organ Company: Van Allen Bradley (1957) gives a history of the company. On November 17, 1857 William Wallace Kimball traded some land in Iowa for four pianos owned by a piano dealer in Chicago. He began a piano dealership in downtown Chicago, selling and renting pianos made by various eastern manufacturers (including Steinway). The idea was to sell pianos to the rapidly growing population of the Midwest. Kimball became dominant among the 15 musical instrument dealers in Chicago. Then his store was completely destroyed in the Great Chicago Fire of 1871—but his credit was good and he was able to restock in makeshift accommodations. The business recovered, but the panic of 1873 set the company back for several years. Business was booming by 1880, when the company sold 12,000 reed organs and pianos. At this point Kimball worked to fulfill his dream of manufacturing his own organs and pianos. The first organ and piano factory opened in 1881, and it was followed by a piano factory in 1887. The Kimball organs were successful from the start, but Kimball upright pianos were not well-regarded until they were redesigned and made in the newer factory. During this period Kimball geared up to sell his pianos. Among other things, in 1885 he hired one John McDonald, a concert pianist from Waterford, Ireland, to demonstrate the product and teach piano playing. This pianist is my great-grandfather, the man who brought my family to Chicago in 1885. The company moved its offices and warerooms to a prominent downtown location on State Street in 1887. This building also included the first "Kimball Hall," a concert hall with a seating capacity of 500. Kimball pianos became a great success in the music world, and were featured in concerts in the Auditorium Theatre—Chicago's premier concert venue built in 1889. Grand pianos were added in 1891, the same year in which the company moved its downtown offices, warerooms, and concert hall to a new seven-story building on Wabash Avenue. This building still stands with W.W. Kimball painted in large lettering still visible on the south outside wall. This building now houses the DePaul University School of Law.

Spatial patterns in Chicago

This section introduces some basic measures of the spatial patterns of Chicago that will be used throughout the book, and then describes some important historical developments related to the changes in those patterns. The fundamental idea is that a growing city "grows up" and "grows out." Growing up is reflected in increasing land values and building heights in and near the central business district, and growing out is shown in land value increases and occupation of sites by urbanites farther away from the center.

Hoyt (1933) provided a detailed history of land values in Chicago, and his estimates can be used to illustrate the changes in land values at different distances from the center. Table 2.7 displays nominal land values per acre for the central peak and at distances of three and five miles from the center for 1857, 1873, and 1892. Peak land value increased enormously as downtown Chicago became the commercial and financial center for a large portion of the nation. The development of the skyscraper building in Chicago is discussed below.

Table 2.7 displays estimates of land values for different Chicago locations— lakefront North and South, inland North, West, and inland South. Land values on and near the lakefront consistently had higher land values compared to the nearby inland locations, and during the nineteenth century the land values on the south side were higher than those on the north side. Lower land values on the north side can be attributed to the fact that one had to cross the Chicago River to reach downtown. The river was a very busy port, so the draw bridges were almost always in the "up" position to permit ships to pass, making access from the north side very difficult. Industrial and commercial development was taking place primarily on the south side (stockyards, packing plants, steel mills, and so on). Also, the near south side became the location of choice for the mansions of the business leaders of Chicago. Table 2.7 shows that land values dropped off sharply

Table 2.7 Land values in Chicago (per acre)

Distance to Peak	1857	1873	1892
Peak	$25,000	$70,000	$1,000,000
Three miles			
Lakefront North	$5,000	$25,000	$30,000
Inland North	1,400	10,000	11,000
West	2,000	18,500	30,000
Inland South	4,000	15,000	25,000
Lakefront South	7,500	40,000	150,000
Five miles			
Lakefront, North	$800	$7,000	$20,000
Inland North	400	2,000	4,000
West	300	3,000	18,500
Inland South	500	6,000	12,500
Lakefront South	600	20,000	60,000

Source: Compiled from Hoyt (1933, pp. 114, 187, and 221).

with distance to the center. Indeed, the central land value of $1 million per acre in 1892 reflects the fact that a location in the central business district conferred great advantages for the commercial, legal, and financial firms of the day. Land values in 1892 were a very high plateau in the center, and can be likened to falling off a cliff a short distance away from the center because the downtown area was hemmed in by the Chicago River on to the North and West and by rail yards to the South. Land values at three miles (away from Lake Michigan) were only $11,000 to $30,000 per acre (1.1 percent to 3 percent of the peak value), depending on direction. Land values on the lakefront to the South took a large jump between 1873 and 1892 because the first rapid transit line was being built in that direction for the World's Columbian Exposition of 1893.

Hoyt (1933, p. 484) provided population estimates by mile zones for 1870, 1880, 1890, and 1900. These data are displayed in Table 2.8. Given that the figures are all round numbers, it is obvious that these are only estimates—perhaps rough estimates. In addition, spatial patterns of the population can be described by a simple device—the population density gradient. Population density is measured as resident population per square mile, where the measure of area includes all uses of land. This figure is known as gross population density, in contrast to net population density that is population per square mile of land devoted only to residential use. The mile zone data are converted to gross population density, and estimates of the density gradient are shown in Table 2.8. The gradients are estimated omitting the density in the 0–1 mile zone because land in this zone increasingly was given over to non-residential use.

Note that the population in the 0–1 mile zone changed very little over the 30 years, and that population in the next zone (1–2 miles) stopped increasing after 1890. Population growth was very rapid in all of the other mile zones. During the 1870s the increase in population was being accommodated near the center of

Table 2.8 Population in Chicago

Mile zone	1870	1880	1890	1900
0–1	70,000	70,000	80,000	80,000
1–2	115,000	170,000	250,000	250,000
2–3	70,000	140,000	303,000	400,000
3–4	35,000	87,000	175,000	295,000
4–5	20,000	50,000	100,000	180,000
5–6	1,000	10,000	70,000	175,000
6–7		2,000	48,000	105,000
7–8		1,000	30,000	95,000
8–9			25,000	55,000
9–10			15,000	30,000
10–11			5,000	20,000
11–12			2,000	10,000
12–13				5,000
Density gradient	−127%/mi.	−120%/mi.	−66%/mi.	−55%/mi.

Source: Hoyt (1933, p. 484).

the city up to a distance of about five miles. The Great Chicago Fire of 1871 mainly destroyed the downtown area, but it also made 90,000 out of 320,000 people homeless. Housing was constructed with smaller lots and at greater heights near the center to handle the population growth of the 1870s. In contrast, the density gradient fell from 120 percent to 55 percent per mile between 1880 and 1900. Even taller residential buildings were built near the center, but also population density at 5–6 miles multiplied by seven times and by 24 times in the 6–7 mile zone. And some people whom Hoyt (1933) considered to be living in the urban area were located perhaps 10–12 miles from the center. What changed? Chicago developed a sophisticated mass transit system during the 1880s and 1890s that greatly reduced the time needed to travel to the central business district. The effect of this system is seen clearly in the data. Also, the development of employment centers brought urban workers to live at such great distance from downtown.

The population data in Table 2.8 fail to provide details about the nature of population growth. As is well known, most of the population growth consisted of immigrants from abroad. These immigrants tended to cluster in their own ethnic communities—German, Irish, Italian, Swedish, Czech, and so on. Wealthier Chicagoans established up-scale neighborhoods on the near north, west, and south sides. These details primarily are the province of urban sociology, but one pattern emerged that is more purely economic in nature. As people found work and their incomes increased, they tended to buy or rent new houses that were being built at progressively greater distances from downtown. Developers created subdivisions that catered to the new middle class, many of whom worked in the offices and shops in the downtown area. This ability to "suburbanize" was, of course, facilitated by the expanding and improving transit system. Some households had started to suburbanize in the 1850s along the main rail lines to places such as Evanston to the North and Hyde Park to the South.

The movement of employment away from the central area of Chicago began very early. A major example was the founding of the Union Stockyards in 1865, which created a major center of employment at the existing fringe of the urban area. The McCormick Harvesting Machine Company moved to a new plant in 1873 that was located about three miles southwest of downtown. The steel plants and other industrial facilities in the Lake Calumet area (south Chicago) and the Pullman Palace Car factory and town are other examples of major employment centers miles from downtown in the nineteenth century. The federal government began to improve Calumet Harbor in 1869, and the first cargo ships arrived in 1871. These sites had immediate access to the railroad network. Population clusters grew up around the employment centers.

Development in the central business district before and after 1880 was distinctly different as well. After the Great Chicago Fire of 1871 the downtown area was rebuilt with the same type of buildings as before—four- to five-story walk-up buildings. Beginning in 1882 these buildings were steadily replaced by "skyscrapers," defined here as elevator buildings of at least ten stories. The story of how downtown Chicago became the "Loop"—the first downtown dominated by skyscrapers—involves several technological breakthroughs. These are as follows, in rough chronological order:

- Technical changes improved travel times in the city. The first horse-drawn trolleys were introduced in 1859. These were replaced by cable cars beginning in 1882. Then electric trolleys were introduced beginning in the early 1890s. The first elevated line was built for the World's Columbian Exposition of 1893, and the Loop elevated and was completed in 1897. These developments reduced commuting times dramatically, permitting workers to live at some distance away from the downtown jobs. Rapid transit also meant that downtown could become a mecca for retailing in the growing city.
- Bell invented the telephone in 1876. This device meant that a company's office workers could communicate with its production facilities from a distance. Office workers could now be located downtown, the better to meet with firms that provide legal, financial, freight, and other providers of business services. Firms could also house showrooms and sales forces downtown. For example, the Kimball company, discussed above, had its plants located four miles from downtown on the west side and its offices and showroom downtown. Pullman, Armour, McCormick, and many other businesses moved their office workers downtown in the 1880s.
- The steam elevator was invented by Elisha Otis in 1853, but the breakthrough that made tall buildings possible was the hydraulic elevator patented by C. W. Baldwin in Chicago in 1878. This innovation was adopted immediately in New York and Chicago.
- Several changes in building technology made skyscrapers possible. The first skyscrapers were built entirely with masonry frames. The Montauk block, competed in 1882, was ten stories tall and had such a frame. The next generation of skyscrapers used partial iron framing bolted together. The 12-story Home Insurance Building was completed in 1885, and is considered to be the first modern skyscraper. Within a very few years the new structural steel from Pittsburgh changed building technology forever. The Rand McNally Building of 1890 was the first tall structure that had a frame entirely of steel. This innovation by Burnham and Root meant that buildings of the twentieth century could be ten times taller than the skyscraper buildings of the 1880s.
- The problem of foundations for tall buildings in Chicago had to be solved before any of these buildings could be built. Bedrock was below 90 to 150 feet below the surface and could not be reached with existing foundation techniques. The water table was only 15 feet below ground. John Root's design for the Montauk Block included a concrete and steel raft—a "floating foundation"—that spread the load of the columns safely. Modern foundations do reach bedrock, but the original generation of skyscrapers was built on Root's floating foundations.

While many of the old buildings have been torn down, downtown Chicago remains the best outdoor museum of skyscrapers.

The location patterns of manufacturing in 1873 were studied by Raymond Fales and Leon Moses (1972). The year 1873 was chosen for study because much of the industrial areas in the city had been destroyed by the fire, so firms could make location decisions anew. They used an industrial directory to locate 659 manufacturing firms that made up 75 percent of manufacturing employment in the city. They computed gross employment density (employment divided by area of the zone) for 129 zones of ¼ square mile each, and 61 of them contained some manufacturing employment. They hypothesized that, because manufacturing was more concerned about the cost of assembling inputs (input oriented) rather than market oriented, manufacturing employment would have located near transportation facilities. And, to reduce the cost of information, firms would locate in the central business district. They indeed found that their measure of employment density was positively related to whether a river passes through the zone, the number of rail terminals in the zone, and whether the zone is located in the central business district. They also found that manufacturing employment density was negatively related to the population in the zone, which suggested that manufacturers were out-bidding residential developers for land in these locations. As we shall see, this pattern of land use has persisted.

A map indicating the location of Chicago industries in 1886 prepared by the Mayor's Committee on Economic and Cultural Development (1966) shows that many printing and garment establishments were located in the central business district. Metal processing firms, meat packing, and other food processing businesses, agricultural implement plants, furniture factories, and other industries primarily were located near the two branches of the Chicago River. Most of these also had access to a rail line, and those that did not locate near the river all had a rail line nearby.

Early suburbanization and annexation

The movement of population and employment away from the central area proceeded much more rapidly than did the boundaries of the city of Chicago. Keating (2002) shows that early suburbs were created to provide the services demanded by the people who lived there. Repeating points made in Chapter 1, some suburbs provided an extensive set of services (water and sewer systems, police and fire protection, and so on), while other suburbs provided very few, if any, services. Instead, this second group provided cheap land and no taxes. However, most of these early suburbs were annexed by the City of Chicago in 1889, and six more were added by 1893. Those annexed in 1889 were mainly large townships with diverse populations. The suburbs that were providing the more extensive set of services thought that joining the City of Chicago would reduce costs and/or improve services as the population increased. And, by that time, people who demanded municipal services had moved into the suburbs with few services. Joining the City was the more expedient solution, and a majority of the voters voted for annexation. At the same time, several other suburbs were already happy with the basket of services provided and did not wish to join the

City. These suburbs were smaller units with pretty homogeneous populations. Very little annexation by the City of Chicago took place after 1893 because at that point the City was mostly surrounded by these smaller suburbs such as Oak Park, Riverside, Evanston, and Cicero.

This record of annexation and formation of independent suburban municipalities is consistent with the "vote with the feet" model of local government invented by Tiebout (1956). In this model households choose among local jurisdiction based on the basket of services offered and taxes imposed. Something akin to a market for local government services (with the prices for those services) is suggested that overcomes the problem of public goods identified by Samuelson (1954). A pure public good is one that is supplied to all citizens jointly, and from which no one can be excluded. The standard example is national defense. The problem is the lack of a market mechanism to determine how much of the good the public is willing to "buy." Asking people to contribute voluntarily will not work because the individual cannot be excluded from the good once it is supplied. In the Tiebout model the services provided by local government are provided only to the residents of the local jurisdiction, and all households in the jurisdiction pay the same amount in taxes, thus overcoming the Samuelson problem. The Tiebout suburb will contain households that are alike in their demands for public services (and probably income levels and other characteristics as well). The decision to expand services will be made unanimously. As Tiebout recognized, the real world of suburban government is much more complex than his model. For example, households do not actually pay the same amount in taxes and businesses also pay local taxes. Nevertheless Keating's finding that the smaller, more homogeneous suburbs did not seek annexation by Chicago is roughly consistent with the Tiebout model. The larger jurisdictions with more heterogeneous populations voted to join the City. Voters who did not wish to be annexed worried that they would pay higher taxes, but they were outvoted by the voters who wanted the more extensive set of services provided by the City.

Conclusion

This chapter has provided a short summary of the history of Chicago from its earliest days to 1900. The pioneer days certainly were over by 1900 (perhaps before that). The Old Northwest had reached a mature status in just 70 years, and Chicago had emerged as the railroad, industrial, banking, and commercial capital of the region and second city of the nation. This modern city of 1.7 million had a sophisticated mass transit system and a downtown filled with skyscrapers, and it had played host to the world at the World's Columbian Exposition in 1893. The world's fair took place seven miles from downtown at the lakefront on the south side of the city, and provided the impetus for the construction of the first elevated transit line. Daniel Burnham was the architect for much of the "White City," and later he prepared a plan for the entire city. The mile-long Midway Plaisance adjacent to the University of Chicago campus was the midway for the Bazaar of Nations. The beautiful, but largely temporary buildings of the fair were in stark contrast to conditions in much of the rest of the city. This city, Chicago, was a place that as recently as the 1840s still had a few travelers who used the Chicago Portage through Mud Lake.

Notes

1   The definition of the North Central region used by the Census Bureau includes North Dakota, South Dakota, Nebraska, and Kansas. These are not included in Table 2.3.
2   A steamboat company sued the bridge company when one of its boats hit the bridge and was destroyed. Abraham Lincoln was one of the attorneys for the bridge company at the civil trial. The trial resulted in a hung jury, and the plaintiff decided not to pursue the case further.
3   The Comptroller of the Currency was authorized to redeem the national bank notes of a bank that could not meet its obligations, and could reimburse himself by selling the U.S. bonds that had been deposited and had first lien on any remaining assets of the bank should the bond sale prove inadequate. Only holders of that national currency were protected. The bank's depositors were not.
4   Banking history of the late nineteenth century is a complex topic in itself that is beyond the scope of this book. This history includes the resumption of the gold standard in 1879, which led to an inelastic currency and long-term deflation that advantaged creditors and harmed borrowers (e.g. farmers). This deflation was one cause of the populist movement, which advocated the inclusion of silver in the monetary base of the nation. This movement culminated in the "Cross of Gold" speech given by presidential candidate William Jennings Bryan at the 1896 Democratic National Convention in Chicago. Bryan lost and the nation remained on the gold standard, but discoveries of gold in Alaska and other places permitted the monetary base to expand as the century ended. See Friedman and Schwartz (1963) and James (1938) for detailed accounts of this history.
5   Alvah Roebuck sold out to Sears in 1895 for $25,000, a case of the worst possible investment timing. He was hired back by the company when he needed a job in the Great Depression. When he applied for the job he was asked whether he was related to the co-founder of the firm, and he replied that he *is* Roebuck.

Appendix

Table A.2.1 Chicago population and area: 1830–1900

	Chicago	Chicago foreign born	6-county area*	Area of city (sq. mi.)
1830	50 (est.)			0.417
1832	200 (est.)			
1831	350			
1835	3,265			
1837	4,170			
1840	4,479		35,616	10.186
1843	7,589			
1845	12,088			
1847	16,859			
1849	23,047			
1850	29,963		115,285	9.311
1854	65,872			

	Chicago	Chicago foreign born	6-county area*	Area of city (sq. mi.)
1855	80,023			
1859	95,000			
1860	112,172	50.0%	259,384	17.492
1862	138,186			
1864	160,353			
1866	200,418			
1868	252,054			
1870	298,777	48.4%	493,531	35.152
1872	367,396			
1880	503,185	40.7%	771,250	35.152
1890	1,099,850	41.0%	1,391,890	178.052
1900	1,698,575	34.6%	2,084,750	189.517

Sources: U.S. Bureau of the Census, Cutler (1976), Hoyt (1933), Mayer and Wade (1969).

Note
*Cook, DuPage, Kane, Lake, McHenry, and Will counties. Area 3,730 sq. mi.

3   The second city

1900–1930

Introduction

The city of Chicago entered the new century with a population of 1.7 million and an economic base consisting of industry and trade that was supported by the nation's largest railroad system. At the end of the next 30 years the population of the city reached 3.38 million, which is very nearly the maximum number of 3.62 million in 1950. The population of the metropolitan area more than doubled during this time, from 2.09 million to 4.71 million. Immigrants in large numbers arrived from abroad and from other locations around the nation, especially from the South. They were drawn by the rapid growth in employment opportunities in manufacturing, trade, and transportation. But as Chicago grew, its economy was transformed into its modern form. By 1930 (or before), Chicago could no longer be considered "nature's metropolis" because substantial parts of the original economic base had declined and been replaced by newer industries such as electrical machinery (e.g. telephone equipment, electrification equipment, radios, and so on). Streets were filled with trucks and automobiles, and the horses were retired. And the city looked to the future by adopting a plan (the Burnham Plan) and made a serious attempt to control the negative effects of chaotic urban growth by adopting a comprehensive zoning ordinance.

Infrastructure development

An urban area can grow in terms of population and employment (nominal growth) without having economic growth in real terms. Many cities around the world have experienced rapid population growth as people migrate from rural areas into crowded and unhealthy urban areas. All of these many millions of people were not wrong. They were better off in the cities than in the rural areas, but the standard of living in the cities may not have been improving. The real economic growth of an urban area, growth that produces increases in the real incomes of people, depends upon several factors:

- export demand,
- availability of critical natural resources,
- private capital,

- public capital (infrastructure),
- labor quality,
- technical change,
- agglomeration economies,
- entrepreneurship, and
- amenities (quality of life factors).

The relative importance of these factors varies over time. As we have seen, the rapid nominal and real growth of Chicago in the second half of the nineteenth century was a result of available natural resources (such as fertile farmland, iron ore, coal, and lumber), private capital investments (railroads, etc.), rapid technical change, demand for exports from Chicago to the rest of the nation, and entre-preneurship (Ogden, McCormick, Armour, Ward, et al.). Indeed, Gavin Wright (1990) found that non-reproducible natural resources were the most distinctive feature of American industry during the latter decades of the nineteenth century and first decades of the twentieth century. For example, the iron ore of the Mesabi Range in Minnesota (discovered in 1866) meant that steel production could incre-ase rapidly, which meant that railroads could be constructed and machinery and machine tools produced, which form the basis for many manufacturing indu-stries.[1] Agglomeration economies—increases in productivity that result from the concentration of economic activity in one location—were a strong factor in the case of the railway network. The Granger railroads made the mainline rail-roads more productive, and vice versa, because all could benefit from network externalities and economies of scale. These factors attracted immigrants in vast numbers, which led to further growth. The old question is, "Do people follow jobs, or do jobs follow people?" The answer is "both." In addition, Chicago did manage to provide public infrastructure that facilitated growth.

The quality of the labor force as conventionally measured was not as important to the economy of the nineteenth century as it is in modern times. While the Land Ordinance of 1785 designated one section in each township of 36 square miles for public education, many people had little formal education. Necessary skills were learned through experience on the job. For example, a prominent Illinois attorney of the 1850s had only about one year of classroom schooling. Later he managed to save the Union and free the slaves. My great-grandfather, one William O. Freeman, was a veteran of the Civil War from Dayton, Ohio. He received a pension from the federal government, and underwent a review of his continued eligibility for the pension in 1886. Depositions were taken from several people, including his wife Julia King Freeman. Her testimony was duly transcribed by a stenographer, and she signed by making her mark. Mrs. Freeman apparently was illiterate—in Dayton, Ohio, in 1886. Mr. Freeman, who was literate, continued to receive his pension until he passed away in 1937.

Cities that grow rapidly play catch-up with public infrastructure, and Chicago was no exception. Chicago was blessed with its strategic location, but it is well to remember that public investments created the first city—the canal project and the opening of the Chicago River to navigation. However, the rapid population growth that resulted created a serious sanitation problem in the city with a water table just below the surface. The city had no sewer system and drew its water supply from Lake Michigan, into which the badly polluted Chicago River emptied. The city was the scene of a devastating cholera epidemic in 1854 that claimed 1,424 victims, and had experienced epidemics of typhoid fever and dysentery. Local citizens demanded action, and a Board of Sewerage Commissioners was formed in 1855. Over the next 15 years the city constructed the first comprehensive sewer system in North America (above ground, running in the middle of the streets), dredged the Chicago River, and built a new water supply system. The sewer system meant that the streets and buildings had to be raised 15 feet. The dredging of the river supplied the dirt to raise the streets, but private owners were responsible for raising the buildings. George Pullman got his start in Chicago in 1859 raising buildings. The water supply system included a "crib" built far out in Lake Michigan and a sloping tunnel that was supposed to bring clean water to the pumping station—the famous Water Tower that was completed in 1869. But the water system never worked as well as hoped. There was an attempt to reverse the flow of the Chicago River in 1871, but this project did not work effectively. Another cholera epidemic occurred in 1873, and smallpox and dysentery outbreaks were frequent. According to Mayer and Wade (1969, p. 274), the typhoid death rate was 174 per 100,000 people in 1891. The next round of infrastructure investments was gigantic. The Illinois legislature created the Sanitary District of Chicago (now called the Metropolitan Sanitary District) in 1889 with its own body of elected officials and taxing authority. The district originally covered 185 square miles, and included all of the city and most of the western suburbs. This was an early form of metropolitan government, and illustrates the fact that some public services must be provided on a massive scale. The project, which was financed by a bond issue, finally reversed the flow of the Chicago River and replaced the Illinois and Michigan Canal with the Sanitary and Ship Canal. The project was completed in 1900 and involved moving more earth than the building of the Panama Canal. As Miller (1996, p. 131) stated:

> Chicago was made possible by the largest engineering project undertaken in an American community up to that time, the river reversal and the installation of a new sewage and water system. Now the fourth-largest city in North America, it was capable of doing big things and doing them well, and this became part of its permanent reputation.

Urban infrastructure has many other components, some of which are supplied by private businesses. The city of 1900 required an internal transportation system, communication systems, utilities such as electricity and gas, and public buildings and parks. Chicago relied on private businesses to provide the internal transportation system that by 1900 included the famous elevated transit system and the electric trolleys. Licenses were granted to build and operate components of the system, and the system was not made fully public until 1947, when the Chicago Transit Authority was formed. The commuter rail system was supplied by the railroads from the earliest days. The electric and gas utilities were (and still are) private businesses that operate under public regulation. The telegraph and the telephone systems were also supplied privately. The public sector built its own buildings, of course, although public agencies often rent space in private buildings. Chicago is notable for its park system that was designed by Frederick Law Olmsted, who began his work in Chicago for the Township of Hyde Park before it was annexed to the city. Later he designed Lincoln Park along the lake on the north side. Grant Park, to the east of downtown, was created by filling in the space between the lakeshore and the Illinois Central trestle (and further into the lake) with the debris from the Great Chicago Fire. Grant Park is the place that A. Montgomery Ward declared shall be "forever open and free." The existence of Grant Park as a beautiful public space distinguished Chicago from other cities such as Cleveland and Toronto. Other parks were built to be a system that ringed the city. Lastly, Chicago needed a better port than the Chicago River, which was still badly congested in 1900. The river as a port facility started to be phased out with the development of the Calumet River and Calumet Harbor on the south side. As noted in Chapter 2, the project began in 1869, and the first ships used the port in 1871. These were also public investments. The massive South Works of Illinois Steel, the Pullman factory and town, and many other industrial facilities located there.

So, in 1900 Chicago was a city with water and sanitation systems, a transit system, telephone and telegraph, electricity and gas utilities, public buildings and parks. Critical parts of the infrastructure had been built by the government. Chicago was ready for the new century, or was it? Perhaps it is ironic that Chicago, in particular the Department of Economics at the University of Chicago, became the home of free-market economics. Milton and Rose Friedman (1980, p. xix) are famous for writing:

> In the government sphere, as in the market, there seems to be an invisible hand, but it operates in precisely the opposite direction from Adam Smith's: an individual who intends only to serve the public interest by fostering government intervention is "led by an invisible hand to promote" private interests, "which was no part of his intention."

As we shall see, the Chicago business community of the early twentieth century apparently did not believe the Friedmans' theorem.

Make no little plans

While a street grid had been established in 1830, it is fair to say that the development of Chicago largely was unplanned and pretty chaotic. The Progressive Movement, supported by muckraking journalists, emerged in the early twentieth century to advocate good government. The City Beautiful Movement was a part of the Progressive Movement. The story of the Progressive Movement as described by Richard Hofstadter (1956) and many others is complex. Nevertheless, as a part of that movement, in 1906 a local business association, the Merchant's Club (later the Commercial Club), formed a committee to examine the physical conditions of the city. They saw an overcrowded and inefficient city with bad traffic congestion and that lacked amenities. Urban planning had been used in several other cities, and it so happened that one of the world's leaders in the field was a Chicagoan. Daniel Burnham, the chief designer of the World's Columbian Exposition of 1893, had developed plans for Washington, DC, Cleveland, San Francisco, and cities in the Philippine Islands. Burnham and his associate Edward Bennett were hired by the business group to produce a plan for Chicago.

The longer version of the famous Burnham statement about making no little plans, as included in the recent printing of Burnham and Bennett (1970, p. v), is:

> Make no little plans; They have no magic to stir men's blood and probably themselves will not be realized. Make big plans; aim high in hope and work, remembering that a noble, logical diagram once recorded will never die, but long after will be a living thing, asserting itself with evergrowing insistency. Remember that our sons and grandsons are going to do things that would stagger us. Let your watchword be order and your beacon beauty.

The *Plan of Chicago* certainly is not little. Burnham and Bennett (1970, p. 4) stated their fundamental objectives as follows:

> The plan frankly takes into consideration the fact that the American city, and Chicago preeminently, is a center of industry and traffic. Therefore attention is given to the betterment of commercial facilities; to methods of transportation for persons and goods; to removing the obstacles which prevent or obstruct circulation; and to the increase of convenience. It is realized, also, that good workmanship requires a large degree of comfort on the part of the workers in their homes and surroundings, and ample opportunity for that rest and recreation without which all work becomes drudgery.

The major elements of the Plan (working to the interior from 60 miles out), along with whether that element was implemented, are:

- A system of circumferential and radial highways for the territory within 60 miles of Chicago; the system was eventually constructed in the 1950s and 1960s, and does loosely resemble the Plan;
- An encircling system of forest parks; the idea was not original with Burnham and Bennett, and the forest preserves do follow the Plan;
- A plan for improving the internal rail freight system, including a freight center: Plan partially adopted, but Chicago still struggles with the internal handling of freight;
- A plan for rail passenger terminals; partly implemented;
- An elaborate plan for subways in the downtown area; only partly implemented and at first opposed by commercial interests outside the central area;

- A plan for city streets that includes residence streets, avenues (traffic streets), diagonal streets, and boulevards; largely implemented;
- A plan for downtown streets and for bridges over the Chicago River; widening Michigan Avenue, construction of the Michigan Avenue Bridge, and other aspects of the Plan were implemented;
- A plan for downtown and lakefront parks; largely implemented; and
- A plan for an east–west "grand axis" (Congress Street) with a massive civic center; Congress Street became the Eisenhower Expressway in the 1950s, and the massive civic center became the Chicago Circle interchange, where the radial expressways meet.

The Plan was published in 1909, and adopted by the city in 1910. The Chicago City Plan Commission was formed, with Charles Wacker as chairman. Wacker wrote a manual of the Plan, which was used in the eighth and ninth grades in the Chicago public schools for many years thereafter to teach its basic principles.

The Plan has been criticized on several points. There was no provision for automobile parking other than on the street in spite of the fact that much of the Plan was designed to facilitate auto and truck traffic. The Plan did not propose a consolidated passenger rail terminal but rather included seven terminals, four of which were never built. The Plan included no discussion of the mixing of incompatible land uses and the inability of the law of nuisances to address this problem. Perhaps the greatest omission from the Plan was consideration of ideas for improving the slums, other than two paragraphs that advocated "remorseless enforcement of sanitary regulations." Nevertheless, city planning became a regular part of life in Chicago. The regulation of land use and buildings is discussed in the "Land use and zoning" section later in this chapter.

The Burnham Plan (1970, p. 33) contains a statement regarding future population: "Chicago is now facing the momentous fact that fifty years hence, when the children of to-day are at the height of their power and influence, this city will be larger than London: that is, larger than any existing city." At that time (1911) the population of Greater London was 7.16 million, Inner London residents were 4.23 million, and the entire metropolitan area (including outer rings) housed 9.25 million. In 1960 the population of the city of Chicago was 3.55 million, and the metropolitan area population was 6.22 million. The statement by Burnham and Bennett was not wildly off base, but so began a tradition of making population projections for Chicago that were/are too high.

Industrial giant

Employment data from the Census show that the total employment of Chicago residents more than doubled from 1900 to 1930 (121.0 percent increase), compared to a population increase of 99.0 percent (from 1.70 million to 3.38 million). Table 3.1 displays the broad industry categories of employed Chicagoans for 1900, 1920, and 1930. (The 1910 Census did not collect the same data. Indeed, employment data were not collected in a consistent manner from Census to

Table 3.1 Industries of Chicago residents (1000s) (data by place of residence)

Industry	City of Chicago 1900	City of Chicago 1920	City of Chicago 1930	Metro area 1920	Metro area 1930
Total employment	705	1,231	1,559	1,561	2,083
Agric. & mining	8	10	5	33	34
	1.1%	0.8%	0.3%	2.1%	1.6%
Manufacturing	265	590	683	752	923
	37.6%	47.9%	43.8%	48.2%	44.3%
Trade &	204	383	541	453	691
transportation	28.9%	31.1%	34.7%	29.0%	33.2%
Service	228	254	330	323	434
	32.3%	20.6%	21.1%	20.7%	20.8%
Professional	45	86	111	109	156
service	6.4%	7.0%	7.1%	7.0%	7.5%
Domestic &	183	140	187	168	235
personal	26.0%	11.4%	12.0%	10.8%	11.3%
Public service	n.a.	28	31	46	43
		2.3%	2.0%	3.0%	2.1%

Source: U.S. Bureau of the Census for 1900, 1920, and 1930, and Mitchell (1933, pp. 74–76).

Note: For 1920 Mitchell spread employees listed as clerical among the three large broad industry categories in proportion to the employees in each category. Metropolitan area defined as Cook, DuPage, Kane, Lake, and Will counties in Illinois and Lake County, Indiana.

Census, and industries were called occupations.) These figures show that Chicago was booming as a manufacturing center and as a center for trade. Manufacturing employment increased from 265,000 in 1900 to 683,000 in 1930, an increase of 158.0 percent; 43.8 percent of employed Chicagoans worked in manufacturing in 1930, which was down from 47.9 percent in 1920. Employment in trade (both retail and wholesale) and transportation boomed from 204,000 in 1900 to 541,000 in 1930 (up 165.0 percent). Service occupations declined from 32.3 percent in 1900 to 21.2 percent of the total employment of Chicagoans in 1930 as employment in domestic and personal service workers increased by only 16.0 percent.

The figures for the metropolitan area in 1920 and 1930 show that employment was growing much more rapidly outside than inside the city of Chicago. Total employment of Chicago residents grew by 26.7 percent (328,000), while employment of residents outside the city increased by 58.2 percent (194,000). Manufacturing employment of Chicago residents increased by 15.8 percent (93,000) and increased by 48.2 percent (78,000) for residents outside the city.

Manufacturing employment in the metropolitan area grew rapidly. The 1900 Census reported manufacturing employment of 357,900 for five counties in Illinois (Cook, DuPage, Kane, Lake, and Will) and Lake County, Indiana. Of this total 317,500 jobs were located in the city of Chicago (89.0 percent). The Census of Manufactures reported 663,900 manufacturing jobs for this same area in 1929, an increase of 85.0 percent over 29 years. The city of Chicago was the location for 491,200 of these jobs in 1929 (74.0 percent of the total). Manufacturing employment located in the city of Chicago had increased by 55.0 percent as the metropolitan area increased manufacturing jobs by 85.0 percent. This pattern is typical; rapid growth of the metropolitan area in population or employment produces growth in the central city, but at a slower pace, unless the central city annexes territory. As shown below, a major reason for manufacturing growth outside the city of Chicago during this time was the emergence of Gary, Indiana, as a center for the iron and steel industry.

The Statistical Abstract of the U.S. reported that wage earners in manufacturing (i.e. production workers) located in the city of Chicago increased from 314,000 in 1914 to 404,000 in 1919, declined to 311,000 in 1921 (year of a deep postwar recession), and bounced back to 386,000 in 1923 and 370,000 in 1925 and 1927. Wage earners in manufacturing employed in the city totaled 404,000 in 1929.

Manufacturing employment had grown rapidly, but the mix of industries changed over these years. Table 3.2 shows employment in the largest manufacturing industries located in Chicago for 1900–1929. The clothing industry (both men's and women's clothing) was the largest industry in Chicago in 1900, and this industry grew in the first two decades of the new century. However, employment in the industry declined after 1919. Somewhat similarly, employment in slaughtering and meat packing increased sharply from 1900 to 1919, and then fell between 1919 and 1929 by 24,400. During the 1920s meat packing was being

Table 3.2 Employment in manufacturing (data by place of work)

Industry	1900 City of Chicago	1909 City of Chicago	1919 City of Chicago	1923 City of Chicago	1929 City of Chicago	1929 Chicago Industrial Area*
Total	317.5	357.0	502.1	385.7	491.2	663.9
Clothing	36.8	45.0	49.1	49.3	33.6	34.4
Slaughter & meat packing	29.4	27.1	52.4	30.4	28.0	28.1
Foundry & machine shop	23.1	36.9	32.1	23.0	31.1	43.4
Printing & publishing	18.5	33.4	39.3	27.5	49.1	57.7
Rail cars	15.6	22.5	26.4	26.3	13.6	22.5
Agric. implements	13.6	n.a.	n.a.	7.3	n.a.	n.a.
Furniture	8.7	11.1	10.1	11.0	16.9	18.4
Lumber products	n.a.	11.7	n.a.	5.1	4.9	5.4
Iron and steel	7.5	7.7	n.a.	9.7	15.9	50.0**
Electrical machinery	5.8	7.3	17.1	16.8	69.8 (Cook)	70.8
Automobile and parts	—	1.5	6.3	n.a.	n.a.	6.6

Source: U.S. Bureau of the Census, 1900, 1910, 1920, 1923, and 1930.

Notes
  * Chicago Industrial Area included Cook, DuPage, Kane, Lake, and Will counties in Illinois and Lake County, Indiana.
** Lake County, Indiana, employment was 26,600.

decentralized to smaller cities such as Omaha, Kansas City, and East St. Louis. The industry was becoming more resource oriented, i.e. located closer to the live-stock as the cost of shipping packed meat fell relative to the cost of shipping live animals. The rail car industry was the other Chicago industry in which employ-ment increased and then declined by a significant amount.

Employment in these industries was replaced largely by two industries—electrical machinery and printing and publishing. The electrical machinery industry added about 50,000 jobs in the 1920s as consumers bought telephones, radios, and other modern products and as firms converted to equipment run by electricity.[2] Employment in printing and publishing did not increase as spectacularly, but grew by 165.0 percent from 1900 to 1929.

Employment in the iron and steel industry increased in the city of Chicago from 7,500 in 1900 to 15,900 in 1930, but the largest increase in the metropolitan area took place across the state line in Gary, Indiana. As of 1929 employment in the industry in Lake County, Indiana, was 26,600. The largest employer was U.S. Steel, the descendant of Illinois Steel. John Hekman (1978) studied the change in the location of iron and steel production in the U.S. and found that the share of national output for metropolitan Chicago increased after 1910. He found that the demand for steel products in the market area covered by the industry in the Chicago area grew in relative terms. Hekman (1978) also indicated that the elimination in 1924 of the Pittsburgh Plus basing point pricing system stimulated production in Chicago. These effects were larger than changes in relative pro-duction costs, so Hekman (1978) concluded that the relative growth of iron and steel production in the Chicago area was exogenous to the local economy. Automobiles and parts was another growing industry, but unfortunately a figure for 1929 was not reported (included in the "other" category).

As noted above, the Census Bureau in 1929 reported manufacturing employ-ment for the Chicago Industrial Area (six counties, including Lake County, Indiana). These figures in Table 3.2 provide a snapshot of the composition of manufacturing for the larger Chicago metropolitan area. These figures document that iron and steel was the main industry with a major presence outside the city of Chicago.

The Chicago Industrial Area in 1929 had the second-largest total manufacturing employment among the industrial areas in the nation with 6.5 percent of the national total of 10.2 million jobs. The New York Industrial Area was the leader with 1.12 million jobs (11.0 percent of the nation), and Philadelphia was in third place with 438,900 jobs (4.3 percent of the nation). Detroit came in fourth with 331,900 jobs (3.3 percent of the nation).

The financial sector in Chicago grew along with the local economy. The banking system of the nation was reformed in 1913 with the creation of the Federal Reserve System, which was designed to be the lender of last resort to the members of the system. Regional Federal Reserve banks were created in Chicago, St. Louis, Minneapolis, Cleveland, Kansas City, and eight other cities around the country (including New York, of course). The First National Bank of Chicago immediately joined the Federal Reserve System. The role of the Federal

Reserve in the Great Depression is discussed in the next chapter. Data from Hoyt (1933, p. 489) show that bank clearings in Chicago increased from $6.80 billion in 1900 to $15.4 billion in 1912, the year prior to the creation of the Federal Reserve System. With the production boom during World War I and the advent of the Federal Reserve System, bank clearings in Chicago more than doubled to $32.7 billion in 1920. After a decline to $25.9 billion in 1921 as a result of the postwar recession, bank clearings resumed their growth and reached $37.8 billion in 1928.

Trucks, automobiles, and other modern conveniences

In 1900 intra-urban freight was moved by horse and wagon, and people mainly rode in trolleys. The first three decades of the twentieth century were the years in which all of that changed. Hoyt (1933, p. 485) provided data on passenger automobiles, motor trucks, and horse-drawn vehicles registered in the city of Chicago:

	Passenger automobiles	Motor trucks	Horse-drawn vehicles
1910	12,926	709	58,114
1920	89,973	22,833	27,937
1930	409,260	56,751	9,351

The number of registered motor trucks exceeded the number of registered horse-drawn vehicles for the first time in 1921. Automobile registrations increased by 32,000 per year during the 1920s. And by 1930 most of the horses had been retired, although some milk was still delivered to homes by horses who could remember the route and junk men patrolled neighborhoods by horse and wagon. The number of passengers carried by rapid transit increased up through 1926, but then began to decline (Hoyt, 1933, p. 491):

	Rapid transit passengers
1900	81.275 million
1910	164.876 million
1920	190.639 million
1926	228.813 million
1927	226.212 million
1928	207.864 million
1929	196.774 million
1930	182.955 million

Some of the decline in rapid transit passengers in 1930 may have been caused by the overall economic decline after 1929, but automobile registrations increased to 425,294 in 1931—and then declined to 398,376 in 1932.

The explosion of automobile registrations in the 1920s facilitated the move-ent of population to remoter areas of the city and to the suburbs. An examination of population and housing patterns is provided in the next section. But the purchase of an automobile did not necessarily mean a move to the suburbs. My grandfather (also John McDonald) lived on the south side of Chicago and owned a Cord automobile in the 1920s, but he rode the rapid transit to work while the car stayed in the garage to be used only on Sundays.

A study by Leon Moses and Harold Williamson (1967) hypothesized that prior to the introduction of trucking for the movement of intra-urban freight in the second decade of the new century, the spatial pattern of urban industry was tied to access to rail terminals in or near the central business district. Moses and Williamson (1967, p. 214) examined the fragmentary data on freight rates for 1910 to 1920 and found that "the data do give rough evidence that the intro-duction of the motor truck reduced the cost of moving goods during a period when the cost of moving people was relatively constant." They gathered data on 473 manufacturing firms in Chicago that could be identified in 1908 and 1920, and found that 285 of those firms had moved. The average distance from downtown for those 285 firms increased from 0.92 miles to 1.46 miles, i.e. 59.0 percent greater. The average origin distance for firms that moved was less than that for the firms that did not move. They conclude that these results are consistent with the hypothesis that the introduction of the motor truck fostered the decentralization of business, and had a greater impact on businesses located in the core of the urban area.

However, while trucking obviously had a major impact on the spatial pattern of industry, the city was already undergoing significant decentralization of industry because of the railway system of belt lines and classification yards. Some of the most important industrial location decisions which involved major decentralization occurred before the truck could have been a factor. These include the Chicago Stockyards (1865), Pullman (1881), Illinois Steel South Works (1889), the Hawthorne Works of Western Electric (1903), and U.S. Steel in Gary, Indiana (1906). As time passed and truck registrations continued to climb in the 1920s, firms found that less-than-carload loads of freight could be moved inside the metropolitan area more cheaply by truck than by the belt railway system and, as Thor Hultgren (1948) found, the truck was an effective competitor against the railroads in hauling such smaller loads of inter-urban freight. This was true even though trucks lacked many of the safety features that subsequently were introduced and the highway system of the 1920s had obvious deficiencies. Regulation of interstate trucking was initiated in 1935 under the Motor Carrier Act.

Chicagoans and residents of major cities were afforded many other modern conveniences during the 1900–1930 period. The city became electrified. Commonwealth Edison customers purchased 10 million kilowatt hours (kwh) of electricity in 1893, and by 1930 this electricity purchased had grown to 4.19 billion kwh. The figures by decade from Hoyt (1933, p. 493) are:

KWH
_____

1900	39 million
1910	615 million
1920	1.83 billion
1930	4.19 billions

The principle use of electricity of course was for electric lights, but the general availability of electricity also meant that other modern items such as radios, electric heaters, refrigerators, and other modern products could be sold in large quantity. For example, Lizabeth Cohen (1990, p. 134) reported that in 1930, 73.7 percent of households in four middle-class Chicago neighborhoods owned radios and that 44.3 percent of households in five working-class neighborhoods did so as well.

Telephone service also grew rapidly. Telephones as reported by Illinois Bell in Hoyt (1933, p. 490) are:

1890	6,518
1900	26,661
1910	239,083
1920	575,840
1930	981,325

In short, the city was being transformed into its modern version. No more horses, no more gas (or candle) lighting. Modern plumbing was pervasive, except in the worst slums.

Population and housing

During the 30 years from 1900 to 1930 the population of the city of Chicago doubled from 1.699 million to 3.376 million. During this same time period the population of the metropolitan area (five counties in Illinois plus Lake County, Indiana) more than doubled from 2.094 million to 4.68 million. In other words, the big city gained a population of 1.677 million while the rest of the metropolitan area increased by 909,000. These and other data are displayed in Table 3.3. The first task of this section is to gain some perspective on this rapid growth.

First of all, the population of the nation grew rapidly during the first three decades of the century—from 76.2 million to 123.2 million (61.7 percent, an average of 17.4 percent per decade). Chicago's Midwestern region, as defined previously in Chapter 2 (definition repeated in Table 3.3), grew in population from 23.1 million to 34.0 million (47.2 percent, an average of 13.7 percent per decade). The region as a share of the nation's population fell continuously from 30.4 percent in 1900 to 27.5 percent in 1930. But metropolitan Chicago outpaced both the nation and its region by a sizable margin. The metropolitan area as a share of the nation's population increased from 2.75 percent to 3.79 percent over these same 30 years. Agriculture was declining as a share of employment,

Table 3.3 Population of the U.S., the region, and metropolitan Chicago with decadal percentage changes: 1900–1950

	U.S. (mil.)	Region (mil.)	Metro area (1000s)	Chicago city (1000s)	Chicago city foreign-born national (1000s)	Region as % of U.S.	Metro area as % of U.S.	City as % of metro area
1900	76.2	23.08	2,094	1,699	588	30.36	2.75	81.14
1910	92.2	25.84	2,753	2,185	784	28.03	2.99	79.37
Change	21.0%	12.0%	31.5%	28.6%	33.3%			
1920	106.0	29.67	3,522	2702	808	27.99	3.32	76.72
Change	15.0%	14.8%	27.9%	23.7%	3.1%			
1930	123.2	33.96	4675	3,376	861	27.54	3.79	72.21
Change	16.2%	14.5%	32.7%	24.9%	6.6%			
1940	132.2	35.74	4826	3,397	676	27.04	3.65	70.39
Change	7.3%	5.2%	3.2%	0.6%	−21.5%			
1950	151.3	39.96	5,495	3,621	536	26.41	3.63	65.90
Change	14.4%	11.8%	13.9%	11.8%	−20.7%			

Source: U.S. Bureau of the Census.

Note: Region consists of the states of Illinois, Indiana, Michigan, Ohio, Wisconsin, Iowa, Minnesota, and Missouri. The metropolitan area consists of Cook, DuPage, Kane, Lake, and Will counties in Illinois and Lake County, Indiana.

population was moving to the cities, and Chicago was a big part of the urbanization trend. The population growth of the metropolitan area of 2.58 million was 5.5 percent of the nation's population growth.

As discussed in Chapter 2, Chicago attracted large numbers of immigrants from Europe. Foreign-born immigrants continued to be a large source of population growth during the first decade of the new century. During that decade the population of the city of Chicago increased by 469,000, and 41.4 percent of that growth (194,000) consisted of foreign-born immigrants. According to Hoyt (1933, p. 284), 45.2 percent of the increase was natural population growth (births over deaths), and the migration from other parts of the U.S. contributed only 13.4 percent of the increase. The sources of population growth changed substantially in the next two decades. Migration from other parts of the U.S. surged, while foreign-born immigration contributed only about 5 percent to the city's population growth in each of these two decades. The figures from Hoyt (1933, p. 284) for the city of Chicago are as follows. (Hoyt's figures differ slightly from the official census data in Table 3.3.)

Decade	Natural increase	Foreign-born migration	Migration from U.S.
1900–1910	212,000	194,000	63,000
1910–1920	200,000	24,000	301,000
1920–1930	233,000	37,000	405,000

Migrants from the rest of the U.S. included an increasing number of African-Americans; 14,000, 65,000, and 146,000 in the first, second, and third decades, respectively. This group is discussed in detail below.

The 1900–1910 decade was the last decade in which foreign-born immigrants accounted for such a large increase in the population of the city. The top nations of origin of the 784,000 foreign-born Chicago residents in 1910 were:

Germany	182,000
Austria	132,000
Russia	122,000
Ireland	66,000
Sweden	63,000
Italy	45,000

Together these six countries accounted for 77.9 percent of the foreign-born population of the city. Next in line were Canada (31,000), England (28,000), and Norway (24,000).[3]

In 1900 the city of Chicago was 81.1 percent of the population of the metropolitan area, and the more rapid growth outside the city in percentage terms meant that the city's share of metropolitan population fell to 72.2 percent in 1930. Rapid growth in the population of the metropolitan area meant slightly less rapid growth in the central city by an average of 5.3 percent per decade even though the city annexed a small amount of territory in those years. In other words, on average for the three decades:

City Pop Growth Percent = Metro Pop Growth Percent – 5.3%.

This sort of relationship will be shown to hold for the subsequent decades as well, including the decades when slow population growth at the metropolitan level means population decline in the central city. But the overwhelming fact is that the city added an average of 560,000 people in each decade, including an increase of 674,000 in the 1920s. How did the city manage to do this?

The answer is that employment was growing rapidly and the city had a great deal of vacant land in 1900 that had been made accessible to downtown by the transit system and the commuter railroads and later by the automobile. And, as has been noted, some major employers had established major growing centers of employment outside the central area. Subdivisions were created and houses and apartment buildings were built for those who could afford a better residence than most could find in the older parts of the city. Hoyt (1933, p. 484) shows that the population of the city within four miles of downtown declined slightly from 1.025 million in 1900 to 1.016 million in 1916, but that the population residing from four to ten miles from downtown increased from 460,000 to 992,000 in these 16 years. The population data for the community areas of Chicago compiled by Evelyn Kitagawa and Karl Taeuber (1963) show that the population within four miles of downtown was 638,000 in 1930, so the central area lost population of 387,000 from 1910 to 1930, nearly all of that after 1916. This large population decline occurred even as the population of the city increased by 1.19 million. The population density gradient as estimated by McDonald (1979) flattened from a decline of 40 percent per mile in 1900 to 28 percent per mile in 1920 and 25 percent per mile in 1930 as population grew rapidly in those areas four miles beyond downtown. Hoyt (1933, p. 476) recorded buildings erected in Chicago for 1912 to 1930; construction of single-family houses averaged 5,000 per year and an average of 3,100 apartment buildings were built during those 19 years. Construction activity was particularly brisk from 1922 through 1928.

What was the condition of the housing in Chicago? With the exception of some high-income areas near downtown, housing conditions within four miles of downtown were, in a word, horrible. The poor of Chicago, including most of the new immigrants, lived in deplorable conditions near downtown. The slums were characterized by overcrowding and lack of proper sanitation. Mayer and Wade (1969, p. 256) cited an unpublished 1900 report by a Dr. Frank Fetter that the average slums in Chicago had 270 people per acre, and the worst slums had 900 people per acre. At a density of 270 per acre, the city of Chicago could house 32 million people, or 42 percent of the population of the nation. Two techniques were used to increase population density in the slums; an old frame house would be moved to the rear of the lot and another house would be built in front, and larger, older single-family houses were cut up into apartments (usually without bathroom facilities for each unit). These techniques continued in use for decades, especially in the African-American parts of the city. About 300,000 Chicagoans were living in slums in 1900. However, even by 1900 many of the early immigrant groups, such as the Swedes, Germans, Norwegians, and Irish, had moved away from the old downtown neighborhoods to better quarters.

As an example of middle-class housing, my grandfather, the proprietor of a small restaurant and with the Cord automobile resting in the garage, owned a house in the 1920s located eight miles directly south of downtown in the Woodlawn neighborhood. The house was built of brick in 1904, contained 1,882 square feet of interior space on a standard Chicago 25' x 125' lot, and was valued at $10,000 in 1930. The house was home to Mr. and Mrs. McDonald, five children, and sometimes a young woman maid. The house at 6426 Drexel Boulevard still stands and has an estimated value of $133,654 in 2014.

The early Great Migration

Rapid population growth in an urban area is the result of migration. Migration has many causes—push factors from the origin and pull factors to the destination. Economic factors are important for both the push and the pull, but they are not the entire story. Economic factors on the push side include low wages, high unemployment, a declining agriculture sector, mechanization of agriculture, and primogeniture in which the oldest son inherits the farm. On the pull side, a growing urban area can provide higher wages and/or lower unemployment as well as a better quality of life in terms of opportunities for education, health care, entertainment, and so on.

The Great Migration in the U.S. refers to the migration of African-American population from the South to the North and the West, and the early portion of this migration from 1910 to 1930 is examined here. However, it is useful to put the early Great Migration to Chicago in perspective. As shown in Table 3.4, the

Table 3.4 Total and African-American population by decade

Location	1900	1910	1920	1930
U.S. population (mil.)	76.2	92.2	106.0	123.2
African-American (1000s)	8,834	9,828	10,463	11,891
Northeast population (mil.)	21.1	25.9	29.7	34.4
African-American (1000s)	385	484	679	1147
Midwest population (mil.)	26.3	29.9	34.0	38.6
African-American (1000s)	496	543	793	1,262
South population (mil.)	24.5	29.4	33.1	37.9
African-American (1000s)	7,922	8,749	8,912	9,362
West population (mil.)	4.1	6.8	8.9	11.9
African-American (1000s)	30	51	79	120
Illinois population (mil.)	4.82	5.64	6.49	7.63
African-American (1000s)	85	109	182	329
Chicago population (mil.)	1.70	2.19	2.70	3.38
African-American (1000s)	30	44	110	234

Source: U.S. Bureau of the Census.

African-American population of Chicago increased from 30,000 in 1900 and 44,000 in 1910 to 234,000 in 1930, a huge increase in percentage terms. The percentage of the city's population that was African-American was just 1.8 percent in 1900 and grew to 6.9 percent in 1930. However, 25.4 percent of the population in Chicago in 1930 was born in a foreign country. The foreign-born population increased from 587,000 in 1900 to 781,000 in 1910, and then to 856,000 in 1930. As of 1930, 260,000 Chicagoans were born in Poland, Russia, or Lithuania, which exceeded the African-American population by 24,000. In short, the first decade of the century saw continuation of a great migration to Chicago from abroad that was followed after 1910 by the Great Migration of African-Americans.

Table 3.4 shows population figures by decade for the U.S., the four major regions, Illinois, and the city of Chicago. As noted above, the population of the nation increased rapidly by 61.7 percent from 1900 to 1930. Migration from abroad was a major factor in this increase. The African-American population increased by 34.6 percent over this same period (from 8.83 million to 11.89 million). Since it is unlikely that many African-Americans had migrated from abroad, this figure is a result of natural population increase. In the absence of inter-regional migration and major regional differences in the rate of natural increase, the African-American population in each region would have increased by approximately 34.6 percent. This did not happen. Total and African-American population growth figures for the 30 years (1900–1930) by region are:

	Total	African-American
U.S.	61.7%	34.6%
Northeast	63.6%	197.9%
Midwest	46.6%	154.4%
South	54.4%	18.2%
West	190.8%	300.0%

Population growth in the Northeast was slightly more rapid than it was in the nation, and population growth in the Midwest and South fell below the nation's growth because of the rapid growth in the West (from a very small population base in 1900).

It is clear that the early version of the Great Migration from the South to the Northeast and Midwest took place from 1910 to 1930. Going decade by decade, we see that the African-American population of the nation increased by 11.3 percent in the first decade, and the increase of this group in the South was slightly lower at 10.4 percent. The African-American population of the Northeast increased by 25.7 percent over this same decade, indicating that migration to this region had begun. However, the actual growth of the African-American population in this region was only 99,000. Significant net migration to the Midwest and the West are not evident for 1900–1910.

The pattern changed in the next decade. World War I created demand for industrial and service workers in the cities of the North, and the African-Americans of the South (among others) responded. The African-American population of the nation increased by just 6.5 percent from 1910 to 1920, but the South saw an increase of just 1.9 percent—far below the rate of natural increase. Population growth of this group was rapid in the Northeast (40.3 percent) and the Midwest (46.0 percent). The West did not attract a large number of African-Americans in this decade, or in the 1920s either.

The demand for workers in the northern cities expanded rapidly after the postwar recession of the early 1920s. This decade brought increases in the African-American population of 68.9 percent to the Northeast and 59.1 percent to the Midwest, compared to 13.5 percent for the nation and 5.1 percent for the South. The net result was that 89.7 percent of the African-American population lived in the South in 1900, and this percentage had declined to 78.7 percent in 1930. The vast majority of the African-American population still resided in the South in 1930 and, as documented by Myrdal (1944) and his research team in *An American Dilemma*, most lived in extreme poverty under conditions of severe discrimination.

The African-American population of Illinois tripled from 1910 to 1930 from 109,000 to 329,000. The vast majority of this population growth (77.9 percent) took place in the city of Chicago, from 44,000 in 1910 to 110,000 in 1920 to 234,000 in 1930. It is time now to examine the location pattern and conditions of life for the African-Americans of Chicago.

The African-American population of the metropolitan area (including five counties in Illinois and Lake County, Indiana) was 285,000 in 1930. The city of Chicago was home to 234,000, while 30,700 lived in Lake County, Indiana (Gary) and 13,000 resided in other parts of Cook County. The remaining four counties in Illinois had only about 7,600 African-American residents. The African-Americans of Chicago largely were confined to one area called the Black Belt (later Black Metropolis) on the south side of the city. This area contained an African-American population of 192,000 (82 percent of the Chicago total and 67 percent of the total for the metropolitan area). Another concentration of African-Americans of 25,200 was located on the near west side of the city. The heart of the Black Belt, with 167,000 African-Americans, was a relatively narrow area that extended from 2600 South to 6300 South (in three community areas: 35 (Douglas), 38 (Grand Boulevard), and 40 (Washington Park)). The remaining 25,000 Black Belt residents lived on the fringe of these three community areas. See the map of community areas for the city of Chicago (Figure I.1).

The African-American population was segregated from the rest of the population, and the rapid growth in its numbers created conflict along the expanding borders of the Black Belt. The classic study *Black Metropolis* by St. Clair Drake and Horace Cayton (1945) recorded these events. Reaction to the invasion of white neighborhoods often resulted in bombs being thrown at African-American homes. Drake and Cayton (1945, p. 64) stated that 58 such bombs were thrown from 1917 to 1921 in and around the Black Belt. The most famous incident was the race riot of 1919 that began when an African-American boy crossed the imaginary line that separated whites and African-Americans on the 29th street beach. The boy was drowned, and pitched battles ensued that lasted for five days.

At least 38 people were killed. White gangs raided the African-American community, and African-Americans engaged in reprisals. The state militia ended the rioting on the sixth day. Drake and Cayton quoted several "Old Settler" African-Americans who stated that race relations were reasonably harmonious prior to World War I, when the Great Migration began. But (1945, p. 73), "The Riot, to them, marked a turning point in the history of Chicago."

The expansion of the Black Belt that took place during the 1920s to the South and East of the original Black Belt is an illustration of both active and passive discrimination. Restrictive covenants in deeds were common. Whites conducted active campaigns that included bombing to prevent African-Americans from "invading" a block, but once the color line had been breached, whites sold out and moved away. Housing units turn over as households move out and others move in for the normal reasons of age, income change, household size change, etc. But at some point (the "tipping" point) the growing percentage of African-American households motivates white households on the block to move out and other white households not to consider moving in—because of race. The prices at which the housing units transact tend to be pushed up by strong African-American pent-up demand, or pushed down by the flight of large numbers of white households. Indeed, unscrupulous real estate dealers can take advantage of the situation by convincing white households to sell to them at low prices, and then to sell to African-Americans at much higher prices. Hence the origin of the term "block busting," meaning that a real estate firm creates panic among the white population by beginning to bring in African-Americans. A housing market that operates in this fashion creates resentment on both sides of the color line.

Drake and Cayton (1945) provided a detailed picture of the employment situation for the African-Americans of Chicago. The occupational distributions for white and African-American men and women in 1930 are shown in Table 3.5. African-American employed men primarily worked as unskilled laborers or servants (58.2 percent), while only 15.5 percent of white men worked in these occupations. And over half of the African-American women who worked were employed as servants, while only 12.2 percent of employed white women were classified as servants. The African-Americans who were classified as professionals

Table 3.5 Occupational distribution: Chicago in 1930

Occupation	Men white	Men Af-Am	Women white	Women Af-Am
Professional & proprietor	16.9%	6.1%	13.2%	4.1%
Clerical	20.7%	6.2%	48.4%	4.9%
Skilled worker	22.0%	9.6%	1.2%	0.3%
Semi-skilled	17.8%	15.4%	21.9%	32.2%
Unskilled	11.5%	33.1%	1.2%	2.0%
Servant	4.0%	25.1%	12.2%	55.7%
Unclassified	7.1%	4.5%	1.9%	0.8%

Source: U.S. Bureau of the Census, 1930.

or proprietors primarily served the African-American community; the men as lawyers, doctors, and owners of small businesses and the women as teachers and nurses.

In short, the African-American population of Chicago had grown rapidly during the early years of the Great Migration to 234,000 in 1930. However, at 6.9 percent, this group was only a small minority of the Chicago population at this time. African-Americans largely were confined to a well-defined residential area on the south side of the city (the Black Belt), and employed primarily (but not entirely) as unskilled workers or servants. Most of the African-Americans had migrated from the South. Drake and Cayton (1945, p. 100) reported that, in spite of these conditions, the following are responses to the question "What do you like about the North?"

- Freedom in voting and conditions of colored people here . . .
- Freedom and chance to make a living; privileges.
- The schools for children, the better wages, and the privileges for colored people.
- Freedom of speech and action. Can live without fear. No Jim Crow.
- Liberty, better schools.
- More money and more pleasure to be gotten from it; personal freedom Chicago affords, and voting.
- No lynching.[4]

Land use and zoning

As has been discussed, the rapid growth of Chicago was supported by massive investments in urban infrastructure. Land development was influenced strongly by the infrastructure investments and the awarding of franchises for the private provision of mass transit and electricity, but the details of land development were left to the market. Given the very rapid growth, it is difficult to imagine how it could have been otherwise. Some of the residential and industrial land in Chicago was developed as fairly large tracts. For example, the Central Manufacturing District (CMD) was established by the Chicago Junction Railway and the Union Stockyards. CMD started its development activity in 1905 with a square mile adjacent to the stockyards. CMD assembled land, laid out streets, installed utilities, constructed industrial buildings, and provided services to industrial firms that located in the development. CMD created eight other industrial districts in Chicago and others in the nearby suburbs of Cicero, Chicago Heights, and Clearing. Industrial zones were segregated from residential and commercial areas. On the residential side, the expansion of Chicago normally involved the creation of subdivisions and the construction of housing on a fairly large scale. Restrictive covenants in deeds that were enforceable in court were used. Clear tendencies in land use patterns emerged that are discussed below.

Chicago, and most other cities, never relied entirely on the private market to determine the use of land. The City Charter of 1837 prohibited nuisances such as dung and dead animals, and this law was strengthened in 1851 with an ordinance that permitted the City to abate nuisances and punish offenders. Also, in 1850 a downtown zone was designated to require fire-resistant construction. Disastrously, this zone was not expanded until 1875 (after the 1871 fire), at which time the City established a building department to enforce the building code. Other efforts to control land use included a frontage consent ordinance in 1887 that gave the residents of a block authority to disapprove non-residential use on the block, and an expanded building code in 1893 that included side yard requirements and limited the height of multi-family housing structures.

Buildings in the downtown area received special attention. The 1893 building code limited the height of downtown buildings to 130 feet (to protect the public from fire and falling debris). Several buildings already exceeded this limit. For example, the Masonic Temple, which was completed in 1894 but was begun before the new building code, rises to a height of 302 feet. The height limit was raised to 260 feet in 1902, and then reduced to 200 feet in 1915. The City changed its mind again in 1920, and permitted a height of 260 feet again, with an unoccupied ornamental tower on top that could rise to 400 feet. Falling debris—large chunks of ice in particular—continue to be a problem, by the way. One price of progress?

These limited efforts failed to prevent development in the city from including crowded areas consisting of shacks and marred by debris, congestion, noise, and air pollution. The resolution of conflicts involving land uses was left to the law of nuisances. It became increasingly clear that the remedy of filing a lawsuit was entirely inadequate to handle the large problems that had emerged in the rapidly industrializing city. Courts were flooded with cases, and outcomes depended on individual judges.

People in the City Beautiful Movement who were behind the Burnham Plan began to think of methods that could be used to separate and control land uses, and the zoning movement was born. New York City adopted the first comprehensive zoning ordinance in 1916. A zoning ordinance includes text and a zoning map that specifies the allowable use of all parcels of land in a jurisdiction, usually a municipality or a county. Land use categories include residential, commercial, and industrial (and perhaps finer gradations in each category). Some zoning ordinances control both land use and the intensity of land use (e.g. the volume or the square footage of structures). Zoning is based on the police power of government to protect the welfare of the public, not on the law of nuisances. By 1925 nearly 500 cities had adopted zoning codes, but the constitutionality of such laws was not settled until the U.S. Supreme Court ruled in 1926 that the Euclid, Ohio ordinance did not violate the due process and equal protection clauses of the 14th Amendment. The decision was five to four, and stipulated that the zoning ordinance must cover all of the privately owned land in the local jurisdiction.

The history of zoning in Chicago is a major piece of the economic history of the city, and that history is recounted in detail by Joseph Schwieterman and Dana Caspall (2006). The path to the Chicago zoning ordinance of 1923 was rocky. The Illinois legislature passed a residential district bill in 1911, but the governor vetoed the bill on the grounds that it was unconstitutional. The state adopted a zoning enabling law in 1919 that included a neighborhood consent clause, which the advocates of zoning opposed. Then in 1921 the state adopted a new zoning enabling law without neighborhood consent that was drafted by the Chicago Real Estate Board. The City moved quickly to conduct a comprehensive survey of land use in Chicago and to draft a zoning ordinance. It is clear that the motivation for the zoning ordinance was controlling negative external effects, which were thought to have caused land values to decline. The Library, City Planning and Zoning Committee of the Chicago Real Estate Board (1923, p. 12) cited "innumerable instances of the invasion of residential properties by objectionable buildings and uses and shows the importance of prompt action in the prevention of such nuisances in the future."

The 1923 ordinance had three major features:

• The ordinance specified a hierarchy of land uses: single-family residences on top, followed by apartments, followed by commercial use, followed by industrial use. Higher uses could exist in areas zoned for lower uses, but lower uses could not be developed in areas zoned for higher uses. In other words, single-family houses could be located anywhere, but industrial use was permitted only in industrial zones.
• The ordinance controlled the land use and land-use intensity, the latter through the use of volume districts.
• Existing uses that did not conform to the zoning requirement in a zone were permitted to continue to exist, but could not expand and had to be removed upon a change in ownership of the land.

The provision for downtown buildings permitted a height of 264 feet plus a useable tower of no more than one-fourth of the footprint and one-sixth of the volume of the building. In effect, this meant that buildings could rise to 500 feet. The Wrigley Building (398 feet) and the Tribune Tower (462 feet), two iconic Chicago buildings, were built in the 1920s with "zoning law towers." The ordinance also created a zoning board of appeals to handle disputes and exceptions.

The survey of land use in Chicago of 1921 proved to be a valuable resource for research on land-use patterns in a major city before zoning. John McDonald and Daniel McMillen (1998) drew a sample of 943 block faces over the entire developed portion of the city from the survey. They found a substantial amount of mixing of residential and non-residential uses at the block level. Most of the non-residential uses mixed in with residences were commercial, not industrial. The basic land-use data and subsequent zoning designations for these blocks are as follows.

Existing use in 1921	Blocks	Zoning in 1923
100% Residential	300	Residential 273 Non-residential 27
100% Non-residential	244	Residential 6 Non-residential 238
Mixed use	399	Residential 213 Non-residential 186

Mixed use existed on 42.3 percent of the blocks in 1921. Nearly all of the blocks that were 100 percent of one use were zoned for that use, but mixed-use blocks presented a problem. Of these mixed-use blocks 53.4 percent were zoned for residential use, which meant that these blocks included non-conforming non-residential use of some sort. In short, mixed use existed on 399 (42.3 percent) of the blocks, and the zoning ordinance permitted 27+6+399 = 432 (45.8 percent) blocks to have mixed use. Non-conforming uses were a continuing problem, and attempts to address the problem are discussed in subsequent chapters.

The land-use survey documented a substantial amount of mixed land use, but as noted above, there were clear tendencies in the pattern of land use and land values in 1921. McDonald and McMillen conducted detailed statistical analyses of the data, and reached the following conclusions (1998, p. 148):

> Residential land values were higher near Lake Michigan and elevated stations and lower adjacent to elevated lines, rivers or canals, and rail lines. Residential land use closely followed this land-value pattern. Non-residential land values were higher adjacent to main streets, rail lines and rivers or canals, and commercial and manufacturing land use corresponded closely to these land value results.

Also, as expected, land values were found to decline with distance to downtown. And as noted above, population density declined sharply with distance to downtown (28 percent per mile in 1920). McMillen and McDonald (2002) studied the impact of zoning on land values by comparing values from 1921 and 1924. They found that residential land values increased more rapidly than non-residential land values. While the zoning ordinance did not eliminate the problem of mixed land uses as they existed, the more rapid increase in residential land values can be interpreted as reflecting the assurance that the problem of mixed land use would not get worse; a free insurance policy of sorts.

Urban sociology invented in Chicago

The University of Chicago was founded by John D. Rockefeller and William Rainey Harper, and opened in 1892. The idea was to create a full-blown university of the first rank in the world's newest major city, and the effort was a success. The new university included the first department of sociology, and in the 1920s this department became known primarily for its research on the ecological structure of the city. This research involved detailed field work informed by a theoretical structure, and concentrated on studying Chicago. Urban ecological research was led by Professors Ernest Burgess and Robert Park, and many scholars contributed to the work. Robert Faris (1970) provided a history of the department for the years 1920 to 1932.

The ecological pattern of the city was described as consisting roughly of concentric rings:

- downtown (the Loop), dominated by offices and retailing,
- a factory zone just outside the downtown area,
- a zone in transition populated by poor people, many of whom were immigrants, and containing growing commercial businesses and light manufactures,
- a zone of workingmen's homes,
- a residential zone for higher-income households, and
- a commuters' zone.

The process of urban growth operates through this ecological structure. Population growth is driven by immigration, and most immigrants come with lower levels of education and skills. These people can afford only the oldest, most crowded housing that is located in the zone in transition. Earlier arrivers had prospered and moved away, leaving the poorer housing for the new immigrants.

A critical result of the research is that severe social problems exist in the zone in transition regardless of which ethnic group happens to occupy that area at a particular time. This finding flew in the face of the eugenics movement of the time that asserted that certain ethnic groups are more prone to social problems than are other groups. As Faris (1970, p. 57) stated, "It is partly a discovery of the Chicago urban research that the characteristic extremes of poverty, disease, and behavior troubles found everywhere in slum populations are products of social disorganization, rather than of low genetic quality in the populations." He went on the say (p. 57):

> The Chicago research, however, showed that with few exceptions, each racial or national population that poured into the slum areas of the city experienced the same severe disorganization, and that as each of these populations in time prospered and migrated outward into more settled residential districts, the symptoms of disorganization declined.

This basic approach to the study of the city has been highly influential, and can be seen in the modern work of the eminent Chicago urban sociologist William J. Wilson, whose works are discussed in detail in later chapters. Wilson called one of those few exceptions the underclass.

Conclusion

The 30 years from the reversal of the Chicago River in 1900 to the onset of the Great Depression was a time of rapid growth and development in Chicago. Chicago was the newest great city in the world, and its attractions drew large numbers of immigrants from abroad and from the southern and other rural areas of the U.S. Chicago was a manufacturing town that also was the transportation hub for much of the nation. The economy of Chicago changed its composition. The lumber business declined as the north woods of Wisconsin and Michigan were depleted, and the enormous grain elevators at the mouth of the Chicago River were moved to the Lake Calumet area. The grain trade increasingly was moving to smaller nodal cities such as Minneapolis, Omaha, Indianapolis, and Decatur. Chicago was still the largest center of meat packing, but by 1930 some meat packing had been decentralized to smaller cities in the Midwest. This trend would continue until the Union Stockyards were closed for good in 1971. Other industries became the engines of growth. In other words, during these decades Chicago turned from being "nature's metropolis" into a modern industrial and transportation powerhouse. The manufacturing industries that had grown rapidly included electrical machinery, steel, and printing and publishing.

The city and metropolitan area grew mainly by expanding outward as transportation costs within the urban area declined with the construction of transit lines and the introduction of the truck and automobile. The population converted to electricity as the major source of energy, and purchased telephones, radios, and other modern conveniences. The City of Gary, Indiana, was founded in 1906 and built from scratch as a home for U.S. Steel and other steel firms. The Burnham Plan envisioned a city of the future, and Chicago adopted a zoning ordinance in an effort to control the negative externalities of the industrial city. But Chicago and the rest of the nation were in for a shock . . .

Notes

1   Wright (1990) did not discuss industrial location patterns. The importance of natural resources for industrial growth has declined over time.
2   The employment figure for electrical machinery for 1930 is for Cook County because the figure for the city of Chicago was deleted for disclosure reasons. One major employer, Western Electric, was located just to the west of the city in Cicero. This facility, the Hawthorne Works, produced telephone equipment for much of the nation.
3   The nation of Poland did not exist in 1910. The territory that would become Poland after World War I was divided among Germany, Russia, and Austria.
4   Survey conducted in 1920 by the Commission on Race Relations.

4   Depression and war

To understand the Great Depression is the Holy Grail of macroeconomics.

Ben Bernanke (2000, p. 5)

Introduction

The 20 years after the "roaring twenties" were the time of the Great Depression, World War II, and the immediate aftermath of the war. So far this history of Chicago has made only passing reference to some of the business cycles that took place from 1830 to 1929, but the Great Depression must be discussed in some depth. The deep recession and slow recovery that began at the end of 2007 will be given detailed treatment as well in Chapter 8. The available data show that Chicago suffered from the Great Depression more than did the nation as a whole, so this part of the story must be told. Chicagoans whose formative years were the 1930s behaved according to what they had "learned" for the rest of their lives; to be cautious with money and wary of losing a job. Furthermore, the 1930s saw major changes in the role of the federal government in the economy that must be described. The economy did not really recover from the Great Depression before the federal government began the preparations for World War II during 1941–1942. Available data suggest that Chicago played a major role in war production and logistics, and show that the buildup in manufacturing in Chicago continued into the late 1940s after the war.

The population story for the two decades of 1930 to 1950 is not complicated. The population of the metropolitan area grew very little in the 1930s (3.2 percent), and the city of Chicago added just 0.6 percent (21,000 people). This should be no surprise given that employment opportunities were absent. The African-American population increased by 18.7 percent at the metropolitan level and 18.8 percent in the city, but the actual numbers were not large (52,000 at the metropolitan level and 44,000 in the city). Note that the increase in the African-American population of the city was greater than the increase in the city's total population.

The decade of the 1940s is a different story. The wartime boom in employment brought people to Chicago, and the population of the metropolitan area increased by 13.9 percent to 5.5 million in 1950. The population of the city of Chicago reached its all-time high of 3.62 million in 1950, up 6.6 percent from 1940. The

Table 4.1 Population: Chicago metropolitan area (1000s)

Area	1930 total	1930 Af.-Am.	1940 total	1940 Af.-Am.	1950 total	1950 Af. Am.
Metro area	4,675	278	4,826	330	5,495	587
City of Chicago	3,376	234	3,397	278	3,621	492
Suburbs	1,299	44	1,429	52	1,874	95

Source: U.S. Bureau of the Census.

Note: Metropolitan area is defined as Cook, DuPage, Kane, Lake, and Will counties in Illinois and Lake County, Indiana.

African-American population grew rapidly—by 77.9 percent in the metropolitan area and 77 percent in the city. The addition of 214,000 African-Americans to the population of the city created great racial tension, which is discussed in detail in Chapter 5. The increase in the African-American population accounts for almost all of the city's total population increase of 224,000, and by 1950 the population of the city was 13.6 percent African-American. The city was home to 84 percent of the African-American population of the metropolitan area in all three census years. The population of the rest of the metropolitan area (the suburbs) increased by only 10 percent in the 1930s, and then added 31.1 percent in the 1940s. Rapid growth was underway in the suburbs in the 1940s, even though no expressways had yet been built. The basic population data are shown in Table 4.1.

The changes in the spatial pattern of population can be described simply by the gross population density gradients. Gradients estimated by McDonald (1979, p. 122) include:

Year	Central density	Gradient
1920	79,500/sq. mi.	−28% per mile
1930	83,200/sq. mi.	−25% per mile
1940	78,700/sq. mi.	−24% per mile
1950	74,800/sq. mi.	−22% per mile

These estimates show that the central density increased and the gradient became flatter during the 1920s as the population grew and spread out. The central density declined in the 1930s as population growth fell to a low number. The central density declined and the gradient flattened during the 1940s. A comparison of 1950 with 1920 shows a decline in the central density of 5.9 percent and a marked flattening of the gradient.

The suburbs of metropolitan Chicago were concentrated in suburban Cook County in 1950. Suburban Cook County had a population of 888,000 in 1950 compared to 618,000 in the four nearby suburban counties of DuPage, Kane, Lake, and Will. However, population in these four counties was dominated by the old satellite cities of Waukegan, Elgin, St. Charles, Aurora, and Joliet. Exclusion of these satellite cities and their close-in suburbs leaves a population of 198,000, so by this accounting suburban Cook County contained 81.8 percent of the suburban population of Chicago in 1950. The Cook County suburbs provided a wide variety of options for households. As one would expect because of the concentration of jobs in Chicago, most of the suburbs could be classified as dormitory suburbs (employment well below employed residents), but a few such as Cicero on the near west side and Chicago Heights and Harvey on the south side were employing suburbs (employment exceeded employed residents). Suburbs varied widely in size and income level. The nature of land-use regulation strongly influences the nature of housing that can be constructed. As McDonald (2004b) showed, of the 88 Cook County suburbs in existence in 1946, 54 had adopted a zoning ordinance and 34 had not. Minimum lot sizes for single-family houses had been adopted by 44 of the 54 suburbs with zoning, and those minima varied widely from 2,178 square feet to one-half acre.[1] In effect, 50 percent (44, 34 plus 10) of the suburbs in Cook County did not require a minimum lot size. Of those 54 with zoning, 52 permitted some multi-family housing with minimum land per housing unit that ranged from 350 square feet to one-quarter acre. A minimum lot area of 833 square feet per housing unit is needed for the construction of a standard six-flat building on a conventional suburban lot of 5,000 square feet. Twelve suburbs met this standard. In short, the suburbs of metropolitan Chicago provided opportunity for people to "vote with their feet." However, based on the facts from Table 4.1 that only 16.2 percent of African-Americans lived outside the central city in 1950 compared to 36.3 percent of other groups, the ability to exercise that franchise was restricted.

The depression years

The Great Depression of the 1930s was both the deepest and longest depression in the nation's history. This section provides a brief review of the facts and theories that have been advanced as explanations for this economic disaster. Some of the same themes are pertinent to the first decade of the twenty-first century. A great number of economists and historians have weighed in on the Great Depression, of course, and there is no consensus on the main cause of the depression. However, there does appear to be agreement that there were several causes and exacerbating factors.

Most macroeconomists divide into two main schools of thought—Keynesian and Monetarist. According to John Keynes (1936) a depression is the result of aggregate demand that is deficient to employ the resources of a nation. Demand consists of four categories: private consumption, private investment, government purchases of goods and services, and net foreign trade in goods and services. These four add up to the Gross Domestic Product (GDP), the total measure of the value of all final goods and services produced during a year. In a nutshell, Keynes thought that private investment was the volatile component of aggregate demand because it depended on expectations of future profits, and those expectations can change abruptly according to "animal spirits," the willingness (or unwillingness) to take risks. If firms look ahead and conclude that future profits are not there, then investment spending on plant and equipment will drop quickly. Likewise, builders of housing (also a component of investment) decide to cut back based on their expectations. Employment falls, so household income falls, which in turn causes declines in consumption spending and further declines in employment and income. This process is the Keynesian multiplier.

When the economy turns down, Keynes insisted that the government must step in to stimulate investment through monetary policy and to stimulate demand directly by increasing government purchases of goods and services. Monetary policy is used to lower interest rates in an attempt to induce investment spending, but Keynes also believed that sometimes this effort will be ineffective. If firms are very pessimistic about the future, lower interest rates may not matter much at all. Indeed, Keynes thought that such was the situation in the Great Depression. Fiscal policy (cutting taxes and increasing government spending) was the effective policy tool. Keynes thought that there was no automatic mechanism that would return the economy to full employment.

Monetarists think about the essential role of money in a market economy. Their basic framework says that

Money Supply times Velocity of Money = Real Output times
Price Level (GDP).

This basic framework is called the Quantity Theory of Money. The money supply consists of the bank accounts of households and firms plus the amount of currency in circulation. The velocity of money is just the ratio of GDP to the money supply. For example, if the money supply is $4 trillion and the velocity of money is three, then GDP is $12 trillion. The velocity of money is just the number of times the money supply is used to buy final goods and services in a year. Here is the catch. Suppose the money supply falls to $3 trillion and the velocity of money remains three, then the GDP will fall to $9 trillion. This decline consists either of a fall in real output or a decline in the price level (or both). On the other side of the coin, so to speak, if the money supply increases to $5 trillion with a constant velocity of money, then Gross Domestic Product increases to $15 trillion—accomplished by an increase in real output or the price level or both. If the economy is at full employment, only the price level increases. As the leading monetarist Milton Friedman said on occasions too numerous to count, "Inflation is always and everywhere a monetary phenomenon."

Friedman and Keynes had very different views regarding macroeconomic policy. Friedman believed that a market economy, if left to its own devices, would return from a downturn to full employment. An automatic adjustment mechanism—called market incentives—would do the trick. Macroeconomic policy, if exercised by fallible humans, could disrupt this mechanism. Therefore, his basic policy conclusion was that the money supply should increase automatically at a rate just slightly above the rate of real economic growth, say 3 percent. Instead a massive wave of bank failures and huge decline in the supply of money occurred from 1929 to 1932, and the Federal Reserve Bank did nothing to prevent this disaster. Discretionary monetary or fiscal policy likely would be badly timed or just plain mistaken.

So there you have it. Keynesians look to a drop in aggregate demand, investment spending in particular, as a basic cause of the depression, and look to fiscal policy to bring the economy back to full employment. Note that the Keynesian remedy includes a sustained increase in the level of public spending until private investment recovers, not a "one-shot" increase to "prime the pump." Oh, and "jump start" and economy do not belong in the same sentence, in my opinion. In contrast, monetarists look for a decline in the supply of money as the major cause of a depression. As it happened, both aggregate demand and the supply of money fell—a lot.

It is useful to know about some of the details of the Great Depression:

- Increased productivity and over-expansion in agriculture caused prices to fall in the late 1920s, which caused loans to farmers to go bad, which in turn made banks in the agricultural areas insolvent. These insolvent banks weakened the rest of the financial system. Banks failed in large numbers from 1929 to 1933 as the depression deepened (and the Federal Reserve did not step in to prevent these failures), which caused a large drop in the supply of money—bank accounts in particular.
- Both consumption and investment boomed in the 1920s, but spending on consumer durables leveled off starting in 1926, and residential construction began to decline after 1926. However, firms continued to issue stock and borrow money in 1928 and 1929 and to produce more consumer durables in the face of the leveling of consumer demand and falling prices. Auto production peaked in June 1929, iron and steel peaked in July 1929, and construction already had peaked in April or May of that same year. Consumption did not increase in 1929, so inventories increased sharply. In short, there was over-investment. Investment spending plummeted by 90 percent from 1929 to 1932.
- Consumer credit was used extensively for the first time in the 1920s. Households undertook historic levels of debt. Home mortgages were of short duration, many just five years, and monthly payments just covered the interest on the loan, so home owners had to refinance upon expiration of the loan. When the economy went into recession and incomes declined and unemployment increased, the house values fell. Many home owners were unable to refinance their home loans and defaulted.
- The stock market boomed as investors borrowed to buy stocks "on margin." The stock market is regarded as a "leading indicator" of the economy. The crash of the stock market in October 1929 was a strong signal of trouble in the real economy. But note that the stock market crash came after the real economy had begun to decline.

The table in the appendix to this chapter shows the severity of the depression in numerical form. GDP fell by 45.6 percent from 1929 to 1933 (26.6 percent in real, deflation-adjusted terms); consumption spending fell by 40.8 percent and investment fell by 90 percent. Government purchases of goods and services actually increased in 1930 and 1931, but as of 1933 had fallen by 7.4 percent compared to its 1929 level. The supply of money (measured as currency held by the public plus demand deposits in banks) fell by 24.5 percent from January 1929 to January 1934. The low point for non-farm employment was 1932, which was off by 24.6 percent from its 1929 level. Manufacturing employment was more strongly affected than was total non-farm employment, and had dropped by 35.2 percent over these same years. The official unemployment rate was 23.6 percent in 1932 compared to 3.2 percent in 1929. Recovery from the depression began in 1934, and the macroeconomic aggregates improved steadily up through 1937. However, the official unemployment rate was still a very high 14.3 percent in 1937. The number of non-farm jobs had almost regained its 1929 total, but the increase in the labor force of 9.8 percent meant that unemployment was still pervasive. Michael Darby (1976) found what he believes to be a flaw in the official unemployment rate data in that people who were employed on public relief jobs were counted as unemployed (presumably because they were looking for "real" jobs). Public relief jobs included the Works Progress Administration and the Civilian Conservation Corps. Darby's correction to the official unemployment rate in 1937 brought it down to 9.1 percent.

African-Americans had higher rates of unemployment than did whites during the depression. William Sundstrom (1992) showed that the unemployment rate for African-American males in the seven largest cities of the North in 1931 was 39.8 percent, compared to 31.1 percent for white males.[2] The corresponding unemployment rates for females were 46.8 percent and 17.9 percent. In 1936 the unemployment rate for African-American male household heads in 83 cities of the North was 17.9 percent, compared to 10.8 percent for whites. Female household heads had corresponding unemployment rates of 24.4 percent and 11.5 percent. Sundstrom (1992) found that the unemployment differential by race for males could be attributed to differences in occupational status. However, for females the unemployment differential existed within specific occupations. Sundstrom concluded that racial discrimination was a factor in producing the unemployment differentials, especially in the case of women in unskilled service sector jobs.

The recovery of the economy was interrupted by a recession in 1938. Declines were recorded in GDP, consumption, investment, and employment. The official unemployment rate popped up to 19 percent. As the table in the appendix shows, the economy had not recovered fully until government spending was increased dramatically from $14.7 billion in 1939 to $62.8 billion in 1942 (using borrowed money) and the unemployment rate was down to 4.7 percent. In real terms GDP had recovered to the 1929 level in 1936, but the official unemployment rate was still 16.9 percent because the labor force had grown.

Chicago in the depression

How did the depression affect Chicago? Unfortunately, complete data do not exist for individual cities, but the available data indicate that Chicago suffered in economic terms more than did the nation as a whole. Mayer and Wade (1969, p. 360) stated that:

> By 1933 employment in the city's industry had been cut in half; payrolls were down by almost seventy-five percent. Foreclosures had jumped from 3,148 in 1929 to 15,201 four years later; over 163 banks, most located in outlying areas, closed their doors. Land values which had reached the five-billion-dollar level in 1928 dropped to two billion dollars at the beginning of 1933. Every index reflected the same grim story.

The land value figures were provided by Hoyt (1933). Cohen (1990, p. 222) also notes the closure of 163 banks in the city of Chicago, out of 199 located outside the downtown area. Data from Hoyt (1933, p. 489) show that bank clearings in Chicago had reached a peak of $37.8 billion in 1928 and fell slightly to $36.7 billion in 1929. Then bank clearings fell by about $8 billion per year and reached $10.9 billion in 1932 (and $8.3 billion for 1933 through November 13).

The bottom dropped out of the Chicago labor market between the spring of 1930 and autumn 1931. The U.S. Department of Labor (1932) reported that, at the time of the U.S. Census of April 1930, there were 1.559 million "gainful workers at work and drawing pay" and 168,000 persons in the city of Chicago out of a job and looking for a job or on layoff without pay. The unemployment rate was 10.8 percent. The number of unemployed Chicago workers increased to 449,000 in January 1931 (28.8 percent).[3]

The U.S. Department of Labor (1932) cited a report from the Illinois Department of Labor that the unemployment rate for Chicago in October 1931 was 40 percent, far worse than the nation. In January 1931 there was an estimated 1.101 million gainful workers at work or drawing pay in Chicago, and 458,000 unemployed (very close to the 449,000 figure from the federal source), for an unemployment rate of 29.4 percent. The number of gainful workers drawing pay fell to 921,500 by October. The number of persons out of a job and looking for a job or on layoff without pay was 624,000 at that time, so 40.4 percent of the Chicago labor force of 1.546 million was unemployed. And autumn of 1931 was not the low point of the depression.

Hoyt (1933, p. 269) reported data provided by the Illinois Department of Labor for employment and payrolls in Chicago manufacturing. These figures are in the form of an index relative to the years 1925–1927, and shown in Table 4.2. The index of manufacturing employment fell from 97.8 in 1929 to 56.5 in 1932 (down 42.2 percent) and 49.3 in 1933 (down 49.6 percent), but the index of payrolls fell from 100.5 to 26.4 (down 73.6 percent). Recall that manufacturing employment in the nation fell by 35.5 percent from 1929 to 1932, so the loss of jobs was steeper in the city of Chicago than in the nation as a whole. The steeper decline in payrolls was the result of moving employees to part-time work as well as cuts in hourly pay. Table 4.2 shows that the largest decline took place from 1930 to 1931 and 1931 to 1932. The monthly data for payrolls also reported by Hoyt (1933, p. 267) show that the index declined from 103.9 in October 1929 to the low point

Table 4.2 Employment and payroll index: Manufacturing in the city of Chicago

Year	Employment index*	Payroll index*
1927	100.9	99.0
1928	93.3	88.9
1929	97.8	100.5
1930	90.0	86.0
1931	74.3	59.8
1932	56.5	35.9
1933	49.3	26.4

Source: Hoyt (1933, p. 269) from Illinois Department of Labor.

Note
*Figures for the month of April for each year.
Monthly average for 1925–1927 = 100.

of 25.7 in March 1933, at which point the index turned up and reached 39.9 in September 1933.

Census data on unemployment by occupation group for the city of Chicago for 1930 and 1931 reported by Cohen (1990, p. 241) show that skilled, semi-skilled, and unskilled workers bore the brunt of the layoffs. Professional and clerical workers suffered less unemployment, at least as of 1931. A summary of these data, broken down by sex, is contained in Table 4.3. At 57.2 percent,

Table 4.3 Unemployment rates by occupation: Chicago residents, 1930 and 1931

Occupational groups	Gainful workers* (1000s)	1930 unempl. rate	1931 unempl. rate
Men			
All occupations	1,152	12.2%	30.7%
Proprietors, managers, professional, clerical	386	5.8%	14.2%
Skilled workers	261	16.8%	40.4%
Semi-skilled workers	198	14.5%	36.6%
Unskilled workers	167	22.3%	57.2%
Domestic workers	63	9.0%	26.9%
Women			
All occupations	407	6.6%	23.7%
Proprietors, managers, professional, clerical	221	5.0%	15.3%
Skilled workers	7	6.0%	20.2%
Semi-skilled workers	88	10.1%	35.4%
Unskilled workers	9	9.3%	33.7%
Domestic workers	69	7.7%	37.7%

Source: Cohen (1990, p. 241) from U.S. Bureau of the Census.

Note
* Gainful workers defined as persons who usually followed a gainful employment even though they may not be employed at the time of the census.

Table 4.4 Unemployment of Chicago residents, January 1931

	Male total	Native white	Foreign-born white	Af.-Amer.	Other
Male population (1000s)	1,711	1,126	452	115	17
Gainful workers (1000s)	1,153	649	405	85	12
Looking for work	25.1%	23.4%	24.6%	40.3%	22.3%
On layoff	3.8%	2.8%	6.6%	2.3%	4.4%
All unemployment	28.8%	26.2%	31.2%	42.6%	26.7%
Female population (1000s)	1,666	1,149	390	118	79
Gainful workers (1000s)	407	285	77	44	<1
Looking for work	20.2%	16.9%	12.0%	55.4%	17.6%
On layoff	3.5%	3.6%	3.5%	3.1%	1.7%
All unemployment	23.7%	20.5%	15.5%	58.5%	19.3%

Source: U.S. Bureau of the Census, 1930, Unemployment, Vol. 2, p. 474.

Note: The population includes everyone aged ten and over.

the highest rate of unemployment in 1931 was among men classified as unskilled workers.

A special census of unemployment for Chicago and other major cities was conducted in January 1931. This study broke down unemployment by race and sex, and shows that the unemployment rates for African-American workers were much higher than for white workers. The unemployment rate (counting those looking for work and on layoff) for male African-American workers was 42.6 percent compared to 26.3 percent for male native white workers. The comparable figures for female workers are 58.5 percent and 20.5 percent. Details of the special census are shown in Table 4.4. Note that the special census of unemployment included everyone aged ten and over, which accounts for the fact that the percentage of the native white population who were considered to be gainful workers was only 57.6 percent for males and 24.8 percent for females. Presumably native white children had the largest school attendance percentage compared to the other groups. The special census also included data on the duration of being out of work. The vast majority of workers on layoff had been out of work for less than one week (65,000 out of 79,400, or 81.9 percent). In complete contrast, among those who were looking for work, only 800 out of 371,000 had been out of work for less than one week, and only 9.4 percent had been out of work for four weeks or less. Among this group 29.6 percent had been out of work for five weeks to 17 weeks, 17.5 percent for 18 to 26 weeks, 32 percent for 27 to 52 weeks, and 10.8 percent for more than a year. In short, the problem of long-term unemployment had emerged and was in evidence in January 1931.

Hoyt (1933, pp. 470–493) also contains other indices of economic activity for 1932 or 1933 for Chicago, but he stopped his research sometime in late 1933. The number of property transfers in Cook County fell from 102,399 in 1928 to 43,635 for the first ten months of 1933. New mortgages and trust deeds in Cook County were:

Year	Number	Amount of consideration
1927	126,389	$1.046 billion
1928	120,346	$1.039 billion
1929	94,671	$759,000
1930	63,161	$425,000
1931	48,159	$265,000
1932	23,043	$143,000
1933	11,630	$74,000 (first ten months)

In other words, the mortgage market had collapsed completely. New construction in the city of Chicago had peaked in 1925 with 17,501 buildings ($361 million in value) and fell continuously to 1929 (6,146 buildings with a value of $202 million). But then the bottom dropped out. New construction in 1932 was 467 buildings, with a value of $3.8 million (and 412 buildings with a value of $3.4 million in the first ten months of 1933). The value per new building in 1925 was about $21,000 compared to $8,000 in 1932.

The value of manufactures in the city of Chicago was $3.884 billion in 1929 and fell to $2.20 billion in 1931, a decline of 43.4 percent. The vacancy rate in the downtown office buildings was a low 5.3 percent in 1927, increased to 14 percent in 1929, and then doubled to 27.8 percent in 1933. The number of trucks registered in Chicago declined by 9.2 percent from 1929 to 1932, and the number of telephones in Chicago fell from 988,000 in 1929 to 799,000 in 1933. Apparently some 19 percent of the telephone customers stopped paying their phone bills. The number of passengers carried by Chicago Rapid Transit Company declined from 229 million in 1926 to 197 million in 1929, and then dropped to 127 million in 1932 as far fewer people needed to go to work or to go shopping downtown. In my judgment, this recitation of data from Hoyt (1933) makes the 50 percent decline in industrial employment in the city a believable estimate. The available data show that the decline in manufacturing employment was somewhat less severe at the metropolitan level.

The response by relief agencies to the Great Depression was minimal. A survey conducted by the Russell Sage Foundation found that 18 public and private relief agencies in Chicago dispensed about $8 million in relief funds from January to September 1931, about $2.40 per Chicago resident. This amount put Chicago near the bottom of major cities; the relief provided per resident of Detroit was $6.60, in New York it was $4.69, agencies in Los Agencies provided $3.40 per resident, and the amount in Philadelphia was $2.87 per resident. However, clearly none of these cities was providing much relief. Recall that there were 624,000 workers out of work in Chicago in October 1931; the relief per out-of-work worker was $12.80 for the previous nine months. The U.S. Department of Labor on January 3, 1933 reported to a subcommittee of the Committee on Manufacturers of the U.S. Senate that these relief agencies in Chicago were able to step up their funding during the first nine months of 1932 to $25.7 million ($7.60 per resident). New York had increased to $8.40 per resident, and relief in Philadelphia moved up to $3.85 per

Table 4.5 Wage earners in manufacturing: Chicago industrial area*

Year	*Wage earners in manufacturing*
1929	551,000
1931	383,000
1933	333,000
1935	430,000
1937	539,000
1939	484,000

Source: Statistical Abstract of the U.S.

Note
* Cook, DuPage, Kane, Lake, and Will counties in Illinois and Lake County, Indiana.

resident, but the amounts declined by $1.60 in Detroit and by $0.90 in Los Angeles. It was still clear that more help was needed.

The Statistical Abstract of the U.S. (various issues) reported wage earners in manufacturing for the Chicago industrial area for every other year from 1929 to 1939.

These figures are shown in Table 4.5. The decline in wage earners was 39.6 percent from 1929 to 1933, but nearly all of those jobs had been regained by 1937. As shown in the appendix to this chapter, manufacturing employment in the nation fell by 30.8 percent between 1929 and 1933, and had begun to increase from 1932 to 1933. As of 1939 the number of wage earners in the Chicago industrial area was less than its 1929 figure by 12.2 percent. It makes sense that the city of Chicago would have lost a larger percentage of its manufacturing jobs than did the Chicago industrial area as a whole during the severe downturn because it was likely that the older facilities were located in the city. Furthermore, it is likely that the recovery phase was less robust in the city compared to the entire industrial area. Manufacturing employment located in Chicago was 491,200 in 1929 and 402,800 in 1939 (down 18 percent). Manufacturing production workers located in Chicago were 344,000 in 1939 compared to 405,000 in 1929 (down 15.1 percent), compared to 12.2 percent for manufacturing wage earners in the entire Chicago industrial area. Production workers in Lake County, Indiana, were 50,000 in 1939 compared to 58,000 for ten years earlier (down 13.8 percent).

The Census of Business provides data for retail and wholesale trade for 1929, 1935, and 1939. Retail trade employment in Chicago was 200,600 in 1929 and 159,200 in 1935 (down 20.6 percent), while employment in wholesale trade dropped from 135,100 to 83,400 (down 38.3 percent). Retail trade employment, with 184,000 jobs, had not recovered fully by 1939. Wholesale trade jobs had bounced back to 138,000 jobs in 1939.

Why was the Great Depression more severe in Chicago than in the nation as a whole? The answer is pretty clear; Chicago specialized in manufacturing, especially the manufacture of durable goods such as machinery, iron and steel, metal products, rail cars, furniture, and so on. Purchases of durable goods can be postponed, and the collective decision to postpone these purchases hit Chicago. Indeed, manufacturing in the city of Chicago and in the metropolitan area was hit harder than was manufacturing in the nation as a whole.

1940–1950: The war and early postwar years

As we have seen, the national economy really did not recover from the Great Depression before the federal government began its big wartime buildup. The data in the table in the appendix to this chapter show that, during the war years of 1942 to 1945, the unemployment rate averaged 2.4 percent (with 1.2 percent in 1944). During those four years 44.1 percent of the Gross National Product was government purchases of goods and services. However, personal consumption expenditures increased in each year; consumption was 47.9 percent greater in 1945 than in 1941 (but just 9.7 percent greater in real terms). Private investment spending was held back, falling from $18.1 billion to $6.1 billion in 1943. The manufacturing buildup began in 1941, and employment of 17.6 million in 1943 was 60.2 percent higher than in 1940.

Wartime production was organized by the War Planning Board, which was led by Donald Nelson, a former executive with Sears, Roebuck. Early in 1942 production of some 600 consumer goods was halted, leaving firms with a great deal of idle capacity. Those firms, including hundreds in Chicago, eagerly bid for defense work. That work was organized through the use of subcontractors working at the direction of the government and a lead firm. The use of many smaller firms boosted morale, used existing equipment and workers, involved shorter start-up time, and made disguising the nature of the final product easier.

Military service and wartime production made for major changes in the size and allocation of the labor force. In particular, millions of men were in uniform and millions of women joined the workforce. Data from Table 4.6 show that the male civilian labor force fell from 41.48 million in 1940 to 35.46 million in 1944, and the female civilian labor force increased from 14.16 million to 19.17 million over these same years. Males in military service in 1944 were 11.06 million. The number of women employed in civilian work increased from 11.97 million in

Table 4.6 U.S. male and female labor force during World War II (millions)

Year	Male civilian labor force	Female civilian labor force	Male civilian employment	Female civilian employment	Male armed forces	Female armed forces
1940	41.48	14.16	35.55	11.97	0.39	0.00
1941	41.27	14.64	37.35	13.00	1.47	0.00
1942	40.30	16.11	38.58	15.17	3.81	0.01
1943	36.84	18.70	36.27	18.20	8.76	0.11
1944	35.46	19.17	35.11	18.85	11.06	0.20
1945	34.83	19.03	34.21	18.61	11.04	0.24

Source: Historical Statistics of the U.S.

1940 to 18.85 million in 1944 (as the number of unemployed women fell from 2.19 million to 0.32 million). The total female population over the age of 14 in 1944 was 52.65 million, of whom 18.85 million (36 percent) were employed in civilian work. Because Chicago was a major center of wartime production, it is likely that the employment rate for women in the metropolitan area exceeded the national figure: Perry Duis and Scott LaFrance (1992, p. 9) stated that the metropolitan Chicago percentage for 1944 was 43 percent.

Chicago had a high density of manufacturing firms, and so participated in war production and logistics in many respects, from food and uniforms for the military personnel to airplanes. Duis and LaFrance (1992) estimated that over 1,400 companies in metropolitan Chicago were engaged in production for the war effort, and that the war production of these companies was second only to Detroit. Chicago industries and their wartime products as noted by Duis and LaFrance (1992) included the following:

Food products	rations with high-energy and low bulk, chow kits to mail to service members
Apparel	uniforms
Textiles	fabric products: barracks bags, gun slings, mosquito nets
Basic metals	basic steel, cast armor plate, aluminum plate
Fabricated metals	landing ships, subchasers, troop sleepers and other rail cars adapted to military use, Sherman tanks
Consumer products	antennas, portable showers, metal cabinets, radar, sonar, gun director equipment, the small walkie-talkie
Watches and jewelry	delicate parts for fuses
Electronics	electric autopilot, gauges, control panels
Pharmaceuticals	anti-malarial compounds, serum to limit blood loss, new muscle relaxant

Western Electric (at the Hawthorne Works) and Zenith played important roles in the development of sonar and radar, and Galvin Co. (later Motorola) created the small walkie-talkie (five pounds, waterproof, runs on two small batteries). With their regular products halted, Chicago Roller Skate Co. made bomber nose sections and parts for guns, Radio Flyer (toy wagons) made gas cans, and Rockola (juke boxes) made M-1 rifles.

Dozens of Chicago companies produced ammunition, hand grenades, and aerial bombs. Torpedoes, the most complex ordnance with 5,000 parts, were produced by International Harvester at the old tractor plant in Chicago and by Amertorp Company at a location just west of Chicago. The 17,000-acre Amertorp facility became the Forest Park Mall. Military electronics gear was produced in 60 local plants with about 40,000 workers. The companies were members of the Radar-Radio Industries of Chicago organization, a group that produced 50 percent of all electrical equipment in the U.S. About 100,000 workers were employed in aircraft plants of various types. The Buick Division of General Motors built Pratt and Whitney airplane engines at a location west of the city, and Studebaker built a new plant to produce machined magnesium parts for the Wright Cyclone engine.

Chrysler-Dodge-Chicago built a new plant on the southwest side that used 32,000 workers to produce 10,000 engines for B-29 bombers in 15 months. The site became a shopping center. A location to the northwest of the city called Orchard Place became the site for the Douglas Aircraft production of the C-47 and C-54 transport planes. These airplanes used engines from the Buick plant, wings manufactured by Pullman Standard on the south side, and other parts made by dozens of Chicago firms. The Orchard Place site became the military facility of O'Hare Airport, which explains its airport code of ORD.

The Central Manufacturing District on the west side of the city was a logistics center for the Quartermaster Corps. Training centers included the Great Lakes Naval Center and Fort Sheridan for the army to the north of the city along Lake Michigan. Glenview Naval Air Station trained over 20,000 carrier pilots. And, on December 2, 1942, the first controlled atomic chain reaction took place under the grandstand at the University of Chicago's Stagg Field. The atomic age began in Chicago.

The impact of war production on the movement of jobs away from the center of the city was sizable. As indicated above, major war production facilities were built at the edge of the city or in the suburbs, especially the near western suburbs. Duis and LaFrance (1992) showed that some housing for war workers was built at the edge of the city and in suburban Cook County, but that many workers "reverse-commuted" to work with great difficulty. Automobile production had been halted, and public transit was not set up to reach the more remote locations. A major factor in the suburbanization of employment was made when the Orchard Place site was chosen for the new airport. This problem with getting to a job came up again later, and is discussed in Chapter 7.

Many people, including prominent economists, worried that the economy would re-enter the depression after the war as government spending was cut. Indeed, government spending was cut drastically in 1946 to $39.8 billion from $93.2 billion in 1945. Wartime production ceased, and the military personnel were discharged and sent home. War production workers were laid off abruptly in 1945. According to Duis and LaFrance (1992, p. 116), Chrysler-Dodge-Chicago cut half of its 30,000 workers, Buick shut down the airplane engine plant in August 1945, and Douglas closed its aircraft plant with 20,000 workers in October 1945. The unemployment rate did increase from 1.9 percent in 1945 to 3.9 percent in 1946, and GDP did fall by 11.1 percent in real terms (but not in current dollar terms as price controls were lifted). Private consumption increased as rationing ended, and private investment increased, making up for much of the reduction in government spending. Net exports also provided some strength for the nation as well. Manufacturing employment had been cut back to 15.5 million in 1945, and fell again to 14.7 million in 1946, but came back to 15.6 million in 1948. There was pent-up demand for American goods such as automobiles and other items, a fact that had been overlooked by those who worried about a postwar depression. The economy of the late 1940s was growing briskly. Real economic growth was 12 percent from 1946 to 1950. The immediate postwar years were a time of transition to a reasonably prosperous peacetime economy.

Table 4.7 Employment: Data by place of work (1000s)

Area	Manuf. 1939	Manuf. 1947	Wholesale 1939	Wholesale 1948	Retail 1939	Retail 1948
Metro area*	478** 610***	756** 946***	102	155	236	354
City of Chicago	344** 403***	532** 668***	95	138	184	249
Rest of metro area	134** 207***	224** 278***	6	17	52	105

Source: U.S. Bureau of the Census, Censuses of Business.

Notes
  * Cook, DuPage, Kane, Lake, and Will counties in Illinois and Lake County, Indiana.
 ** Production workers
*** All employees

Little data on the overall picture are available for metropolitan Chicago for the war years (the economic censuses were not conducted), but the economic censuses of 1947 and 1948 provide information by place of work for manufacturing, wholesale trade, and retail trade compared to 1939. These figures are shown in Table 4.7. Manufacturing production workers in the metropolitan area increased by 58.2 percent from 1939 to 1947, while wholesale trade employees increased by 52 percent and retail trade added 50 percent to jobs over this same time period. The city of Chicago registered large employment gains in these industries as well. Total employment in manufacturing located in the city increased from 403,000 in 1939 to 668,000 in 1947. One imagines with some difficulty where all of these workers were located inside the city limits. Alas, as we shall see in later chapters, this level of manufacturing employment in the city could not be sustained.

The steel industry of metropolitan Chicago quickly shifted to civilian production. The local electronics industry resumed production of telephone equipment, radios, record players, and radar for civilian use. And by 1950 the Chicago firms Zenith, Admiral, and Motorola were the leaders in the production of television sets. Local firms produced the kitchen appliances, furniture, cookware, cosmetics, and plastic products demanded by consumers with money to spend accumulated during the war.

The population censuses for 1940 and 1950 provide a complete enumeration of employment by industry by place of residence. The data are shown in Table 4.8. The total number of employed residents of the metropolitan area had increased by 25.7 percent (compared to population growth of 13.9 percent). Manufacturing employment had increased by 19.9 percent, and 37.5 percent of employed residents worked in manufacturing in 1950 (compared to 25.8 percent for the nation as a whole). The number of employed residents of the city of Chicago was up 19.5 percent even as the population of the city had increased by only 6.6 percent. City residents working in manufacturing increased by 28.6 percent, a remarkable change given that the increase was 19.9 percent for the metropolitan

Table 4.8 Employment by industry: Data by place of residence (1000s)

Industry	Metro area 1940	City of Chicago 1940	Metro area 1950	City of Chicago 1950
Total	1,880	1,352	2,363	1,615
Construction	73	52	108	66
Manufacturing	738	461	885	593
Transportation	133	99	172	125
Communication	28	20	37	25
Utilities	26	17	32	19
Wholesale trade	68	54	98	74
Retail trade	332	256	377	270
Finance, ins., real est.	96	73	109	79
Business, repair serv.	45	34	65	46
Personal services	157	115	128	94
Amusement, rec. serv.	20	15	24	16
Professional services*	136	92	182	116
Government	67	48	93	68

Source: U.S. Bureau of the Census.

Note
* Includes public school personnel.

area as a whole. Employers were placing jobs in the city rather than in the suburbs, perhaps because the City of Chicago had zoned a great deal of land for manufacturing. Another reason is that much of the growth in manufacturing employment was in non-production workers. Table 4.6 showed that non-production workers in the city increased from 59,000 in 1939 to 136,000 in 1947, and it is likely that many such jobs would have been located downtown. Detailed scrutiny of Table 4.8 reveals that only in manufacturing did the percentage increase in employed residents in the city exceed the percentage increase in employed residents for the metropolitan area as a whole. Total non-manufacturing workers residing in the metropolitan area increased by 29.4 percent and 14.7 percent for workers residing in the city.

Table 4.8 shows that employment in transportation and wholesale trade totaled 270,000 in 1950. The movement of goods and people was the second-largest industry in the metropolitan area, behind manufacturing. Transportation included railroads, trucking, and by 1950 air transportation. Midway Airport, just one mile square, was the busiest airport in the world. Chicago was the stop-over place for people traveling by rail or air from one coast to the other, and Chicago hotels and restaurants took advantage of this travel pattern. Chicago was the most popular location for the national political conventions.

Manufacturing employment in the metropolitan area reached a high point in 1947 with 945,000. It is useful to have some idea of the amazing variety of manufacturing industries at that time. Table 4.9 shows details of the manufacturing sector for the metropolitan area arranged by the Standard Industry Classification (SIC) system at the two-digit level, with some examples for the largest industries.

Table 4.9 Manufacturing employment in metropolitan Chicago: 1947* (1000s)

Industry code	Industry	Employment 1947
	Manufacturing	945.0
20	Food products	96.8
	Meat	31.9
	Bakery	16.0
	Confections	17.1
22	Textile mills	7.8
23	Apparel	48.1
24	Lumber products	7.3
25	Furniture and fixtures	23.4
26	Paper and allied products	22.2
27	Printing and publishing	63.5
	Commercial printing	34.3
28	Chemicals	37.8
	Drugs and medications	7.1
	Paints	7.4
	Toilet preparations	2.3
29	Petroleum and coal products	23.3
	Petroleum refining	13.8
30	Rubber products	3.3
31	Leather and leather products	12.9
32	Stone, clay and glass products	17.0
33	Primary metals	137.8
	Blast furnace and steel mills	73.8
	Iron and steel foundaries	14.4
	Forgings	7.1
	Wire drawing	5.2
34	Fabricated metal products	90.2
	Tin cans	10.7
	Cutlery	8.3
	Hand tools	4.3
	Structural metal products	13.7
	Metal rolling and stamping	19.9
	Light fixtures	8.4
	Fabricated wire products	7.5
	Bolts, nuts, rivets, washers	7.3
35	Non-electrical machinery	133.5
	Engines	8.6
	Tractors and farm equipment	18.6
	Construction and mining Equipment	6.6
	Metal working machinery	18.5
	Special industry (food products, printing)	14.8
	General industry (pumps, compressors, power transmission)	18.4
	Office and store machinery	9.7
	Service and household (laundry, refriger.)	15.5
	Valves and fittings	14.9

(Continued)

Table 4.9 (Continued)

Industry code	Industry	Employment 1947
36	Electrical machinery	116.8
	Communication equipment	80.4
	Electrical appliances	11.2
	Electrical industrial apparatus	16.2
37	Transportation equipment	42.2
	Motor vehicles	13.7
	Railroad equipment	24.8
	Bicycles and motorcycles	2.3
38	Instruments	25.2
	Medical instruments	5.8
39	Miscellaneous	34.3
	Musical instruments	3.0
	Toys and sporting goods	4.9
	Office supplies	4.1
	Plastics	6.4
	Signs and advertising display	3.3

Source: Census of Manufactures, 1947.

Note
* Metropolitan area defined as Cook, DuPage, Lake, Kane, and Will counties in Illinois and Lake County, Indiana.

The largest industries were, in order, primary metals (137,800 employees), nonelectrical machinery (133,500), electrical machinery (116,800), food products (96,800), and fabricated metals (90,200). Printing and publishing (63,500) and apparel (48,100) come next. The metropolitan area had a concentration in the production of durable goods. By far the largest employment figures for sub-categories are communication equipment (80,400) under electrical machinery and blast furnace and steel mills (73,800) under primary metals. The former category was dominated by the Hawthorne Works of Western Electric, and the latter category includes U.S. Steel, Wisconsin Steel, Republic Steel, Inland Steel, and the other steel firms in Gary and Chicago. But the metropolitan area had over 18,000 people working in numerous industries such as meat products, furniture and fixtures, paper, commercial printing, petroleum and coal products, metal rolling and stamping, tractors and farm equipment, metal working machinery, general industrial machinery (e.g. pumps, compressors, power transmission equipment), electrical industrial machinery (e.g. wiring devices), railroad equipment, and instruments. There were 17,100 workers making confections (e.g. Brach candies, Tootsie Roll), 15,500 producing washing machines and refrigerators (e.g. Homart appliances for Sears), 10,700 making tin cans, and 4,300 making crafting hand tools (e.g. craftsman tools for Sears).

So the decade of the 1940s ends with a Chicago economy dominated by manufacturing and the related supporting industries such as transportation and wholesale trade. The unemployment rate in the metropolitan area was 4.2 percent, and unemployment among city residents was only slightly higher at 4.8 percent. Chicago was still the "second city" and the second metropolitan area as well, but the Los Angeles metropolitan area surpassed metropolitan Chicago in population during the 1950s. A new era for Chicago was about to begin.

The New Deal

The nation elected Franklin D. Roosevelt as President in 1932, and in his inaugural address on March 4, 1933, he stated: "This nation asks for action, and action now." A complete catalog and history of the New Deal policies enacted under FDR is too lengthy to discuss here. The policies that are important to our story that still survive are:

- Federal insurance of bank deposits, to stop the bank runs and bank failures;
- Regulation of banks and security markets;
- The Social Security pension system that also included Aid to Families with Dependent Children (AFDC) and unemployment insurance;
- The National Labor Relations Act;
- Institution of a federal minimum wage;
- The Tennessee Valley Authority and rural electrification;
- Federal public housing program; and
- Federal insurance of mortgage loans (FHA).

In addition, the federal Home Owners' Loan Corporation (HOLC) made loans so that people could keep their homes, and many people worked on the public emergency jobs provided by agencies such as the Works Progress Administration and the Civilian Conservation Corps, including this author's father and grandfather.

The creation of confidence in the banking and financial system was critical to the recovery of the nation's economy, including the Chicago economy. As noted above, the banking system in the Chicago area had collapsed, and lending and construction were at a standstill. Home foreclosures were epidemic. Federal insurance of bank deposits and financial regulation did much to restore confidence. The financial system of the first decade of the twenty-first century will come under detailed scrutiny in Chapter 8.

The National Labor Relations Act of 1935 guaranteed the right of employees in the private sector to form unions and engage in collective bargaining. This law was the impetus for turning Chicago into a "union town." Unionization in Chicago after 1935 had its conflicts; a major strike took place in 1937 that included deadly violence at the Republic Steel plant. Cohen (1990) provided a detailed history in Chicago of the lack of unionization in the 1920s and the unionization wave after 1935. In the 1920s industrial workers tended to cluster along ethnic lines and looked to their own churches and other organizations for help when needed. However, the ability of these groups to assist people was seriously diminished during the Great Depression. The Congress of Industrial Organizations (CIO) was able to organize workers along industrial lines and win certification elections in most of the major plants. The CIO was successful in the Chicago steel, farm equipment (i.e. the International Harvester tractor plant on the west side of the city), packinghouse, and apparel industries. The CIO union was rejected by the workers in the Western Electric Hawthorne Works in Cicero and the Wisconsin Steel plant on the far south side in favor of the "company" union. These two plants had histories of more benevolent treatment of workers, and were rather isolated geographically and culturally from the other industrial areas of Chicago.[4]

The Social Security system and AFDC did not play important roles in the Chicago economy until much later. Unemployment insurance benefits began to be paid in 1937. Also, the federal minimum wage and rural electrification were not particularly important for Chicago—except that electrical machinery was manufactured in Chicago, of course. The federal minimum wage of 25 cents per hour in 1938 had a major impact on the South, and according to Wright (1986), was a factor in forcing the South to make the transition to a more modern economy.

The housing programs had significant impacts on Chicago almost immediately. The Home Owners' Loan Corporation (HOLC) was a New Deal housing program that was created in 1933. HOLC sold bonds and used the funds to purchase mortgage loans from lenders. Those loans had been made to borrowers who were having difficulty making the payments through no fault of their own. HOLC refinanced the loan for a longer term (20 years) and a lower interest rate (but not with a lower remaining principal), so monthly payments were reduced. HOLC made loans to about one million households during 1933 to 1935. The loans were amortizing; about 800,000 of those loans were repaid (foreclosures were made on the other 200,000), and the agency went out of business in 1951. According to Cohen (1990, p. 274), HOLC granted loans to 45,500 Chicago area households between June 1933 and June 1936, which was about half of the homes threatened by foreclosure.[5]

The public housing program was enacted in 1937, and provided federal funds to support the construction of public housing projects proposed by local housing authorities. Chicago began to participate in the program immediately, and had constructed 9,719 units by 1950. Most of the units were constructed from 1938 to 1945; only 2,208 units were added from 1946 to 1950. The program expanded dramatically in the 1950s, and the story of public housing in Chicago will be told in Chapter 7. The title of the best book on the subject by D. Bradford Hunt, *Blueprint for Disaster* (2009), gives you some idea about how the story goes.

The program to insure home mortgages had a major impact on urban areas. The program was enacted very early in the Roosevelt administration in 1934. Prior to the creation of Federal Housing Administration (FHA) insurance, home mortgages were of relatively short duration (five to seven years were common), loans were a relatively low percentage of the purchase price (50 percent to 65 percent in many cases), and a new loan had to be secured to pay off the old loan because most of the loans were "interest only," which means that the borrower pays only the interest each month and does not reduce the principal. In short, home loans were regarded as risky. The FHA program charged the borrower a fee for the insurance against the borrower's default, but allowed the loan to be up to 20 years in duration (raised to 25 years in 1938). The maximum loan amount could be up to 80 percent of the price of the house (raised to 90 percent in 1938) up to a maximum of $16,000. The maximum interest rate allowed was 5 percent (lowered to 4.5 percent in 1940 and 4.25 percent in 1950). And the loans had to be fully amortizing, meaning that the level monthly payments were sufficient to pay off the loan over the duration of the loan. In other words, the FHA mortgage insurance created a new business model for home lending that consisted of fully amortizing loans of long duration and high loan-to-value ratios.

A similar program of mortgage insurance was created for veterans in 1944 under the Servicemen's Readjustment Act, otherwise known as the GI Bill. The Veterans Administration (VA) loan insurance program covered up to 60 percent of the loan with virtually no fee, and veterans could borrow up to 100 percent of the home value.

These mortgage insurance programs clearly facilitated home construction and purchase. As McDonald (2008, p. 24) noted, in 1950 there was a total of $45 billion in outstanding mortgage debt on family houses of one to four units, and $19 billion of that total was insured either by FHA or VA. These programs were quite successful in making home loans available to middle-class families and veterans, but FHA was subject to criticisms. The idea was to insure "sound" loans. The FHA underwriting manual of 1938 included the statement that FHA property evaluators were to consider whether the home to be insured was located in an area not subjected to "adverse influences." These included business and industrial uses, lower class occupancy, and inharmonious racial groups. The manual also advocated the use of restrictive covenants for new subdivisions. These provisions, which later were changed, resulted in limited lending in older areas of a city and lending to minority groups. In fact, restrictive racial covenants were declared unenforceable by the Supreme Court in 1948, but it is clear that the FHA was concentrated on newer, suburban housing during these first years of the program.

Planning for the future

By the late 1930s the people of Chicago realized that plans for infrastructure investments were needed, and that housing conditions and land use policy needed to be improved. A transportation plan was drawn up during 1937 to 1939 that included subways under downtown and super highways radiating from downtown. The State Street subway was completed in 1943, and the Lake-Dearborn subway opened in 1951. These remain the only two subways in Chicago. A master plan for new highways grew out of the earlier plan and was completed in 1943. This plan was implemented in the 1950s and early 1960s.

A survey by the Works Progress Administration (WPA—the depression-era public jobs program) conducted in 1939–1940 found that 76,000 housing units in Chicago (8 percent of the total) were unfit for use. This survey also found that residential areas were congested, and renovation of many units was desperately needed. As noted above, the City had already started to build public housing; 4,072 units were completed during 1938–1941, and 3,732 more units were added from 1942 to 1945. This effort was only scratching the surface of the problem. The city still contained a considerable amount of vacant land zoned for housing, but private housing construction in the city of Chicago averaged just 4,500 units per year during 1939 to 1941, and then declined to 4,000 units per year during the war years of 1942 to 1945. Significant amounts of housing construction had to wait until the end of the war. During the five years from 1946 to 1950 8,700 units were constructed in the city per year, including 16,200 in 1950. The City of Chicago established the Chicago Land Clearance Commission in 1947 with the power of eminent domain for compulsory purchase of property. The first urban renewal project was begun in 1948. The federal government became aware of the poor condition of the nation's housing, and passed the Housing Act of 1949. This act established the goal "to provide a decent home and suitable living environment to all Americans." The programs established under this act are discussed in subsequent chapters.

The Chicago zoning ordinance underwent a revision in 1942. Non-conforming uses had continued to be a problem, and thousands of individual variances to the zoning map had been granted. The new zoning ordinance addressed the problems of congestion and non-conforming uses. Allowable densities were reduced, and requirements for off-street parking were introduced. The zoning ordinance now stipulated that non-conforming uses must be eliminated over a period of years, which varied with the type of use. This was called the amortization of non-conforming use. While this provision was not enforced uniformly, it did succeed in eliminating some non-conforming uses. In addition, the amount of land zoned for industry was increased and land zoned for residential and business use was reduced. The maximum height for downtown buildings was set at 144 times the size of the lot, which translates into a ratio of floor space to land area of about 12. In other words, a building that occupied 33 percent of the lot could be 36 stories tall.

Zoning ordinances were numerous in the suburbs. Oak Park, immediately to the west of Chicago, adopted its ordinance in 1922—before the City of Chicago. However, zoning was not universal. As noted previously, of the 88 suburbs in Cook County in 1946, 54 had adopted a zoning ordinance—but 34 had not. Of those 54, 52 permitted multi-family housing in some locations. Cook County in 1940 adopted a zoning ordinance that covered the areas not within a municipality. Some of the areas zoned for single-family housing required lot sizes of five acres. The intention of such a provision was not to exclude certain types of people. Rather, the idea was to discourage development outside municipal boundaries by requiring a very large lot size. Cook County provides services to unincorporated areas, and was forcing those who wished to develop land outside municipal boundaries to create an incorporated municipality with its own taxing authority, or join one, so that the county was not responsible for the provision of local government services.

Conclusion

Chicago had been hit hard but survived the Great Depression and contributed mightily to war production. Duis and LaFrance (1992, p. 121) summarized wartime Chicago in the following way:

> The military sacrifices of Chicagoans, the superhuman effort in the defense plant, their patriotic willingness to do without, and their realization that fairness and unity were needed—all of these cannot help but evoke a sense of awe from the generations of Chicagoans that have followed.

Such sentiments apply to many other cities as well, of course. Chicago re-established itself as a great center of manufacturing and transportation after World War II. The second phase of the Great Migration from the South had begun, and the African-American population was growing rapidly. Rapid suburban growth began in the late 1940s as people who had served in the war returned home and restarted their lives. Plans for the expressway system were on the drawing board awaiting the means to go ahead. Housing conditions were not good. The 1950 census found that 22 percent of all housing units in metropolitan Chicago were substandard, meaning that a unit lacked hot running water or private toilet and bath, or was dilapidated. Some units had all three deficiencies, but one was enough to rate the unit substandard. The next chapter is a more detailed look at the state of the metropolitan area in 1950.

Notes

1   Minimum lot size for single-family houses in the City of Chicago was 3,125 square feet (25x125).
2   The cities are Chicago, Manhattan, Philadelphia, Pittsburgh, Cleveland, Detroit, and St. Louis.
3   The modern definition of unemployment is that a worker is out of a job and actively looking for work. Workers who are on layoff without pay, but not looking for work (presumably because they expect to be recalled to their employers), are not counted as unemployed. Under this definition the unemployment rate in April 1930 was 9.5 percent.
4   None of the large industrial facilities studied in detail by Cohen (1990) existed 50 years later. Swift and Armour stopped slaughtering livestock in Chicago in the 1950s, the International Harvester tractor works shut down in 1969, Wisconsin Steel closed in 1980, Hawthorne Works followed in 1983, and the US Steel South Works shut down for good in 1992 after a decade of job cuts.
5   Some analysts of the financial crisis of 2008, such as Alan Blinder (2013, p. 325), have suggested that a new version of HOLC should have been initiated.

Appendix

Table A.4.1 Macroeconomic data: 1929–1950

Year	GDP $ bil.	Consump $ bil.	Investment $ bil.	Gov't purchases $ bil.	M1 $bil.	Real GDP $1,996 bil.	Non-farm empl. (million)	Manuf. empl. (million)	Unem. rate %	Darby unem. rate %
1929	103.7	77.5	16.5	9.4	26.1	822	31.3	10.7	3.2	3.2
1930	91.3	70.2	10.8	10.0	25.7	752	29.4	9.6	8.7	8.7
1931	76.6	60.7	5.9	9.9	24.6	704	26.6	8.2	15.9	15.3
1932	58.8	48.7	1.3	8.8	21.5	612	23.6	6.9	23.6	22.9
1933	56.4	45.9	1.7	8.7	20.6	603	23.7	7.4	24.9	20.6
1934	66.0	51.5	3.7	10.6	19.7	668	25.9	8.5	21.7	16.0
1935	73.3	55.9	6.7	10.9	23.6	728	27.0	9.1	20.1	14.2
1936	83.7	62.2	8.6	13.1	27.1	822	29.1	9.8	16.9	9.9
1937	91.9	66.8	12.2	12.8	30.6	866	31.0	10.8	14.3	12.5
1938	86.1	64.2	7.1	13.8	29.3	836	29.2	9.4	19.0	11.3
1939	92.0	67.2	9.3	14.7	31.7	904	30.6	10.3	17.2	9.5
1940	101.3	71.2	13.6	15.1	36.5	981	32.4	11.0	14.6	
1941	126.7	81.0	18.1	26.6	42.6	1149	36.5	13.2	9.9	
1942	161.8	88.9	10.4	62.8	49.4	1360	40.1	15.3	4.7	
1943	198.4	99.7	6.1	94.9	64.4	1584	42.4	17.6	1.9	
1944	219.7	108.5	7.8	105.5	78.4	1714	41.9	17.3	1.2	
1945	223.0	119.8	10.8	93.2	93.8	1693	40.8	15.5	1.9	
1946	222.3	144.2	31.1	39.8	102	1506	41.7	14.7	3.9	
1947	244.4	162.3	35.0	36.4	109	1495	43.9	15.5	3.9	
1948	269.6	175.4	48.1	40.6	113	1560	44.9	15.6	3.8	
1949	267.7	178.8	36.9	46.8	110	1551	43.8	14.4	5.9	
1950	294.3	192.7	54.1	46.9	110	1687	45.2	15.2	5.3	

Sources: Historical Statistics of the U.S., Friedman and Schwartz (1963), and Darby (1976).

Note

* M1 is the supply of money consisting of currency held by the public and demand deposits. Figures are for January of each year. The low point of $19.4 billion was reached in April 1933.

5   Chicago in 1950, and a look ahead

Introduction

In this chapter we pause to provide further details for the picture of Chicago and its metropolitan area as of 1950 at the end of two momentous decades. Chicago was entering the second half of the twentieth century as the nation's second city and metropolitan area, with a huge manufacturing and transportation base and a growing downtown financial and business services sector. Suburbanization was underway as two-thirds of population growth in the 1940s was located outside the city of Chicago. The metropolitan area was about to embark on the construction of the expressway system and a new airport, and the City of Chicago had begun urban renewal projects and a major expansion of public housing in an effort to address housing problems. The University of Illinois in 1946 had opened a two-year branch campus on Navy Pier, and State Senator Richard J. Daley had proposed a complete U of I campus for the city as early as 1945.

It is fair to say that no one foresaw what would unfold in the second half of the century. The second purpose of this chapter is to provide a broad outline of trends over the next 60 years and how they affected Chicago. Population and economic growth in the nation shifted to the South and West, and the nation changed from being an economy mainly of goods production to one of the production of services. The major metropolitan areas of the North experienced growth from 1950 to 1970, but the growth may have masked underlying problems that broke out in the late 1960s and produced an urban crisis that lasted about 20 years. Major parts of the North were turned into the "rust belt." Chicago was a full participant in the urban crisis. The North experienced a much better decade in the 1990s, and Chicago was one of the best northern urban areas at taking advantage of the opportunities in the decade. But Chicago ended the twentieth century in a state that no one could have imagined in 1950, and then the first decade of the new century brought recession, slow recovery, financial crisis, and deep recession.

An American dilemma in 1950 (Myrdal updated)

In 1937 the Carnegie Corporation hired Professor Gunnar Myrdal of the University of Stockholm to conduct a "comprehensive study of the Negro in the United

States, to be undertaken in a wholly objective and dispassionate way as a social phenomenon" (Myrdal, 1944, p. lix). The project was well funded, and produced a massive report that is summarized in *An American Dilemma: The Negro Problem and Modern Democracy*. The Royal Swedish Academy of Sciences cited this work as a primary reason for awarding the Nobel Prize in Economics to Professor Myrdal in 1974.

An American Dilemma depicts the lives of African-Americans up to 1940, and Myrdal's summary of the situation (1944, p. 205) is to the point:

> The economic situation of the Negroes in America is pathological. Except for a small minority enjoying upper or middle class status, the masses of American Negroes, in the rural areas of the South and in the segregated slum quarters in southern and northern cities, are destitute.

African-Americans in the South were subjected to unrelenting discrimination and segregation. Myrdal concluded that the entire legal, political, social, and mythical system of the South had but one purpose—to create and sustain white supremacy. Some African-Americans had migrated to cities of the North, primarily New York, Chicago, Philadelphia, Detroit, Cleveland, Pittsburgh, Baltimore, Washington DC, and St. Louis. As Drake and Cayton (1945) indicated, real economic opportunity did exist in the North, but Myrdal noted that this opportunity often was exaggerated by labor agents and newspapers. He also described the high degree of segregation in the cities of the North as of 1940, and included a more detailed discussion of the Black Belt in Chicago.

Myrdal's summary of African-American society in America in 1940 included:

- African-Americans had a relatively high rate of illegitimate births (eight times the rate for native whites).
- School attendance had increased to 64 percent in 1940, but African-American adults had a median of 5.5 years of education compared to 8.8 years for native whites. Fifteen percent of rural African-Americans had no education at all.
- The FBI *Uniform Crime Report* for 1940 shows that the arrest rates for criminal homicide were 19.8 per 100,000 population for African-Americans and 3.2 per 100,000 for whites (and similarly wide differences in arrest rates for other crimes such as robbery and assault).

Myrdal attributed the destitute state of African-Americans to the racial attitudes of white Americans that had grown out of the doctrine of racial inferiority. However, this doctrine ran directly counter to the American Creed that all men are created equal. It was this doctrinal conflict that gave Myrdal hope. He believed that African-Americans had been victimized by a vicious circle in which the poor status of African-Americans fed white beliefs, which in turn created conditions that were worse, *ad infinitum*. He felt that, if government intervention could improve the lives of African-Americans, then a virtuous circle would begin that would upgrade white attitudes toward African-Americans that would in turn lead to further economic and social improvements.

Had there been much change in the lives of African-Americans between 1940 and 1950? For the vast majority of this group, the answer is "no." However, the second phase of the Great Migration had begun. About 1.7 million African-Americans migrated from the South in this decade, which is 11.3 percent of the entire African-American population of 15 million in 1950. The states of New York, New Jersey, Pennsylvania, Illinois, Indiana, Ohio, and Michigan were the destinations for one million of the migrants. Migration from the South meant that the African-American population of the region increased only 1.5 percent to 9.52 million in 1950. Unemployment rates were higher for African-American workers than for whites in the northern cities and housing segregation remained extreme, but median earnings were much higher than in the South. For example, the median earnings for African-American men in Chicago in 1950 were $2,361 compared to $1,457 in Atlanta. The unemployment rates for African-American men in the two cities were 10.9 percent and 4.5 percent, respectively. The African-American population was on the move. As noted in Chapter 4, 13.9 percent of the population of the city of Chicago was African-American in 1950.

Industrial base

As we have seen, the wartime boom and early postwar years generated substantial employment growth in metropolitan Chicago. Table 5.1 repeats data from Chapter 4, and provides a detailed picture of the composition of employment in

Table 5.1 Employment in metropolitan Chicago (employment in 1000s, data by place of residence)

Industry	Metro area 1950	City of Chicago 1950
Total	2,363	1,615
Construction	108	66
Manufacturing	885	593
Transportation	172	125
Communication	37	25
Utilities	32	19
Wholesale trade	98	74
Retail trade	377	270
Finance, ins., real est.	109	79
Business and repair services	65	46
Personal services	128	94
Amusement, rec. services	24	16
Professional services*	182	116
Government	93	68

Source: U.S. Bureau of the Census.

Note
*Includes public school personnel.

Table 5.2 Largest manufacturing industries: Metropolitan Chicago (employment in 1000s, data by place of residence)

Industry	Metro area 1950	City of Chicago 1950
Primary metals	125	53
Electrical machinery	105	76
Non-electrical mach.	104	70
Food products	100	82
Fabricated metals	84	58
Printing and publishing	79	59

Source: U.S. Bureau of the Census.

the metropolitan area and in the city from the 1950 Census. The data are by place of residence. As we have seen, 37.5 percent of the residents of the metropolitan area were employed in manufacturing, and a similar percentage of employed residents of the city of Chicago (36.7 percent) got their pay from a manufacturing firm. Table 5.2 lists the largest manufacturing industries in order for metropolitan area residents and residents of the city.

These top six industries accounted for 67 percent of total manufacturing for both employed metropolitan area residents and employed residents of the city. Less than half of the workers in primary metals (including the iron and steel industry) lived in the city of Chicago, but otherwise residents of the city dominated the other top manufacturing industries. Durable goods—primary and fabricated metals and machinery—are four of the six top industries.

The roster of top firms in the Chicago metropolitan area for 1950 included the following:

- Metals:

    o   U.S. Steel, Republic Steel, Inland Steel, Wisconsin Steel, Bethlehem Steel, Youngstown Sheet and Tube.

- Electrical and non-electrical machinery:

    o   International Harvester, Illinois Tool Works, W.W. Grainger, Motorola, Western Electric, Zenith, Ace Hardware, Cotter and Co. (True Value), Abt Electronics, Klein Tools.

- Food products:

    o   Swift, Armour, Kraft Foods, Cudahy (meat packing), E. J. Brach (confections), Kitchens of Sara Lee.

- Printing and publishing:

    o   R. R. Donnelley, Rand McNally, World Book (Field Enterprises), Chicago Tribune, Encyclopedia Britannica, Follett Corporation, Replogle Globes.

- Clothing and other consumer products:

  o Hart, Schaffner, and Marx, Oxford Clothes, Radio Flyer, Wilson Sporting Goods, Lyon and Healy (harps), W. W. Kimball (pianos and organs), Brunswick (boats and bowling equipment).

- Pharmaceuticals:

  o Abbott Laboratories, Baxter Laboratories.

- Retail:

  o Montgomery Wards, Sears Roebuck, Walgreen, Jewel Food Stores.

- Transportation:

  o Illinois Central Railroad and other railroads, Chicago Corporation (gas transmission, became Tenneco).

- Finance and insurance:

  o First National Bank, Continental Bank, Chicago Board of Trade, Federal Reserve Bank of Chicago, Allstate Insurance (part of Sears).

- Others:

  o Union Stockyards, Pullman Standard, Standard Oil, Commonwealth Edison.

Not all of these firms were headquartered in Chicago, but all had major facilities in the metropolitan area.

The principles of business location within the urban area had changed somewhat from the 1920s. Much of heavy industry was still tied to the availability of water and rail transportation. Rail still dominated inter-city freight (and passenger) transportation, but inter-city trucking was growing rapidly. Trucks were used primarily for transporting goods within an urban area. Trucks continued to make it possible for light manufacturing to locate in a more dispersed pattern as long as there were adequate major streets. The major mail-order retailers such as Wards and Sears had their major facilities in the city not far from downtown with access to the rail network. And the public transit system, along with improving high-rise building technology, meant the centralization of office jobs in the central business district. Shopping-goods retailing was concentrated downtown as well, but suburban shopping districts were growing with the suburban population.

Population and housing patterns

As noted in Chapter 4, Chicago in 1950 was the second city and the second metropolitan area. The metropolitan areas in the nation with at least 900,000 residents at that time are shown in Table 5.3. All but three of the top 16 metropolitan areas were located in the North (counting Washington, DC). Los Angeles

Table 5.3 Major metropolitan areas of the nation, 1950

	Metropolitan population (1000s)	Central city population (1000s)	Old Northwest
New York	13,318	7,892	
Chicago	5,495	3,621	yes
Los Angeles	4,650	1,970	
Philadelphia	3,671	2,072	
Detroit	3,016	1,850	yes
Boston	2,370	801	
San Francisco/Oakland	2,241	775	
Pittsburgh	2,213	677	
St. Louis	1,681	857	yes
Cleveland	1,466	915	yes
Washington, DC	1,464	802	
Baltimore	1,337	950	
Minneapolis/St. Paul	1,117	833	yes
Buffalo	1,089	580	
Dallas/Ft. Worth	976	434	
Cincinnati	904	504	yes

Source: U.S. Bureau of the Census.

and San Francisco are the other two with at least one million residents. The 15th metropolitan area on the list, Dallas-Ft. Worth, did not quite have one million residents. No metropolitan area in the South—not Dallas-Fort Worth, Atlanta, Houston, or Miami—had one million people. In 1950 there was only one major league sport, baseball. All 16 teams were located in the North in cities on this list: New York (three teams), Chicago (two teams), Boston (two teams), Philadelphia (two teams), St. Louis (two teams), Detroit, Cleveland, Cincinnati, Pittsburgh, and Washington, DC. Much would change in the coming decades.

The metropolitan areas of the Old Northwest are noted in Table 5.3. Thanks to the auto industry, war production, and the Great Migration, Detroit had taken over as the second metropolitan area of the Old Northwest by a large margin over St. Louis and Cleveland. Minneapolis-St. Paul was a rising metropolitan area but had a population of just 1.12 million, and Cincinnati lagged behind the others. Metropolitan Chicago was six times larger than the Cincinnati metropolitan, the first real city of the Old Northwest.

The state of housing in the Chicago metropolitan area, and in the rest of the nation, was not good in 1950. Only 2.60 percent of the 1.66 million units in the metropolitan area were vacant, when a more normal vacancy is about 7 or 8 percent. Some 21.8 percent of the units were substandard—units lacking plumbing or crowded or in a dilapidated condition. That means there were about 362,500 substandard units in the metropolitan area. Very few units had been built during the Great Depression; housing starts in the nation averaged only 348,000 per year for the ten years from 1935 to 1944. Housing starts jumped to an average of 1.08 million units per year from 1945 to 1949, but only 11.5 percent of the units in metropolitan Chicago had been built since 1940. As noted above, 9,719 public housing units had been constructed, just 0.59 percent of the total stock of housing units. African-Americans were 10.7 percent of the population and occupied 9.5 percent of the units. As stated in Chapter 4, the nation passed the Housing Act of 1949 in an effort to improve the nation's housing. The urban renewal and public housing programs that were started will be discussed in later chapters.

Slum housing was still a major problem in Chicago in 1950 (and in the rest of the nation, as well). The term "slum" does not have a precise definition, but it means housing of poor quality. Poor quality can include dilapidated condition, lack of plumbing, and crowding. It can also include a neighborhood of low quality involving poor sanitation, pollution, noise, crime, crowded land use, lack of public services (parks, street lights, or paved streets). The causes of slums have been debated for many years, but the fundamental cause is poverty. In the first half of the twentieth century slums were located in the older parts of the city as older housing was converted to low-quality housing to accommodate the influx of poor people. Muth (1969) conducted detailed empirical studies of inner-city housing in Chicago in 1950. His main results are summarized here.

Muth's (1969) basic point is that slums are created by poverty. Although the problems of slums may be exacerbated by the spatial concentration of poor people, the fundamental cause is poverty. Muth (1969, p. 256) found that the percentage of housing units in a census tract that was substandard in 1950 was strongly negatively related to the median income of the households who lived there and less strongly positively related to the percentage of housing units that were built before 1920. Given that income and presence of older housing were included in the model, the race of the residents was not a significant factor. The median income of households in a census tract, treated as a dependent variable, was strongly negatively related to the percentage of African-American households in the census tract and the percentage of substandard housing units, and less strongly related to the percentage of housing units built before 1920. These results say that the income level in a census tract is lower if that tract is occupied by African-Americans and contains old and substandard housing. And substandard housing is occupied by households with low incomes and tends to be old. Muth's main policy conclusion is that the problem of slums can be reduced by reducing the incidence of poverty, not by tearing down slums or building public housing. Indeed, his results showed that dwelling unit condition so measured was highly sensitive with respect to income, and he pointed out that dwelling unit conditions improved substantially during the 1950s as incomes increased.

The housing market in Chicago remained highly segregated as the African-American population increased by 77 percent from 1940 to 1950. As computed by Karl Taeuber and Alma Taeuber (1965, p. 39), the segregation index for the city of Chicago was 95 in 1940 and 92.1 in 1950.[1] Arnold Hirsch (1998, p. 23) states that a report in the *Chicago Defender* newspaper in 1947 reported that 375,000 African-Americans in the main Black Belt lived in a housing stock intended for no more than 110,000 residents. In 1950 24 percent of non-whites in Chicago lived in overcrowded conditions, defined as more than one person per room.

Table 5.4 Community areas with an African-American population

Area	1930 Total	1930 Af.-Am.	1940 Total	1940 Af.-Am.	1950 Total	1950 Af.-Am.
8 Near North*	79,554	4,231	76954	5,158	89,196	17,813*
27 West*	63,353	1,848	65,789	2,900	70,091	11,695*
28 Near West	152,457	25,839	136,518	25,774	160,362	65,520
29 West*	112,261	374	102,470	380	100,489	13,146*
33 Near South	10,416	2,474	7,306	5,370	11,317	3,449
34 South	21,450	4,058	18,472	4,062	23,294	10,920
35 Black Belt	50,285	44,644	53,124	49,804	78,745	76,421
36 South*	14,962	4,317	14,500	3,209	24,464	18,926*
37 South*	14,437	1,093	15,094	1,438	17,174	8,545*
38 Black Belt	87,005	82,329	103,256	101,339	114,557	113,374
39 South	26,942	1,146	29,611	1,552	35,705	3,024
40 Black Belt	44,106	40,460	52,736	51,281	56,856	56,178
42 South*	66,052	8,578	71,685	12,107	80,699	31,329*
49 Far South*	43,206	1,256	44,009	1,828	56,705	10,430*
67 Far South	63,845	1,967	64,171	2,479	62,842	3,756
68 South*	89,063	1,126	92849	2,008	94,134	9,857*
69 South	60,007	254	61,554	276	61753	3,575
75 Far South	12,747	4,466	15,645	6,185	22,618	8,984
54 Far South*	1,486	0	1,509	6	9,970	8,242*

Source: Kitagawa and Taeuber (1963).

Notes: Black Belt community areas are in bold type.

* Other community areas with large increases in African-American population, 1940–1950.

Table 5.4 is a detailed list of the community areas in the city of Chicago with at least 1,000 African-American residents. See the map of the community areas of Chicago (Figure I.1). The original Black Belt on the south side consisted of Community Areas 35, 38, and 40, and a second concentration of African-Americans lived in Community Area 28 on the near west side. These four community areas were home to 193,000 African-Americans in 1930, which was 82.5 percent of the total of 234,000 who lived in the city. These four areas were 57.9 percent African-American. As we have seen, the 1930s did not see a large increase in the African-American population. These same four community areas housed 228,000 African-Americans in 1940, which was 82 percent of the total of 278,000 in the city. Some community areas adjacent to these four areas experienced small increases in African-Americans during the 1930s.

The 1940s tell a much different story. The African-American population of the city increased to 492,000, and the original four community areas could not hold most of this large increase of 214,000 people. The African-American population of the original four community areas increased to 311,000, an increase of 83,000. Two of these community areas, number 38 (Grand Boulevard) and number 40 (Washington Park), had little new private construction during the 1930s or 1940s, and yet the population increased by 30.8 percent in the two areas combined. This increase was accomplished by dividing existing houses into multiple units—many without full plumbing facilities. Also, 1,251 public housing units had been built in Community Area 38 as of 1950. Community Area 35 (Douglas) experienced an increase in population of 28,500 (56.6 percent) from 1930 to 1950. The African-American population accounted for 111.5 percent of the increase. This area is the site of about 1,800 public housing units that were built during the 1940–1950 decade, and nearly all of these units were occupied by African-Americans. The public housing replaced old houses that had become slum tenements. Community Area 28 (near west side) experienced a very large increase in the African-American population of 39,726 from 1940 to 1950 as the total population of the area increased by 23,844. The area is one that contained small apartment buildings and old houses that were modified to hold the larger population, and 1,861 public housing units that were built there during 1938–1943.

Where was the remaining increase in the African-American population? Table 5.4 provides the answer. The Community Areas with large increases from 1940 to 1950 are denoted by an asterisk in the table. These include an area just to the north of downtown (site of 586 public housing units built in 1942), one area on the west side adjacent to the near west African-American area, five areas on the south side adjacent to the Black Belt, and two areas on the far south side. Of these last two, Community Area 54 (Riverdale), is the site of a major public housing project with 1,500 units that were built in 1943–1944. The other is Community Area 75 (Morgan Park), which had a significant African-American population in 1930 of 4,466 (35 percent). These eight areas account for an increase in the African-American population of 81,189 (61.8 percent of the remaining increase from 1940 to 1950). In addition, Community Area 29 (North Lawndale) was a site of what appears to be an influx of African-Americans to an area that was not adjacent to an existing concentration of this group. A small public housing development of 128 units was built in the neighborhood in 1943. The other areas listed in Table 5.4 (including North Lawndale) account for an increase of 26,550. The community areas listed in Table 5.4 account for 191,000 of the total increase of 214,000 African-Americans in the city from 1940 to 1950.

The construction of public housing during 1938 to 1950 was a factor in determining the location pattern of African-Americans as of 1950. Of the 9,719 units in place as of 1950, 7,247 had been built in areas that were at least 50 percent African-American at that time. Of course, these areas contained some of the worst slums in the city and therefore were likely targets for public housing construction. The construction of public housing that involved the movement of racial boundaries generated protests. Hirsch (1998) provides a detailed discussion of these incidents. A small riot took place in 1943 at the site of a public housing project on the near north side when it was announced that most of the units would be allocated to African-American war workers. Larger riots of whites occurred around a public housing project on the south side in 1947 and in a south side neighborhood that was beginning to make the transition to African-American occupancy in 1949. The construction of a small public housing project on the southwest side near Midway Airport created a major riot of white residents. Individual incidents were common. Hirsch (1998, p. 52) recounts that there were 357 racial housing incidents between 1945 and 1950, and that 64 percent of those incidents took place in areas immediately adjacent to the old Black Belt. Those incidents often involved arson or bombing.

The adjustment of racial boundaries followed a pattern. At first whites protested, sometimes violently. This was the active form of discrimination—refusal to permit African-Americans to enter a white neighborhood. White residents of a particular neighborhood knew that whites in similar neighborhoods would defend the racial boundary, and that the neighborhood that allowed any African-American entry therefore would be lost to whites. Active discrimination by whites in individual neighborhoods at the racial boundary was sort of "rational," but collectively this response across all neighborhoods created an irrational system. However, the demand pressure created by the large increase in the African-American population, coupled with increases in their employment and income, made the shifting of the racial boundary all but inevitable. Once the transition had begun and a "tipping point" had been reached, whites avoided moving into the neighborhood, and white owners began to sell. The increase in construction of housing in the more remote areas of the city and in the suburbs facilitated the decision to relinquish the neighborhood. This was the passive form of discrimination—avoidance. Hirsch (1998) and others document that there was a substantial rent and price differential between the white and African-American areas at the racial boundary. Many of the white sellers dealt with middlemen who provided cash for the property (but below market value). White sellers had an aversion to dealing directly with African-Americans. These middlemen then found African-American buyers, and the usual transaction was a land contract, often at an inflated price, in which the buyer made a monthly payment but did not obtain title to the property until the full terms of the multi-year contract had been fulfilled. This arrangement was necessary because of the lack of mortgage financing available in such areas.

A look ahead

We turn now to a brief summary of the breathtaking changes that have occurred over the subsequent 60 years. The population of the nation was 151 million in 1950, and over the next 60 years it doubled to 307 million. But not everything just doubled in size—far from it. Those for whom 1950 is within living memory realize, if they think about it, that life in 1950 was quite different from life today. The economy was dominated by the production and distribution of goods. The distribution of wage and salary workers by broad industry categories is shown in Table 5.5. The percentage of workers employed in manufacturing fell from about 34 percent in 1929 and 1950 to 8.9 percent in 2010. There were 10.5 million workers in manufacturing in 1929, and 11.5 million in the much larger economy in 2010 (up to 12 million in 2013). The percentage of workers who provided private services (including education, health, financial, business, leisure, and

Table 5.5 Wage and salary workers in the U.S.

Year	Total employment	Manufacturing percent	Construction, TCU*, Trade percent	Services percent	Government percent
1929	31.0 mil.	33.9	41.5	14.9	9.9
1950	44.1 mil.	33.7	38.0	14.9	13.4
1970	71.0 mil.	25.1	26.0	31.0	17.9
1990	109.5 mil.	16.2	26.2	40.8	16.8
2010	129.8 mil.	8.9	23.8	50.1	17.3

Source: U. S. Bureau of Labor Statistics.

Note
* Transportation, communication, and utilities.

information) increased from 14.9 percent in 1929 and 1950 to 50.1 percent in 2010. The percentage of workers employed by the government increased from 9.9 percent in 1929 to 17.9 percent in 1970, but did not increase further.

There were few four-lane highways in 1950, and only 10 percent of households owned television sets. A substantial amount of the housing stock was considered substandard, but now the Bureau of the Census does not bother in the decennial census to measure the variables used to rate a housing unit substandard because so few would qualify.[2] As noted above, all but two of the major metropolitan areas were located in the North. And those two metropolitan areas, Los Angeles and San Francisco, did not have major league baseball teams. There were five African-American major league baseball players. In 1950 vast changes were about to occur. This section provides a brief overview of some of those changes using population data, with particular reference to metropolitan Chicago, as a preview for the remainder of this history.

Population figures by region provide a basic picture. These data are shown in Table 5.6. Population over the second half of the century shifted to the South, and especially to the West. In 1950 58 percent of the population of the nation was located in the North, 29 percent in the South, and 13 percent in the West. Sixty years later the percentages were 42.2 percent, 35 percent, and 22.8 percent, respectively. It is helpful to consider blocks of 20 years. From 1950 to 1970 the population was headed to the West in net terms. The population of the nation increased by 34.1 percent, and the population of the North fell short of the national growth with an increase of 26.9 percent. Population growth in the South of 31.8 percent did not match the national growth rate either. The population in the states of the Old Northwest increased by 29 percent. The West recorded growth of 71.9 percent. Since the North was the mature region, perhaps it is to be expected that its rate of population growth would be below average. However, the South was not yet experiencing booming population growth even as it was making a transition to a more modern economy. The population figures for the African-American population show the reason. The population increase for this group in the South was only 11.9 percent over the 20 years as the later version of the Great

Table 5.6 Population of the U.S.: 1950–2010 (millions)

	1950	1960	1970	1980	1990	2000	2010
USA Total	150.7	178.5	202.1	225.2	247.1	279.6	306.7
USA Af.-Am.	15.0	18.9	22.6	26.5	29.9	34.6	38.9
North Total	87.4	100.6	110.9	113.4	116.5	124.6	129.5
North Af.-Am.	4.96	7.46	10.23	11.69	13.03	14.60	15.70
South Total	43.7	50.7	57.6	69.9	79.4	93.6	107.3
South Af.-Am.	9.52	10.32	10.65	12.54	14.13	17.01	19.78
West Total	19.6	27.2	33.7	41.8	51.1	61.4	69.9
West Af.-Am.	0.57	1.07	1.68	2.23	2.78	3.03	3.38
Old NW Total	40.0	46.7	51.6	53.6	54.3	58.6	60.9
Old NW Af.-Am.	2.13	3.32	4.42	5.16	5.51	6.27	6.68

Source: U.S. Bureau of the Census.

Note: North includes New England, Mid-Atlantic region, East-North-Central region, West-North-Central region, Delaware, Maryland, and the District of Columbia. The South includes the 11 states of the Confederacy plus Kentucky, Oklahoma, and West Virginia. West includes the Mountain and Pacific regions (excluding Alaska and Hawaii). The Old Northwest includes the states of Ohio, Indiana, Illinois, Missouri, Michigan, Wisconsin, Iowa, and Minnesota.

Migration was in full swing. African-Americans in the North increased by 106.2 percent. The total increase of African-Americans in the nation was 7.6 million, and 5.3 million of that growth occurred in the North.

The next 20 years are a very different story. Population growth from 1970 to 1990 in the nation had slowed down to 22.3 percent, but growth in the North was only 5 percent, a difference of 17.3 percent, compared to the 7.2 percent difference for the previous 20 years. The Old Northwest grew by 5.2 percent. One reason for this change in pattern was that the Great Migration was coming to an end, although the African-American population of the North did increase by 27.4 percent (compared to national growth for this group of 30.6 percent). Total population growth was 37.8 percent in the South and 51.6 percent in the West. What was going on? The South was joining the modern economy and its urban areas were growing rapidly, a story I have told in detail elsewhere in *Postwar Urban America* (2015). In the West the major California metropolitan areas (Los Angeles, San Francisco, San Diego) were booming, and urban areas in other western states such as Seattle, Phoenix, Las Vegas, and Denver were growing rapidly as well. At the same time the manufacturing base of the North was eroding rapidly. The North had a bad "mix" of industries for those years. And the urban areas of the North were the primary (but not the only) locations for the urban crisis that resulted in part from the loss of manufacturing jobs.

The shift of population to the South and West continued during 1990–2010, but at a slower pace. National population growth was 24.1 percent, roughly the same as 1970 to 1990, but population growth in the North was 11.1 percent—more than double the increase of 5 percent from 1970 to 1990. The population growth of the South was 35.1 percent, and the West grew by 36.8 percent. In contrast to the previous decades, African-American population growth was concentrated in

Table 5.7 Population of metropolitan Chicago: 1950–2010 (1000s)

Year	City of Chicago total	City of Chicago Af.-Am.	Metro area (1950) total	Metro area (1950) Af.-Am.	Metro area (2000) total	Metro area (2000) Af.-Am.
1950	3,621	492	5,495	584	5,761	585
1960	3,550	813	6,650	982	7,017	984
1970	3,363	1,102	7,413	1,343	7,883	1,346
1980	3,005	1,188	7,478	1,544	8,053	1,547
1990	2,784	1,076	7,553	1,525	8,182	1,532
2000	2,896	1,054	8,316	1,676	9,098	1,691
2010	2,696	888	8,504	1,584	9,461	1,618

Source: U.S. Bureau of the Census.

Note: Metropolitan area as of 1950 is Cook, DuPage, Kane, Lake, and Will counties in Illinois and Lake County, Indiana. Metropolitan Area (MSA) as of 2000 adds DeKalb, Grundy, Kendall, and McHenry counties in Illinois; Jasper, Newton, and Porter counties in Indiana; and Kenosha County, Wisconsin.

the South. The growth of the African-American population in the South was 40 percent compared to national growth of 30.1 percent for this group. The North and West had roughly equal increases of 20.5 percent and 21.6 percent, respectively. African-Americans were drifting back to their original region, but now as urbanites.

What is the population picture for the Chicago metropolitan area? The data are in Table 5.7. This table provides population figures for the city of Chicago and the metropolitan area as it was defined in 1950 (six counties) and in 2000 (14 counties). The total population data for the metropolitan area reflect the regional data; substantial growth during 1950 to 1970 that was actually greater than regional growth, very slow growth for 1970 to 1990, and growth for 1990 to 2010 that was slightly ahead of regional growth. The African-American population of the metropolitan area increased by 130 percent from 1950 to 1970, only 13.3 percent over 1970 to 1990, and just 4.1 percent for 1990 to 2010. The African-American population actually declined in the 1980s and in the first decade of the new century.

The figures for the city of Chicago tell a pretty dramatic story. It can be argued that the population of the city in 1950 was artificially inflated by the influx of migrants coupled with the lack of housing construction during the 1940s. Over the next 20 years the population fell by 258,000 (7.1 percent). During this time the African-American population of the city more than doubled to 1.102 million, to make up 32.8 percent of the residents of the city (up from 13.6 percent in 1950). Over the next 20 years from 1970 to 1990 the city lost population of 579,000 (17.2 percent of the total in 1970)—greater than the population of the state of Wyoming. What happened? As we have seen, the metropolitan area population growth was only 1.9 percent (or 3.8 percent, depending on the definition of the metropolitan area). And the expressway system was completed in the 1960s. The city was hit by this "double whammy"—very little population growth in the metropolitan area coupled with a substantial reduction in travel costs. Urban economics provides a simple explanation for the decline in the city. Suburban population growth was 17.8 percent (19.4 percent for the 2000 metropolitan area definition). During these decades the African-Americans were among those moving to the suburbs in substantial numbers. The suburban African-American population increased from 241,000 in 1970 to 456,000 in 1990 as their population in the city fell by 12,000 (after an increase during the 1970s). Oh, and the city of Chicago experienced a major urban riot in the wake of the murder of Dr. Martin Luther King, Jr. in 1968.

During the 1990s the city experienced its first increase in population since the 1940s. But this increase of 4 percent was reversed in the next decade, so the city had 88,000 fewer people in 2010 than in 1990. However, the loss was only 3.2 percent over 20 years. As Chapter 8 will show, the two decades of 1990 to 2000 and 2000 to 2010 are very different; the earlier decade was one of economic growth, while the later decade was one of slow growth followed by financial crisis, deep recession, and mortgage loan foreclosures. Nevertheless, the population of the city may have been somewhat stabilized by the population growth in the metropolitan area and the ending of the effects on population movement of opening the expressway system (coupled with the lack of further expressway construction).

The 60 years from 1950 to 2010 brought a sizable reshuffling in the list of the top urban areas. A look at the list provides insight into the changes that have taken place in the nation. The top 16 metropolitan areas in 2010 are shown in Table 5.8. Note that a population of at least 3 million was required to make the top 16, in contrast to 900,000 in 1950. All of the new entrants to the list are in the South or

Table 5.8 Major metropolitan areas, 2010 (population in 1000s)

	Metropolitan population	*Central city population*
New York	19,567	8,175
Los Angeles	17,877	3,793
Chicago	9,461	2,696
Dallas-Ft. Worth	6,372	1,939
Philadelphia	5,965	1,526
Houston	5,947	2,099
Washington, DC	5,636	602
Miami	5,565	399
Atlanta	5,269	420
Boston	4,552	618
San Francisco/Oakland	4,335	1,296
Detroit	4,296	714
Phoenix	4,193	1,446
Seattle	3,440	609
Minneapolis-St. Paul	3,349	668
San Diego	3,095	1,307

Source: U.S. Bureau of the Census.

West: Houston, Miami, Atlanta, Phoenix, Seattle, and San Diego. Gone from the list are metropolitan areas in the North: Pittsburgh, St. Louis, Cleveland, Baltimore, Buffalo, and Cincinnati. Three of these—Pittsburgh, Cleveland, and Buffalo—are located in the area most closely associated with the term "rust belt." Chicago ranked second in 1950, but ranked a distant third in 2010. Indeed, there may come a time in the not-so-distant future when Los Angeles overtakes New York as the nation's largest metropolitan area. Washington, DC is the only metropolitan area in the North that moved up in the ranking, but there is only one national capital, so its experience cannot be replicated by other metropolitan areas.

Conclusion

Chicago entered the second half of the twentieth century as the number two center of manufacturing and trade in the nation. Both the population and employment located in the city itself probably were artificially inflated by the lack of construction during the 1940s. The population of the city was its historic high at 3.62 million, and an amazing 668,000 manufacturing jobs were located within its borders in 1947. Substantial suburban growth had taken place even before the expressway system was opened. The metropolitan area was not in long-run spatial equilibrium in 1950 even assuming that expressways would not be constructed. (But, of course, the expressways were constructed.) The Great Migration was underway, as African-Americans left the South with its backward economy and unrelenting discrimination and responded to the economic opportunity in the North. The housing stock in Chicago left much to be desired, but Muth (1969) was one of the few who thought that a general increase in household incomes would solve most of the problem. The growing African-American population largely was restricted in a segregated housing market that had been unable to expand rapidly enough. The look ahead depicted the massive changes in the economic geography of the nation that were to take place over the next 60 years. Now it is time to look at those changes in detail for Chicago—the topic of the remaining three chapters in this study.

Notes

1   The segregation index indicates the minimum percentage of the minority group that would have to move to a different block in order to have an equal percentage of minority residents in every block.
2   The Bureau of the Census conducts the American Housing Survey that provides very detailed data on the state of the nation's housing.

6 Postwar growth and suburbanization

1950–1970

Introduction

The two decades from 1950 to 1970 were a period of economic boom in the U.S. The American economy largely was unchallenged in the world, and the dollar was the world's reserve currency. Output per worker advanced by 3.3 percent per year from 1947 to 1965, and median family incomes doubled in real terms between 1949 and 1969 (up 99.4 percent). Real GDP increased by 43.4 percent in the 1950s and by 50.4 percent in the 1960s. Over the 20 years population grew by 34.4 percent, while GDP increased by 115.6 percent, bringing GDP per capita up by 60.4 percent. The U.S. Census reports for 1950 and 1970 show that total employment (including agricultural employment) increased by 35.6 percent, in line with population growth. Nonagricultural employment increased from 49.4 million in 1950 to 73.7 million in 1970, an increase of 49.2 percent. This increase in nonagricultural employment that was greater than population growth can be explained by the decline in agricultural employment (especially in the South) and movement of population to urban areas.

The period of rapid economic growth ended in 1973 with the start of a period known as "stagflation," a time of low growth and high inflation. The economy was hit by recessions in 1974–1975 and again in 1980 and 1982. GDP growth was 2.1 percent per year from 1973 to 1983. The recessions are attributed to the two "oil shocks" of 1973 and 1979, and to the actions taken by the Federal Reserve to break the inflation cycle in the early 1980s.

The period of rapid growth had numerous consequences, including the following:

- The baby boom lasted from 1946 to 1964. During this time 76.4 million babies were born. Postwar prosperity was one cause of the increase in birth rates, and the growing population sustained demand for goods and services.
- The education level of Americans increased rapidly. In 1940 49 percent of students graduated from high school; by 1970 this rate had increased to 76 percent. The GI Bill provided funds for veterans to attend college or technical schools, and the modern system of higher education in the U.S. was created. The rising level of education was both a consequence and a cause of rising prosperity.

•   The rising incomes were spent on many things, but houses and automobiles headed the list. These purchases were part and parcel of suburbanization in the urban areas. And consumers bought a myriad of new products such as TV sets, automatic washers and dryers, refrigerators, freezers, stereo systems and long-playing records, frozen foods, Polaroid cameras, vinyl floors, transistor radios, and plastic products. The invention of the transistor in 1947 was the first step in the computer and technological revolution that came later.

Metropolitan Chicago participated fully in the economic boom. Median family income increased by 92 percent, and both population and employment grew briskly. As noted in Chapter 5, the population of the Chicago metropolitan area grew by 34.9 percent (1950 definition) or 36.8 percent (2000 definition) in the two decades from 1950 to 1970. This rate of growth is very small compared to the 1910–1930 period, in which the population grew by 69.8 percent, but is far more than the growth in the 1930–1950 decades of 17.5 percent. However, in both of these previous 20-year periods the population of the city of Chicago increased. Not so for 1950–1970; the city lost 7.1 percent of its population. The era of suburbanization was in full swing. And the Great Migration from the South was in full swing as well. The African-American population of the metropolitan area increased from 585,000 to 1.346 million—a far greater increase than in the entire previous history of the metropolitan area. The increase in the African-American population was concentrated in the city of Chicago. Of the increase of 761,000 at the metropolitan level, the net increase in the city was 611,000 (80.3 percent of the increase), which meant that one-third of the residents of the city were African-Americans in 1970 (up from 13.6 percent in 1950). In other words, the population of the city of Chicago that was not African-American (whites and a few others) fell from 3.129 million in 1950 to 2.261 million in 1970.

Population growth and location patterns

As noted above, using the 1950 definition the population of the metropolitan area increased by 34.9 percent from 1950 to 1970, and more that 100 percent of that growth took place in the suburbs as the population of the city fell. The later Bureau of the Census definition of the metropolitan area includes eight more counties. Population growth in these counties started to be significant in these two decades, so from here on population data will be reported for the city of Chicago, the inner ring of suburbs (the 1950 definition of the suburbs), and the outer ring of suburbs (the additional eight counties). Population data using these designations are shown in Table 6.1.

As discussed in Chapter 5, population declined in the city in the face of population growth in the metropolitan area. As we have seen, this is not the historic pattern. Something new was going on, and the evidence is in the startling population growth of 116.1 percent in the inner ring of suburbs. This was the era of expressway construction, and the displacement that was required. In addition, several other developments conspired to displace population in the city. These

Table 6.1 Population in metropolitan Chicago: 1950–1970 (1000s)

Area	1950	1970
Metro area		
Total	5,761	7,883
African-American	585	1,346
City of Chicago		
Total	3,621	3,363
African-American	492	1,102
Inner suburban ring*		
Total	1,874	4,050
African-American	92	241
Outer suburban ring**		
Total	266	471
African-American	1	3

Source: U.S. Bureau of the Census.

Notes
 * Inner suburban ring: Cook County outside city of Chicago; Dupage, Kane, Lake, and Will counties in Illinois; and Lake County, Indiana.
** Outer suburban ring: DeKalb, Grundy, Kendall, and McHenry counties in Illinois; Jasper, Newton, and Porter counties in Indiana; and Kenosha County in Wisconsin.

include urban renewal demolitions, the construction of public housing and other projects (including the University of Illinois at Chicago Circle campus). The outer suburban ring also gained population of 205,000 (up 77.1 percent). As noted earlier most of the increase in the African-American population was confined to the city of Chicago, but 19.6 percent of the growth of 761,000 took place in the inner ring of suburbs.

Over half of the population loss in the city occurred within four miles of downtown. The population in this area was 638,000 in 1930, and it declined to 581,000 in 1950 (down 9 percent). The next two decades produced a decline of 148,000 inside four miles from downtown, a decline of 25.5 percent. This decline accounts for 57.4 percent of the decline of the population of the city of Chicago of 258,000 from 1950 to 1970. Over the 40 years from 1930 to 1970 the population within four miles had dropped by 205,000 (32.1 percent). McDonald (1979, p. 122) estimated the central density of 74,800 per square mile in 1950 and 41,200 per square mile in 1970, and the density gradient flattened from 22 percent per mile to 14 percent per mile. The two decades from 1950 to 1970 were a time of a rapid spreading out of the metropolitan area—suburbanization.

Empirical studies of land values and population density in Chicago by McDonald (1979) for 1970 showed that net population density (population divided by area of land in residential use) can be described by a simple density function with a density gradient of negative 9 percent per mile. However, the study of residential land values indicated that land value increased with distance to downtown over a range of four to ten miles. Over this range of distance population density fell and land value increased. Attempts to find a correlation between net population density and land value found no correlation. Land values in the city outside the downtown area had collapsed as neighborhoods had begun to lose population. Land values are the capitalization of future land rents, which are based on future housing demand, and the future of those city neighborhoods did not look very good. The idea that land values and population densities could be disconnected during a time of population loss was introduced in Chapter 1.

Transportation infrastructure: Expressways, O'Hare Airport, and the St. Lawrence Seaway

Chicago continued to add to its impressive transportation infrastructure after World War II. These additions included a new highway system, a new airport, expanded port facilities and waterway connections, and new rail yards. With the exception of the rail yards, these new facilities were products of government planning and funding. Once again, public infrastructure development was to play an essential role in the Chicago economy.

The Burnham Plan in 1909 had included a set of expressways, and highway officials were well aware of the need for improvements in the highway system. A detailed plan was drawn in the early 1940s, but completion of the system awaited funding from the Interstate Highway Act, signed into law by President Eisenhower in 1956. The first major part of the system, the Tri-State Tollway that was completed in 1958, did not require federal funding because it was funded by bonds issued by the Illinois Tollway Authority. This highway is a circumferential route which runs around the metropolitan area at a distance of 13 to 20 miles. The radial parts of the system were built as part of the Interstate Highway System, and are:

Northwest	Kennedy Expressway	1961
West	Eisenhower Expressway	1960
Southwest	Stevenson Expressway	1964
South	Dan Ryan Expressway	1962

The Edens Expressway, which is an extension of the Kennedy Expressway that heads to the North, was completed in 1958. The Chicago Skyway, another toll road, connects to the Dan Ryan and runs to the southeast to the Indiana Tollway. An extension of the Eisenhower Expressway in the western and northwestern suburbs was opened in 1971. The Illinois State Tollway system also includes the Northwest Tollway from the end of the Kennedy Expressway to the Wisconsin border, and the East–West Tollway that runs to the West from the Eisenhower Expressway. The metropolitan area had 53 miles of expressways and tollways in 1956, and in 1972 the mileage was 506.

The Chicago trucking industry made a significant jump into the interurban freight business after World War II, prior to the expressway era. By 1949 the metro area had attained national leadership in the inter-urban trucking industry as the largest point of interchange between carriers. Jerome Fellman (1950) showed that the Chicago area was home to more Class I over-the-road carriers than any other metropolitan area. He found that Chicago was a major origin of highway traffic, as well as a point of freight interchange. Heaviest freight volumes moved to the East, although shipments to the North also were heavy. In 1949 intercity truck service was faster than rail service for outbound freight. Fellman (1950) found that 24-hour rail service extended 300 to 500 miles from Chicago, but ten-hour (or overnight) trucking service reached 325 miles in most directions. And pickup by truck service for outbound freight was quicker than rail service.

Freight exchange terminals are the primary destinations for inbound carriers. As of 1950 most of these terminals were located on the near south and southwest sides of the city. Interstate trucking was regulated by the Interstate Commerce Commission (ICC) starting in 1937. The ICC established the Chicago Commercial Trucking Zone (CCTZ), an area where truckers are exempt from ICC regulations. Trucking terminals were located in the CCTZ. Movement of freight from terminal to terminal could be accomplished freely. Also, railroads increasingly used trucks rather than the system of belt railways to move freight between rail yards. The use of trucks for this purpose facilitated the outward movement of primary railway classification yards. However, the outward movement of trucking terminals and rail classification yards was constrained by the existence of the CCTZ and the Chicago Switching District, the zone established by the ICC in which rail traffic was unregulated. These regulations were abolished in the 1980s.

Fellman (1950, pp. 77–78) noted the strong influence of trucking on the location of industry:

> The motor truck has been the most recent and one of the most powerful of several propulsive forces uprooting industry from its established locations within the congested core of the metropolitan area. Freed from the dependence upon trunk-line railway sidings by the development of a successive series of belt railways, Chicago industries are now continuing their peripheral movement in many cases without regard to immediate access to rails.

He reported that 2,500 manufacturing establishments in the city were completely dependent on trucking in 1949. Fellman's study proved to be prophetic.

O'Hare Airport is the other major addition to the transportation infrastructure. The first version of the airport was constructed in 1942–1943 to accompany the Douglas Aircraft plant that produced the C-54 transport planes. The site is located 17 miles to the northwest from downtown Chicago. The Douglas C-54 contract ended in 1945, and the airport took the name Orchard Field Airport. At that time the City of Chicago selected the facility as the site for a new airport that would meet future air transportation demands. In 1949 the airport was renamed O'Hare International Airport in honor of the late Edward O'Hare, Medal of Honor Recipient for his actions at the Battle of Midway in 1942. It soon became clear that Chicago Midway International Airport, the primary airport since 1931, was crowded and unable to handle the jet airplanes that soon would be placed in service. The first commercial passenger flights took off from O'Hare in 1955 and by 1956 the airport was served by ten passenger airlines (including American and United) and two freight airlines. However, growth was slow at first because of the lack of highway access. Midway remained the world's busiest airport. Then the Kennedy Expressway (then named the Northwest Expressway) was opened in 1961. O'Hare now had the expressway connection to downtown Chicago, as well as immediate access to the Illinois Tollway system. The addition of the state-of-the-art Bensenville classification rail yard just to the south of the airport meant that the O'Hare site was a major center of air, truck, and rail freight transportation. Scheduled airline service was moved from Midway to O'Hare by July 1962. Airline operations (takeoffs plus landings) at Midway and O'Hare for selected years are:

	Midway	O'Hare
1958	337,421	66,205
1960	298,582	163,351
1962	46,873	331,090
1964	19,017	389,640
1966	5,090	478,644
1968	26,941	628,632
1970	43,553	598,973

O'Hare had become the world's busiest airport.

The decision to build a major airport at the junction of major highways with room to expand was prescient. The Chicagoans of the day could not have known how important O'Hare Airport would become. The northwest quadrant had been the underdeveloped zone in the urban area, but now it became the growth pole for the metropolitan area. The O'Hare area became a magnet for manufacturing and warehousing—and population. In order to build the airport within the limits of the City of Chicago, the airport land of about 11 square miles was annexed. The airport site was connected to the rest of the city by a thin strip of land. However, the City failed to annex the land around the airport, and thereby did not gain the enormous tax base that developed there.

The nature of water transportation facilities in Chicago evolved from the Chicago River as the port and the Illinois and Michigan Canal as the connection to the interior to a major international port located on Lake Calumet with a new connection to the interior called the Calumet Sag Channel. The development of the Calumet River and Lake Calumet area as a major site for heavy industry in the late nineteenth and early twentieth centuries was discussed in Chapters 2 and 3. A portion of the Illinois and Michigan Canal was replaced by the Chicago Sanitary and Ship Canal in 1900. Also, at that time the Indiana Harbor and Indiana Harbor Channel were opened about six miles from the Calumet River. Plans were made to link the Calumet River to the Sanitary and Ship Canal at a point 21 miles southwest of downtown. This project, called the Calumet Sag Channel, was completed in 1922. The Sanitary and Ship Canal was linked directly to the Illinois River in 1934, thus completely replacing the old canal. This inland waterway system is known as the Gulf to Lakes Waterway. The last major development was the completion of the St. Lawrence Seaway in 1959, which links Chicago to the Atlantic Ocean. The Calumet Sag Channel was widened over the next decade to handle seaway traffic.

Transportation planning in Chicago

Planning for highways did not end with expressway construction. Indeed, transportation planning was institutionalized. The Chicago Area Transportation Study (CATS) was established in 1955 by the City of Chicago, Cook County, and the Division of Highways of the State of Illinois and worked in cooperation with the Bureau of Public Roads of the U.S. Department of Commerce. CATS was funded jointly by these four governments, and all personnel were employees of the State of Illinois. CATS produced a detailed analysis and highway and mass transit plan in 1959, and became a permanent agency because plans should be revised as circumstances change. CATS is responsible for the transportation planning work required by the U.S. Department of Transportation since 1965, and is known as one of the most professional transportation planning agencies in the nation.[1] David Boyce (1980, p. 367) has stated that: "If asked to designate a founding year for the field of urban transportation planning, I would expect many to name 1956, the year in which the Chicago Area Transportation Study conducted its initial surveys." McDonald (1988) provides a detailed retrospective analysis of the initial CATS research and plan. A review of the CATS work provides a sense of the complexities of analyzing an urban area and its transportation needs, and is an important topic in the history of the field of urban economics as well.

CATS was charged with the tasks of analyzing travel behavior, forecasting future needs for the metropolitan area, and devising a long-range plan for highways and mass transit. The initial reports included projections for population and employment for 1960, 1970, and 1980. The CATS final report (1960, p. 8) stated that: "The Chicago metropolitan area probably will grow about as fast as the country because it is still in a good competitive position both regionally and as an urban center." This statement led to the following population projections (1000s):

	Projection	Actual
Metropolitan area (1950 definition)		
1960	6,604	6,650
1970	7,835	7,413
1980	9,500	7,478
City of Chicago		
1960	3,700	3,550
1970	3,700	3,363
1980	3,700	3,005

The projections for the metropolitan area were too high by just 5.7 percent for 1970, but by 27 percent for 1980. And CATS did not include the possibility that the population of the city of Chicago would decline. The projection for the city for 1980 was too high by 23.1 percent. A major reason for the large projection errors for 1980 was the use of the 1959 national population projection from the U.S. Bureau of the Census, which overestimated the 1980 population by 14.4 percent. If CATS had been given the actual population for 1980, their metropolitan population projection would have been 8,132,000—still too high, but by only 8.7 percent. If it is expected that the population of the metropolitan area will increase by 43.8 percent (from 1960 to 1980), then it is reasonable to expect that the population of the central city at least will remain stable. Making local population projections turned out to be a hazardous duty.

Employment projections for 1980 were prepared by the distinguished urban economist Irving Hoch (1959). Hoch's method involved the following steps:

- project a final demand vector for the metropolitan area based on the population and income projections,
- project exports and imports using data on past exports and imports,
- obtain gross output projections by running the demand vector through an input-output model for the metro economy estimated for the purpose, and
- convert output projections to employment projections by industry, after first assuming labor productivity growth.

Hoch used 1947 as his base year for employment. The projected figures for 1980 and the actual non-farm wage and salary employment figures for 1947 and 1980 are shown in Table 6.2.

The employment projections were much too high—by 34.5 percent for total non-farm wage and salary employment. Manufacturing employment was overestimated by 60.6 percent, and the service sector, which in fact grew rapidly, was overestimated by 38.6 percent.

The next step was to project employment location patterns, a task that was undertaken by developing what most likely is the first model of intra-metropolitan employment location for industry. The holding capacity of each zone was determined based on its location, zoning, and net employment density in 1956.

Table 6.2 Actual and predicted employment: 1980 (data in 1000s)

	1947	*1980 actual*	*1980 projected*
Total	2,556	3,432	4,615
Manufacturing	990	874	1,404
Construction, TCU*, Trade	946	1,141	1,631
Services	468	943	1,307
Government	128	461	260

Sources: Hoch (1959) and U.S. Department of Commerce, Regional Economic Information System (1980 actual).

Note
* Transportation, communication, and utilities.

Then the increase in manufacturing employment was allocated to the zones based on distance from downtown (and staff judgment). The model generated an increase in manufacturing employment in the central city, but the estimate was not published. Nevertheless, the model projected a 25 percent increase in land in the city devoted to manufacturing. It was this model of manufacturing employment location that turned out to be the most inaccurate. Instead of increasing, manufacturing employment in the central city fell from 668,000 in 1947 to 569,000 in 1958 to 430,000 in 1972 and to 277,000 in 1982. Total manufacturing employment in the metropolitan area actually held up well from 1947 to 1972 (slight increase from 946,000 to 981,000), but the expansion of the transportation facilities generated a more dispersed pattern. The 1970s brought precipitous decline in manufacturing employment in both the metropolitan area (to 791,000 in 1982) and the central city that is discussed in the next chapter.

The projections of population and employment by zone within the study area were then used to project a travel demand matrix, i.e. a table that shows the trips from each zone to each zone. The zones were arranged in rings around the central area. For example, origins of trips to work during the morning rush hour were based on the population in each zone, and the destinations were based on the amount of employment in each zone and the distance from the residential zone. The trips were assigned to auto or transit based on vehicle ownership and the availability of transit. As it turned out, the CATS projection of total travel demand was reasonably accurate. McDonald (1988, p. 259) estimated that person trips per day in 1980 for the metropolitan area were 19.7 million, compared to the CATS projection of 22.3 million (too much by 13.2 percent). The population and employment projections were much too high, but were offset by under-predictions of vehicle ownership and the propensity of people to travel. In addition, the projection of trips to downtown for 1980 was remarkably accurate—too low by 5.5 percent.

What was the CATS plan? CATS proposed a highway plan to accommodate the projection that vehicle trips would double. The plan envisioned 681 miles of additional expressways beyond the 281 miles that were completed or under construction in 1959. The plan provided for a lattice of expressways that would have covered the entire metropolitan area. Expressways were to be built along major streets in Chicago and the near-in suburbs. The first stage consisted of 109 miles, mainly consisting of circumferential (or "crosstown") expressways. The mass transit plan was not elaborate, and consisted of extending existing transit lines. The transit line from downtown to the Northwest was to be extended to O'Hare Airport, and the line to the South also was proposed for extension. An express bus system was proposed for the Stevenson Expressway to the Southwest, the one quadrant of the city without a transit line. And an elevated line was proposed to connect the line to the South to run to the West and Midway Airport.

What was built? The rather modest transit plan largely was implemented. The main difference is that a transit line was built directly from downtown southwest to Midway Airport in the 1980s (not the express bus line or the elevated line from the South line).[2] However, only one part of the first stage of the highway plan was built—a connecting highway running north and south in the far western suburbs. With one exception, the rest of the highway plan essentially was dead on arrival. The one exception is known as the Crosstown Expressway, which was designed to run north and south at 5000 West along Cicero Avenue from the Kennedy Expressway to the Stevenson Expressway and beyond, and then to turn to the East and connect to the Dan Ryan Expressway. The City of Chicago (in other words, Mayor Richard J. Daley) strongly supported this highway, as long as the federal government would pay most of the cost. The plan that was supported by Mayor Daley was to separate the north-bound lanes from the south-bound lanes by a city block, that would be cleared and become an enormously long industrial park. Numerous community groups opposed the plan, and it died shortly after the death of Mayor Daley in 1976.

The failure of the rest of the CATS highway plan to garner any public support was the result of a lack of federal funding after completion of the original Interstate Highway system (and the lack of local funds as well), and the fact that community interests were not taken into account. The disruptions and displacements arising from expressway construction were fresh in the minds of Chicagoans.

Employment growth and location patterns

The number of employed residents of the metropolitan area increased by 31.6 percent from 1950 to 1970, while the population increased by 36.8 percent. This outcome is in contrast to the figures for the nation, which show that non-agricultural employment grew more rapidly than population. Table 6.3 shows employment by industry by place of residence for the metropolitan area and the city of Chicago. The metropolitan area consists of all 14 counties in the later (2000) definition. Two facts stand out for the metropolitan area. First, employment

Table 6.3 Employment: 1950–1970 (data in 1000s, by place of residence)

Industry	Metro area 1950	City of Chicago 1950	Metro area 1970	City of Chicago 1970
Total	2,455	1,615	3,231	1,390
Construction	114	66	141	44
Manufacturing	922	593	978	404
TCU*	247	169	301	103
Whls. and retail trade	492	344	618	255
Fin., ins. and real est.	111	79	172	81
Bus. and repair serv.	67	46	108	51
Personal services	132	94	120	58
Professional serv.	189	116	462	192
Public admin.	96	68	131	73
Other	84	40	200	129

Source: U.S. Bureau of the Census and HUD State of the Cities Data System.

Note
* Transportation, communication, and utilities.

in professional services increased by 273,000 (35 percent of the total increase), and manufacturing employment held up well, and actually increased by 6 percent. The number of employed residents of the city of Chicago fell by 225,000 (7.2 percent)—in line with the population decline of 7.1 percent. Professional service employment for Chicago residents increased by 66 percent, a sizable increase. However, most of these professionals (58 percent) lived outside the city. The number of city residents employed in manufacturing fell by 189,000 (32 percent), which accounts for most of the decline in employed residents. Sizable employment losses for city residents occurred in transportation, communication, and utilities, in wholesale and retail trade, and in personal services as well.

Employment data by place of work for the whole metropolitan area should be very close to the figures by place of residence. The only differences are the number of residents who worked outside the metropolitan area, and the number of residents outside the metropolitan area who came into it for work. The use of the 14-county metropolitan area should minimize these differences. This assertion cannot be made for the city of Chicago. The number of employed residents and the number of jobs located in the city might be quite different. And unfortunately, complete data on employment by place of work are not available for 1950. Sources can be pieced together to present a less than complete picture.

Manufacturing, wholesale trade, and retail trade employment as recorded in the Census of Manufactures and Census of Business are shown in Table 6.4. The different sources of data for an urban area never match exactly. The figures for manufacturing employment in Table 6.4 are slightly different from those in Table 6.3, but both tables show that employment in this sector did not fall at the metropolitan level, and indeed had increased slightly toward the end of the 1960s/1970. Manufacturing was buoyed by the buildup for the Vietnam War, and then receded by 7.8 percent as of 1972. But manufacturing employment at the metropolitan level was still greater in 1972 than in 1947. However, manufacturing jobs in the city of Chicago fell continuously from 1947 to 1963, increased during

Table 6.4 Employment in metropolitan Chicago: 1947–1972 (data in 1000s)

Year	Manuf. metro	Manuf. Chgo. City	Wholesale metro	Wholesale Chgo. City	Retail metro	Retail Chgo. City	Retail CBD
1947/48	946	668	155	138	354	249	65
1954	942	615	150	131	324	224	49
1958	944	569	166	132	351	225	46
1963	943	509	175	121	373	210	40
1967	1,064	546	203	131	411	218	38
1972	981	430	199	101	454	193	32

Sources: Census of Manufactures, Census of Business, and Meyer, Kain, and Wohl (1965, p. 37) for CBD retail in 1948 and 1954.

Note
* Metropolitan area defined as Cook, DuPage, Kane, Lake, and Will counties in Illinois and Lake County, Indiana.

the Vietnam buildup, and then fell by 116,000 from 1967 to 1972. Overall manufacturing jobs in the city fell by 35.6 percent from 1947 to 1972 even as the jobs at the metropolitan level increased by 3.7 percent. So here we have it once again. Slow growth at the metropolitan level produces decline in the central city—in this case a very large decline.

Employment in wholesale trade increased at the metropolitan level and held up pretty well in the city until 1967. In the end employment in this sector increased by 28.4 percent from 1948 to 1972, and fell by 26.8 percent in the city of Chicago. Retail trade followed a similar pattern. Retail trade employment at the metropolitan level increased by 28.2 percent from 1948 to 1972, and declined by 22.5 percent in the big city. The additional piece of information is retail trade employment located in the central business district (CBD). Employment fell by 50.7 percent, which accounts for 58.9 percent of the decline in the city even though the CBD contained only 26.1 percent of retail trade employment in the city in 1948. Downtown was not doing well by this measure as retailing was shifting to the shopping centers in the suburbs. The employment declines shown in Table 6.4 in the city of Chicago exceed the decline in population of 7.1 percent.

The Bureau of the Census started to collect data on the journey to work in the 1960 decennial census, so we have additional data on employment located in the city of Chicago for 1960 and 1970 as follows:

	1960	1970
Construction	65,000	48,000
Trans., comm., utilities	157,000	118,000
Fin. ins., real est.	101,000	109,000
Services (includes gov't.)	287,000	311,000

Source: Census Journey to Work Survey.

This source shows job losses in construction and transportation, communication, and utilities of about 25 percent (56,000 jobs) in ten years, but gains in FIRE and services of 8.3 percent (32,000 jobs). The service sector as defined here includes business and repair services, personal services, professional services, and public administration. (See Table 6.3.)

The CATS did surveys of travel to work in 1956 and 1970, and found that employment in the CBD fell modestly from 539,000 in 1956 to 514,000 in 1970 (4.6 percent). According to this source, CBD employment in services (including government) increased from 222,000 to 252,000, while employment in manufacturing, trade, and transportation, communication, and utilities fell. Downtown manufacturers cut 19,000 jobs from 134,000 in 1956, trade employment fell from 102,000 to 67,000, and TCU employment dropped to 52,000 from 59,000. The services sector in this data source includes FIRE. Note that the increase of 30,000 service sector jobs reported by CATS is reasonably consistent with the increase of 32,000 for the decade of 1960–1970 from the Journey to Work surveys for the entire central city.

The overall picture for employment from 1950 to 1970 is one of substantial growth at the metropolitan level in line with population growth and a large decline in jobs located in the city of Chicago. The exception for the city is the growth in jobs in the service sector, including financial services, business services, and professional services (legal, medical, etc.). The city was shifting away from its original manufacturing base toward the service economy. The metropolitan area was making this shift as well, but without a loss of manufacturing jobs. Here is an analogy for the change in the location of manufacturing jobs. Between 1947 and 1972 the number of jobs was roughly constant, and it was like pouring a cup of soup from a deep bowl into a shallow bowl.

The decline in manufacturing jobs located in the city and the increase in the suburbs resulted from the following catalog of causes:

- Firms move from city to suburbs
- Firms in city go out of business (deaths exceed births)
- New firms start in the suburbs (births exceed death)

Chicago has a long history of industrial relocation studies. The earliest study was conducted by Mitchell (1933), who examined new plants in the suburbs for 1926–1931. He found that most of the 249 new plants (192, 77 percent) were located in the Chicago Switching District, which (1933, p. 69) "enabled these new industries to enjoy all of the advantages of the superior transportation to be found within the city without suffering the disadvantages of a congested city location." Of these new plants in the Chicago Switching District, 109 (57 percent) had relocated from the city to a suburban location still inside the district. New plants located outside the Chicago Switching District numbered 57, of which 18 (32 percent) had relocated from the city of Chicago. In other words, this first study showed that about half (127) of new plants in the suburbs had relocated from the city of Chicago. The other new plants were entirely new or had moved from suburb to suburb or from outside the urban area.

Mitchell (1933) advocated the suburbanization of industry to escape the crowded conditions in the city. His study led him to conclude (1933, p. 69):

> If, then, by some relatively simple expedient such as the extension of additional motor highways, belt-line facilities, and switching services into the outlying areas of the region these could be made attractive to industry, the result in time might be a rather thoroughgoing decentralization of industry throughout the region without resort to questionable expedients.

It is not clear what the questionable expedients might have been, but Mitchell (1933, p. 69) saw the benefits of decentralization:

> Such efforts would, there is reason to believe, yield vast benefits in improved living standards for industrial workers and at the same time would not do

such great violence to those economic considerations which in the final analysis always have determined where industries should locate.

Urban analysts and reformers of that day had suburbanization as an objective, and one can suppose that the expressway system that was planned in the late 1930s and early 1940s had this goal in mind. Indeed, as Cohen (1990) discussed at length, residential communities had already grown up around centers of employment located at sizable distances from downtown.

The period after World War II brought even more relocation of industrial establishments from the city to the suburbs, and most new firms located in the suburbs as well. Industry was attracted to the northern, northwestern, and western suburbs, areas that had not been heavily developed by industry in the past. The firms that relocated to the suburbs tended to be light manufacturers of durable goods. An interview study by Melvin (1965) revealed that the suburban firms sought spacious facilities, while firms that selected a location within the city were seeking accessibility. Over time the accessible periphery was not so much defined by the Chicago Switching District, but rather by the Chicago Commercial Trucking Zone and the new highway system. The O'Hare Airport area was a major location for industry and warehousing. As noted earlier, it has immediate access to rail, highway, and air transportation.

The most comprehensive study of the 1950 to 1970 period was conducted by the Northeastern Illinois Planning Commission (1965). This study covered components of manufacturing employment change for the years 1955 to 1963 broken down into 38 geographic areas. The data source reportedly covered 99 percent of manufacturing employment, and classified changes in establishments that did not relocate, employment in new establishments, employment in establishments that moved into or out of an area, and employment in establishments that terminated. Total manufacturing employment for the metropolitan area as recorded in this study was 866,000 in 1955 and 835,000 in 1963, a decline of 31,000 jobs. During this eight-year period 1,073 establishments in the city of Chicago moved out of one of the eight zones in the city. Other zones in the city were the destinations for 615 of those establishments, and 458 moved to the suburbs. A total of 688 establishments moved into one of the eight city zones; 625 moved from another city zone; and 63 moved in from the suburbs. (The 615 and 625 figures should be equal of course, but there is a small error.) Establishments that moved out of the city to the suburbs outnumbered those that moved in by a factor of 7.3 to one. Manufacturing employment in the city zones fell from 599,000 in 1955 to 468,000 in 1963. Net relocations accounted for 30.5 percent of the decline in employment of 131,000. The remaining 69.5 percent of the decline was net employment losses in establishments that remained and net deaths of firms. Of those establishments that moved out of the city, 175 went to the western suburbs, 242 had the north and northwest suburbs as their destinations, and only 38 moved to the south and southwest suburbs. A total of 196 establishments moved from one suburban zone to another. Employment changes (1000s) for these three suburban areas are:

	Manuf. 1955	Employ. 1963	Change	Percent due to net relocations
West	154.6	189.4	34.8	38.8
North/NW	65.1	122.2	57.1	63.9
South/SW	43.0	52.0	9.0	20.0

Manufacturing employment almost doubled in the north and northwest suburbs from 1955 to 1963, and the employment growth was mostly due to relocations. Otherwise, changes in employment in the city and the other suburban areas were dominated by employment changes in existing establishments or net firm births (births minus deaths), not relocations.

During the 1950s and 1960s the city of Chicago lost employment in large numbers across the board, with the exception of the service sector. The studies of employment change in manufacturing showed that about 30 percent of the employment loss was due to the relocations of plants to the suburbs and the rest to employment losses in establishments that did not relocate and net firm deaths. Firms were responding to the improvements in the highway system and the opening of O'Hare Airport, and to the suburbanization of the population. The accessible periphery had expanded.

African-American population growth and segregation

The decades from 1950 to 1970 were the peak years for the Great Migration from the South. As the data in Table 5.6 show, the African-American population of the nation grew by 7.6 million (from 15 million in 1950 to 22.6 million in 1970), and that 5.27 million (69 percent) of that growth was located in the North. In 1970 the African-American population was roughly equally divided between the North (45.3 percent) and the South (47.2 percent), with the remaining 7.4 percent in the West. The African-American population of the states of the Old Northwest was 2.13 million in 1950 and 4.42 million in 1970, an increase of 2.29 million. The Chicago metropolitan area was home to 585,000 African-Americans in 1950 and 1.346 million in 1970, an increase of 761,000. In other words, metropolitan Chicago with 11.2 percent of the population of the states of the Old Northwest accounted for 33.2 percent of the increase in the African-American population in the region during these two decades. And the city of Chicago, with 6.5 percent of the population of the Old Northwest, was home to 26.6 percent of the African-American population growth of this region.

Chicago was not the only primary destination for the Great Migration. Tabulations by James Gregory (2005) from census public use micro data show that 418,000 African-Americans born in the South lived in metropolitan Chicago in 1970, but that 601,000 native African-American southerners resided in metropolitan New York. The other top urban areas on Gregory's list are Los Angeles (314,000), Detroit (268,000), and Philadelphia (202,000). An earlier publication by Gregory (1995) showed that a total of 3.48 million African-Americans born in the South lived elsewhere in the U.S. in 1970. These five top metropolitan areas for southern-born African-Americans account for 1.80 million, which is 51.8 percent of this total.

Gregory (1995, 2005) is well known for documenting that the migration of the white population from the South was far larger than that of the African-American population. Whites born in the South living elsewhere in the U.S. were 4.82 million in 1950 and 7.38 million in 1970, compared to 2.59 million and 3.48 million African-Americans in 1950 and 1970, respectively. The main sources of white migrants from the South were the states of West Virginia, Kentucky, Arkansas, and Oklahoma. States of the deep South (Alabama, Mississippi, and North Carolina) provided some white migrants, but far fewer than the top four. The destinations of the white migrants were diverse; California and Florida were the largest recipient states, but the metropolitan areas of the North received large numbers as well. The primary origins of the African-American migrants were states of the deep South (Mississippi, Alabama, South Carolina, North Carolina) and Arkansas. The destination pattern for African-American migrants from the South was less diverse; primary destinations from 1950 to 1970 were California, New York, Illinois, Ohio, and Michigan.

The increase in the African-Americans in the city of Chicago brought about profound changes in the racial geography of the city, but not in the "system" that had been established for expanding the supply of housing available to them. Community areas that were adjacent to existing concentrations of African-Americans were areas where the expansion took place. Refer back to the Chicago community area map (Figure I.1). Those community areas are located on the west side and the south side. The list of community areas that were less than 20 percent African-American in 1950 and equal to or greater than 75 percent African-American in 1970 is shown in Table 6.5. All of these community areas

Table 6.5 African-American population in Chicago community areas: Virtually complete racial transition, 1950–1970

	1950		1970	
	Population	*Pct. Af.-Am.*	*Population*	*Pct. Af.-Am.*
West side				
26	48,328	0%	48,464	97%
27	70,091	17%	52,185	98%
29	100,489	13%	94,772	96%
South side				
39	35,705	8%	21,257	79%
44	40,845	1%	47,287	98%
45	14,358	0%	14,412	83%
68	94,134	10%	89,713	96%
69	61,753	6%	54,414	98%
73	24,488	2%	36,540	75%
Total	490,191		459,044	

Source: Chicago Fact Book Consortium (1995).

Table 6.6 African-American population in Chicago community areas: Fully in the process of racial transition in 1970

	1950		1970	
	Population	*Pct. Af.-Am.*	*Population*	*Pct. Af.-Am.*
8	89,196	20%	70,269	37%
25	132,180	0%	127,981	33%
41	55,206	3%	33,559	31%
43	79,115	0%	80,660	69%
48	9,337	9%	20,123	45%
49	56,705	18%	65,512	55%
50	8,899	0%	10,893	48%
67	62,842	6%	61,910	48%
71	60,978	0%	68,854	69%
Total	554,458		539,761	

Source: Chicago Fact Book Consortium (1995).

experienced large increases in the African-American population. Together these nine account for an increase in African-Americans of 393,000 (out of a total increase in the city of 610,000).

Nine other community areas had not begun the process of racial transition—with 20 percent or fewer African-Americans in 1950, but were fully in the process of racial transition with 30 percent to 69 percent in 1970. Seven of these community areas are located on the south side, one on the west side (CA25), and one (CA8) located on the near north side. The population figures for these nine are shown in Table 6.6. Community Area 25 (Austin on the west side) is a very large area, and had an increase in African-American population of 42,000 and Community Area 43 (South Shore on the south side, just to the south of the University of Chicago) had an increase of 55,500. Together these ten community areas account for an increase of 167,000 African-Americans.

Five community areas began the process of racial transition from 1950 to 1970 and were not fully in the process of transition in 1970. Two are on the west side (CA23 and CA30) and three on the south side (CA46, CA51, and CA53). Their data are displayed in Table 6.7. These areas had a net gain of 38,000 African-Americans. Six other community areas, five on the south side and one on the near north side (CA28), were in the process of racial transition in 1950, with 30 percent to 50 percent African-Americans. This group of community areas is also shown in Table 6.7. Four of these community areas completed or nearly completed the process of racial transition by 1970, but two did not. Portions of Community Area 34 (Armour Square) were demolished to make way for the Dan Ryan Expressway, and about 6,000 people were displaced. In addition, the area attracted Asian-Americans and Mexican-Americans during the 1960s. The net effect was to reduce the African-American population by about 6,700. Community Area 75 (Morgan Park) was a fairly high-income neighborhood on the far south side.

Table 6.7 African-American population in Chicago community areas

	1950		1970	
	Population	*Pct. Af.-Am.*	*Population*	*Pct. Af.-Am.*
Community areas that began racial transition: 1950 to 1970				
23	76,199	0%	71,726	19%
30	66,977	2%	62,895	10%
46	55,715	5%	45,655	22%
51	17,496	0%	19,405	16%
53	29,265	0%	40,318	17%
Total	245,632		239,999	
Community areas in the process of racial transition in 1950				
28	160,362	41%	78,703	72%
33 (CBD)	11,317	30%	8,767	85%
34	23,294	47%	13,058	32%
37	17,174	50%	7,372	97%
42	80,699	39%	53,814	96%
75	22,618	40%	31,016	48%
Total	315,464		192,730	
Community areas that had completed racial transition by 1950: Old Black Belt				
35	78,745	97%	41,276	86%
38	114,557	99%	80,150	99%
40	56,856	99%	46,024	99%
Others				
36	24,464	77%	18,291	99%
54	9,790	84%	15,018	95%
Total	284,412		200,739	

Source: Chicago Fact Book Consortium (1995).

The population growth of 8,400 included an increase of the African-American population of 5,900, but the area continued to attract white households as well. These six areas had a net change in African-American population of 13,000.

The last group of community areas of interest is the group that had completed racial transition in 1950. This group includes the three old Black Belt areas. The data for these five are also shown in Table 6.7. The three old Black Belt areas lost population of 85,600, the result of demolition for the Dan Ryan Expressway and the construction of public housing. Community Area 54 on the far south side (the location of a large public housing project in 1950) experienced a further increase in the African-American population of 6,000 as more public housing units were constructed. Community Area 36 (Kenwood), just to the north of the University of Chicago, lost all of its white population and 800 African-American residents.

The change in the location of the African-American population from 1950 to 1970 therefore can be summarized as follows:

Type of community area	Change in African-Americans
Completed racial transition, 1950	−80,000
Began racial transition 1950–1970, completed by 1970	393,000
Began racial transition 1950–1970, not fully in process of racial transition, 1970	48,000
Began racial transition, 1950–1970, in transition in 1970	167,000
In racial transition in 1950	13,000

The 34 community areas (out of 77) enumerated in this discussion account for an increase in the African-American population of 531,000, which is 87 percent of the total increase in the city of Chicago of 610,000 from 1950 to 1970. A majority of the increase took place in community areas that began and completed racial transition after 1950. Indeed, an increase of 608,000 African-Americans was to be found in those community areas that had begun the process of racial transition during 1950 to 1970. The community areas that had completed transition as of 1950 or that were in transition in 1950 saw a net decline in the African-American population of 67,000.

The 34 community areas in this discussion also lost total population of 258,000, which accounts exactly for the population decline in the city of Chicago from 1950 to 1970 of 258,000. As shown in Tables 6.5–6.7, the largest population losses were among the community areas that fully were in racial transition in 1950 (loss of 123,000) and those that had completed racial transition in 1950 (loss of 84,000). The massive changes in the racial geography of the city included a reduction in the non-African-American population of 868,000—a change that was facilitated by the opening of the expressway system and the movement of jobs and the construction of housing in the suburbs. And much more change would follow.

The African-American population in the metropolitan area outside of the city of Chicago increased from 92,000 to 241,000 over these two decades. Most of the increase of 149,000 can be broken down as follows, as shown in Table 6.8. The satellite cities account for an increase in the African-American population of 77,000, where 54,000 was in Gary, Indiana. The other four old satellite cities increased by 23,000. They were created by railroad junctions, and have formed a ring around Chicago since the late nineteenth century. The south suburbs increased by 18,000 and two suburbs in the West and North together increased by 19,000. These 11 municipalities account for 114,000 of the total increase of 149,000 (77 percent). The southern portion of the metropolitan area, including Gary, accounted for almost half (48 percent) of the increase in the suburban African-Americans.

Table 6.8 African-American population of some major suburbs

	1950		1970	
	Population	*Pct. Af.-Am.*	*Population*	*Pct. Af.-Am.*
Satellite cities				
Gary, IN	133,911	29%	175,415	53%
Aurora	50,576	2%	81,293	10%
Elgin	44,223	2%	55,691	5%
Joliet	51,601	4%	80,378	12%
Waukegan	38,946	6%	65,269	13%
South suburbs				
Chicago Hts.	24,551	17%	40,900	17%
Harvey	20,683	5%	34,636	31%
E. Chgo., IN	54,263	19%	46,982	27%
Hammond, IN	87,594	1%	107,790	4%
West suburbs				
Maywood	27,473	9%	38,036	41%
North suburbs				
Evanston	73,641	9%	79,808	16%

Source: Chicago Fact Book Consortium (1995).

Public housing and urban renewal

Early housing reformers thought that slum housing was a cause of several social problems such as poor public health, disease, juvenile delinquency, and crime. By the 1920s housing advocates could see that the reforms implemented by local governments (building and housing codes) had proved ineffective at reducing the problems. They began to argue that the government should supply housing for the poor directly. Edith Elmer Wood was an influential reformer/economist who wrote several books in which she argued that the private housing market was incapable of supplying decent housing that was affordable by poor families. In one book (1931) she concluded that one-third of families could not afford acceptable housing (rent no greater than 20 percent of income). This book likely was the source of the statement in President Roosevelt's second inaugural address that "one third of the nation is ill-housed." The passage of the Housing Act of 1937 was a victory for Ms. Wood and her colleagues. (The idea that the government might provide the poor with housing vouchers to spend in the private market came much later.)

The first phase of the public housing program in Chicago was discussed in Chapter 4. In 1950 Chicago had 9,719 units standing. The Housing Act of 1949 greatly expanded the public housing program, and initiated the urban renewal program as well. Congress authorized the construction of 135,000 units per year for six years—a total of 810,000 new units to be added to the existing stock of 160,000 to 170,000 units. The cities of the nation responded, and as reported by the National Commission on Urban Problems (1968) in 1968 there were 667,000 units of public housing standing. Construction had fallen short of the goal because some municipalities did not request very many units. In 1967 the Chicago Housing Authority (CHA) had 32,431 units under management. The original idea in the Housing Act of 1949 was to expand public housing units by a factor of 4.75 and the actual expansion was by a factor of 3.92; Chicago expanded its program by a factor of 3.34.

Hunt (2009) provides the locations for the 30,509 CHA family units, and those locations are matched to the community areas. The results of this exercise are:

Community area type	Public housing units
50 percent or greater African-American in 1950	14,579
39 percent to 49 percent African-American in 1950	6,244
17 percent to 38 percent African-American in 1950	6,176
Less than 17 percent African-American in 1950	3,510

One of the community areas (CA54) had been largely vacant until a large public housing project of 1,500 units had been built in 1945, so its African-American population was 84 percent in 1950. A total of 2,000 units were constructed in this area. The famous (or notorious) public housing corridor along State Street contained 7,938 units in two community areas (CA37 and CA38) that together were 92.6 percent African-American in 1950. Another set of public housing projects with 3,239 units was located in two of the other Black Belt community areas (CA35 and CA36). The massive Cabrini-Green projects with 3,606 units were located on the near north side in Community Area 8. The west side (CA27 and CA28) became the site for 7,179 units, including the Jane Addams Homes, the original public housing project in Chicago completed in 1938.

The CHA units were popular in 1967. According to the National Commission on Urban Problems (1968, pp. 131–133) the vacancy rate was 0.5 percent (173 vacant units out of 32,431), and the waiting list had 21,826 households. The ratio of the waiting list to vacancies of 126 was sixth highest in the nation out of the top 50 cities. (The New York waiting-list-to-vacancy ratio was an astounding 762.) During 1966–1967 there were 3,198 units vacated, so the waiting time in effect was 6.8 years. The income limit for a family of four was $4,600 per year, which was 1.34 times the poverty income level for a family of four in 1966. By these basic measures, the public housing program apparently was being run well at that time, except that there were too few units to meet the need.

However, the National Commission on Urban Problems (1968, p. 119) listed several problems with the nation's public housing program:

- Excessive delay in planning, approving, and constructing projects.
- Failure to take advantage of cost-cutting methods.
- "Pronounced" tendency to build extremely high-rise and closely massed projects, which make residents "dwellers in poor town."
- Not enough apartments with more than two bedrooms to accommodate larger families.

- Neglect of services that residents need, including grocery shopping.
- Neglect of attractive design.
- Inadequate training of public housing personnel.

Chicago certainly was guilty as charged on all of the items in the indictment, except that many units were built with more than two bedrooms for larger families. As Hunt (2009) recounts in detail, serious trouble came later.

Data on the location pattern of the CHA projects such as those recounted above motivated a group called Business and Professional People for the Public Interest, led by an attorney Alexander Polikoff, to file a class-action lawsuit in 1966 against the CHA and the Department of Housing and Urban Development on the grounds of racial discrimination. Polikoff argued that the two agencies violated the 1964 Civil Rights Act and the equal protection clause of the 14th Amendment by limiting public housing sites to the "ghetto." The plaintiff was a CHA resident, one Dorothy Gautreaux. The decision of the federal court, after some negotiation between CHA and Polikoff, includes the following provisions:

- The next 700 units were to be built in white areas, and after that only 25 percent of units could be built in African-American areas.
- Half the apartments in white areas would be reserved for white tenants, and the other half would be provided to households on the waiting list, which was 90 percent African-American.
- Projects of more than three stories and more than 120 units were prohibited.
- The concentration of public housing units in a neighborhood was limited, which is a repudiation of much of the program that had been implemented over the prior 30 years.

In response CHA drew up a list of sites for "scattered site" public housing, but this proposal in effect was blocked by the Chicago City Council, which was required to approve each project. The white population of Chicago felt that construction of public housing that would be 50 percent occupied by African-Americans would lead to block busting and the racial transition of a neighborhood. A federal court ruled in 1974 that the requirement of City Council approval was not needed, and the CHA did build a few (900) scattered site units over the next 15 years—just enough to avoid contempt of court citations. The Gautreaux decision in effect had ended the construction of public housing in Chicago. The Housing Act of 1974 included a large expansion of the housing voucher program, so Polikoff changed tactics and sought to obtain vouchers for public housing households.

Arnold Hirsch is well known for his book *Making the Second Ghetto* (1998), a detailed study of race and housing in Chicago that began as a PhD dissertation at the University of Illinois at Chicago. Hirsch argues that the "first ghetto" was formed over a long period from the 1880s to about 1933 almost entirely through private decisions. The period of the formation of the "second ghetto" is 1933 to 1968, and the actions of the public sector are deeply implicated in this new ghetto that replaced the old one. He states (1998, p. 254) that a "key characteristic that distinguished the 'second ghetto': the deep involvement of government." That involvement included redevelopment, urban renewal, and especially the public housing program. The CHA could not act without approval of the Chicago City Council, and the pattern for selecting ghetto sites was clear. However, it is not clear whether the second ghetto hypothesis means that public housing was intended to increase segregation or simply to maintain it. Amanda Seligman (2003) points out that public housing never housed more than 10 percent of the African-American population of Chicago, and that this population grew enormously over these years while the degree of segregation was maintained. She followed up with a detailed study (2005) of racial transition in Chicago neighborhoods that had no public housing. An econometric study by McDonald (2011) found that the change in the segregation index from 1940 to 1960 for 44 major cities was unrelated to the number of public housing units per 1,000 people. This study also found that the number of public housing units per 1,000 people in these cities in 1967 was positively related to the percentage of families with low incomes and the percentage of the African-American population (thus providing indirect evidence that public housing construction was partly motivated by the desire to maintain segregation). Public housing per 1,000 was negatively related to the rate of homeownership and the percentage of housing built after 1940 in the city. The model predicts about 29,600 public housing units for Chicago compared to the actual number of 32,431.

The Housing Act of 1949 also created the Urban Renewal program, later changed to Slum Clearance and Urban Renewal. The program authorized the Department of Housing and Urban Development to approve funds for urban renewal projects proposed by local authorities. The idea was for the local urban renewal authority to assemble property, using the power of eminent domain if necessary, to demolish the blighted structures, and then to sell the land to private developers and public agencies at "use value." The developer had to submit a development plan for the reuse of the site. Sometimes urban renewal sites were allocated to the public housing authority, but it is wrong to think that urban renewal and public housing were the same. While some urban renewal projects were successful and completed in a reasonably timely manner, the National Commission on Urban Problems (1968) was harshly critical of this program. The report (1968, pp. 165 and 167) stated:

> The first great weakness in carrying out urban renewal has been the unconscionable amount of time consumed in the process.
> [. . .]
> The second great weakness in urban renewal is that even if one takes into account all the other programs, it has in itself failed to help the poor and near-poor who make up most of those who have been displaced. . . . But urban renewal has in the past gone its way relatively oblivious to the housing needs of the poor, although it has not been as indifferent as the highway program, which in the past had demolished several hundred thousand homes without showing until recent years the least tangible interest in what happened to the occupants.

The Commission (1968, pp. 166–167) undertook a detailed study of the 194 urban renewal projects completed in the Chicago region as of 1967. On average it took about four years for the contract to be drawn up and approved. Then it took an average of 132 months from the start of property acquisition to completion and disposition of site improvements. In all the process took 15 years on average. Some urban renewal projects on the south side were successful and produced good housing for middle-class households; these include the Lake Meadows, Prairie Shores, and Hyde Park developments. This author resided on the near west side of Chicago from 1971 to 1984, and very large tracts of land in the neighborhood had been cleared and stood vacant from sometime in the 1960s to the late 1970s. But the projects ultimately were completed, and provide middle-class housing (some available to the holders of housing vouchers), a public school, and a hotel.

Suburbanization and central city decline

Powerful forces were unleashed in the 1950s and 1960s that produced rapid suburbanization. Rising incomes permitted households to purchase new houses and cars, land at the urban fringe was inexpensive and plentiful, transportation costs had declined substantially thanks to the new expressways, construction costs were reasonable, and the government facilitated suburbanization through the FHA mortgage insurance program and income tax deductions for interest and local property taxes. Can the federal government, through its highway program and mortgage insurance and tax policies, be "blamed" for suburbanization? Federal policy is certainly part of the story, but so are these other factors—mainly rising incomes. Besides, the federal government was delivering what people wanted.

Rapid suburbanization meant population and employment declines in the city of Chicago, as has been laid out in detail in this chapter. But the central city decline was not just a benign down-sizing of a crowded city. As we have seen, jobs located in the city declined much more rapidly than population, and that population was increasingly African-American. The problems with this pattern were becoming obvious.

First of all, segregation in housing remained extremely high. In 1970 82.1 percent of the African-American population in the metropolitan area lived in the city of Chicago, and a large number of this group that did not live in the central city (93,000 out of 241,000) resided in the heavily African-American city of Gary, Indiana. The segregation index for the city of Chicago was 92.1 in 1950 and 92.6 in 1960, and had declined only to 88.8 in 1970. The "system" for expanding the supply of housing for African-Americans described previously, coupled with their income levels, meant that this group occupied housing of lower quality than the other residents of the central city. More of the housing occupied by African-Americans lacked plumbing, was in deteriorated condition, or was crowded (more than one person per room). The figures from the 1960 Census are as follows.

	African-American	Other groups
Units	233,949	981,494
Lacked some plumbing	19.4%	9.8%
Substandard condition	30.7%	11.6%
Crowded	27.4%	7.3%

African-Americans made up 22.9 percent of the population of the city in 1960, and occupied 19.2 percent of the housing units.

Rents and housing prices were greater in the African-American neighborhoods during their period of rapid population growth in the 1950s and 1960s. Demand growth, coupled with relatively slow supply response, drove up prices in these areas compared to prices for lower-quality units in white areas. This situation was to change dramatically in the 1970s and 1980s as whites continued to move to the suburbs in great numbers and the African-American population stabilized. In fact, rents and prices in many inner-city African-American neighborhoods collapsed and abandonment became rampant. In addition, research from the 1960s showed that African-Americans faced discrimination in the mortgage market. Rates of home ownership were (and are) lower for African-American households relative to comparable white households.

The best study of housing rents in the 1960s is the study by A. Thomas King and Peter Mieszkowski (1973) of New Haven, Connecticut, during 1968–1969. This study included numerous variables to control for the quality of the housing units and the neighborhoods. They found that rents paid by whites were 7 percent lower in the "border" areas compared to rents in the white interior areas. Rents paid by African-Americans in the border areas were equal to the rents in the white interior areas, and 9 percent greater in the interior African-American areas. David Karlen (1968) examined housing prices over time in a portion of the South Shore community area of Chicago (CA43) compared to a control area that was not in the path of the expansion of the African-American population. South Shore had 10 percent African-American residents in 1960, and was 69 percent African-American in 1970. Prices in the study area in South Shore were declining relative to the control area just prior to African-American entry (1956 to 1963), and then increased relative to the control area once racial transition was underway (1963 to 1966). Brian Berry (1976) studied housing prices in Chicago during 1968–1972, and found that prices in white areas near the racial boundary were lower than prices in the white interior. However, prices in zones of recent racial transition were no higher than prices in the white border areas, and were actually lower in the interior minority areas. Berry concluded that suburbanization of the white population, coupled with much slower growth in the African-American population, produced this new pattern. The first detailed studies of race and home ownership are John Kain and John Quigley (1972) and McDonald (1974). These studies confirmed that, holding constant income and other household variables, African-Americans had lower rates of home ownership in St. Louis and Detroit, respectively. The difference was approximately 9 percent to 10 percent. The "raw" difference in the rates of home ownership was much greater, but there was this remaining difference that could not be explained by income and other control variables. The remaining difference was attributed partly to the nature of the supply of housing available to African-Americans, which included fewer single-family houses. Controlling for structure type, these studies reduced the remaining racial difference by about half.

Housing was not the only problem for African-Americans in the 1960s. Retailing in the inner-city neighborhoods was deficient. The well-known book by David Caplovitz, *The Poor Pay More* (1963), showed that poor neighborhoods lacked supermarkets that sell groceries in greater variety and at lower prices than the small "mom-and-pop" stores that served the poor. Chain drugstores also avoided inner-city areas, and banks and savings and loan associations avoided the inner city entirely. Instead the poor had to cash their paychecks at "currency exchanges," which charged a fee for the service. Furniture and appliance stores sold to the poor on credit, often with high rates of interest—presumably because of the high risk. Berry (1963) conducted a detailed study of retailing in Chicago as of the late 1950s. He found sizable differences between the higher- and lower-income areas of the city. Higher-income areas had all types of retail centers including major regional centers and community centers as well as the smaller shopping goods centers and neighborhood centers. Lower-income areas lacked both major regional centers and community centers. Floor space per establishment was markedly smaller in the lower-income neighborhoods, and vacancy rates considerably higher. Indeed, the title of the report includes the word "blight" because that is what happened when the income level of a neighborhood dropped. Berry did not include race as a factor in the study, but the map showing population and income losses for 1950 to 1960 (1963, p. 172) makes it clear that the areas with income losses were the African-American areas as they stood in 1960.

African-Americans faced discrimination in employment. Discrimination can occur at every step in the process: obtaining education and training, searching for work, getting hired, being paid a wage equal to other workers, and getting promoted (or demoted or fired). The Great Migration had opened up job opportunities for African-Americans, but they faced difficulties in the northern cities at every step in the employment process:

- Racial segregation in housing meant that the schools were de facto segregated. Educational outcomes were not equal.
- Job training was not offered on an equal basis by many unions and employers.
- The job search process was not equal. Many jobs were not advertised broadly and filled by word of mouth.
- Hiring was discriminatory. For example, employers might not wish to hire African-American workers to deal with the public, or to work with white workers.
- There was unequal pay for equal work. This rather narrow issue was studied in depth by Stanley Masters (1975), Franklin Wilson (1979) and others. The racial wage differential was well documented.

- There was discrimination in promotion, and since African-Americans often were the last to be hired, they were the first to be fired.

Becker (1957) documented most of these points for 1949 in his first book.

This study will not include a detailed analysis of the very large topic of employment discrimination. Here are some basic labor market outcomes for African-American workers in Chicago as of 1970. The labor force participation rate for males (aged 16 and over) was 73.1 percent compared to 79.7 percent for all men in the nation and 76.5 percent for African-American men in the nation. Labor force participation is a function of the prospects of finding a job and the pay that one earns on that job. The national male unemployment rate was 4.4 percent in this year of low unemployment, while the unemployment rate for African-American men in Chicago was 6.5 percent. The net outcome was that 66.6 percent of African-American men in Chicago were employed in 1970 compared to 76.2 percent for all men in the nation. The earnings of African-American men in metropolitan Chicago were 78.5 percent of the earnings for all men in the Chicago metropolitan area. African-American women participated in the labor force to a somewhat greater extent than all women. Their participation in Chicago was 45.9 percent compared to 43.3 percent for all women in the nation. The female unemployment rate was 7.7 percent for African-Americans in Chicago compared to 5.9 percent for all women in the nation. However, African-American women in Chicago had earnings that were 99.5 percent of all working women in the Chicago metropolitan area. It must be remembered that 1970 was a time of particularly strong demand for workers.

The problems of African-Americans in the northern cities had not gone unnoticed by the leaders of the civil rights movement. On January 26, 1966, Rev. Martin Luther King, Jr. and his wife Coretta Scott King moved with their children to an apartment on the west side of Chicago in the North Lawndale Community Area (CA29). King had selected Chicago for the next phase of the civil rights movement. The passage of the Civil Rights Act of 1964 and the Voting Rights Act of 1965 meant that the civil rights movement could move on to attempt to attack economic discrimination. A huge rally was held at Soldier Field at which Dr. King presented demands for open housing and employment in industries dominated by whites. Mayor Richard J. Daley met with Dr. King and spoke in conciliatory terms. An agreement that pledged an effort for open housing (with follow-up research) was reached at a "summit" meeting between the two in August 1966. The agreement hardly ended segregation, but Dr. King's biographer Taylor Branch (2006) concluded that this meeting did begin a process of change. And Dr. King's move to Chicago made him a national figure.

While he was in Chicago King led open housing marches to the southwest side of the city and to the near west suburb of Cicero. He was hit by a rock in the all-white neighborhood of Marquette Park. The projectile was thrown from an angry crowd of thousands of whites. King's comment was, "I have never seen such hate in my life." Quite a statement, but some of the residents of Marquette Park likely were people who had moved from their former neighborhoods that underwent racial transition.

Trouble had been brewing in many central cities. A riot occurred in New York in 1964, and the Watts Riot of 1965 in Los Angeles took place just days after President Johnson signed the Voting Rights Act. A small civil disturbance took place on the west side of Chicago one day after the beginning of the Watts Riot. More riots in other cities followed in the summer of 1966, and July 1967 was the time of the huge riots in Detroit and Newark. The Detroit Riot was the worst in terms of deaths with 43, and Watts was next worst with 34 deaths. Chicago escaped the worst of the rioting—until Dr. King was murdered on April 4, 1968. What followed was a devastating riot on the west side of the city in the East Garfield Park and North Lawndale areas (CA27 and CA29). These are community areas that had just recently undergone racial transition in the late 1950s and early 1960s. Businesses along the major streets were looted and burned. The urban riots of 1968 in the wake of Dr. King's murder were the peak of the rioting, although some more rioting did take place in 1969, 1970, and 1971. In the eight years from 1964 to 1971 there were 752 civil disturbances that were classified as race riots (289 in 1968). In all 228 people were killed, 12,741 injured, and 69,099 arrested. The vast majority of the incidents were minor; for example, no deaths were recorded in 684 out of the 752 incidents.

The National Commission on Civil Disorders was appointed by President Johnson in 1967, and issued its report in March 1968—before the 1968 riots. The Commission famously concluded that, "Our nation is moving toward two societies, one black, one white—separate and unequal." The report blamed the rioting on racial discrimination in employment, education, welfare, housing, and police practices. More detailed findings include:

- Rioters mainly were young African-American men who were acting against white society and property. Many were high-school dropouts who were unemployed or had menial jobs.
- Civilian African-Americans were the majority of persons killed or injured.
- A series of incidents, capped by a final incident (often involving police actions), led to rock and bottle throwing and sometimes much worse.
- The riots were not planned or led by any organization, but some militant organizations and individuals did add to the violence.
- In addition to those mentioned above, the list of grievances included discrimination in the administration of justice and dissatisfaction with federal programs, welfare programs, consumer and credit practices of businesses, and recreation facilities.

Researchers such as Seymour Spilerman (1970) attempted to discover any patterns in the proximate causes of the riots. The only pattern discernable in the data is that rioting was more prevalent in the North and in cities with larger African-American populations. If the proximate causes of the riots are not clear in terms of statistical significance, the consequences of the riots are very clear. William Collins and Robert Margo (2004, 2005) found that riot zones suffered devastating losses of population, income, and businesses that persisted for decades into the 1970s and 1980s. Such was the case for Chicago.

The great society

The federal government began to measure poverty during the Kennedy Administration after it had become clear that the prosperity of the 1950s was not improving the lives of some Americans. The procedures for measuring poverty were applied to the income data for 1959 from the 1960 Census, and the poverty rate was found to be 22.4 percent (39.5 million poor people). The poverty rate was 55.1 percent for African-Americans, 48.9 percent for persons in households headed by a female, and 70.6 percent for persons in households headed by an African-American female. The poverty rate for metropolitan Chicago (1950 definition) was 11.9 percent, far below the national figure (11.7 percent excluding Lake County, Indiana). However, the poverty rate for African-Americans in the five counties in Illinois was 35 percent (excluding Lake County, Indiana), compared to 7.6 percent for whites. Recall that the vast majority of African-Americans lived in the city of Chicago.

In his State of the Union Address on January 8, 1964, President Johnson declared that this session of Congress was to be "the session which declared all-out war on human poverty and unemployment in these United States." Congress passed the Civil Rights Act that had been submitted to Congress on June 19, 1963, by President Kennedy, and LBJ signed it into law on July 2, 1964. The Civil Rights Act outlawed discrimination in public accommodations, receipt of federal funds, and in any employment. The law set up the Equal Employment Opportunity Commission to investigate, mediate, and file lawsuits on behalf of workers. The law also barred unequal application of voter registration requirements (but did not abolish literacy tests) and authorized the U.S. Attorney General to file suits to force school desegregation.

President Johnson followed up on his State of the Union address by proposing the Equal Opportunity Act of 1964. This act, which passed later in the year, set up the Office of Economic Opportunity (OEO). OEO initiated programs such as the Job Corps and various community action and education programs. The year 1964 also saw passage of the Food Stamp Act that turned a program for the use of agricultural surpluses into a broad, means-tested voucher program to enable poor households to buy more and better food.

In May 1964 LBJ addressed the graduating class of the University of Michigan with these words: "We have the opportunity to move not only toward the rich society and the powerful society, but upward to the Great Society." He set up 135 task forces with the assignment to study a wide gamut of social problems, and after the election in November, he made an enormous set of proposals dealing with medical care for the elderly, poverty, enforcement of the Civil Rights Act, immigration law, education at all levels, crime control, and programs for cities. The Democrats had won an overwhelming majority in both houses of Congress, and here is a partial list of the laws and the programs that were created:

- Elementary and Secondary Education School Act to provide federal funds for schools with high concentrations of poor children, preschool programs (e.g. Head Start), and other school programs.
- Medicare (health care for the elderly) and Medicaid (health care for the poor).
- Manpower Act to provide more funds for job training.
- Public Works and Economic Development Act to provide federal funds to state and local governments for these purposes.
- Law Enforcement Assistance Act to fund local law enforcement.
- National Foundation of the Arts and Humanities Act to fund the arts.
- Amendment to the Immigration and Nationality Act to abolish the restrictive quotas set up in 1924 so that entry could be based on family relationships and occupational qualifications.
- More funding for medical research and the Office of Economic Opportunity.
- Acts to create the Department of Housing and Urban Development and the Department of Transportation.
- Demonstration Cities and Metropolitan Development Act, which created the Model Cities Program to fund programs to improve cities by rehabilitation, social service delivery, and citizen participation. This program generated controversy over the control of federal funds and was ended in 1974.
- The Voting Rights Act of 1965, which put an end to literacy tests and authorized the Department of Justice to send federal voting registrars to localities with a history of denying people the right to vote. This act enfranchised the African-American population of the South.
- The Fair Housing Act of 1968 prohibits discrimination in the sale, financing, or rental of housing based on race, color, religion, sex, handicap, familial status, or national origin.
- The Housing Act of 1968 created a program of low interest loans for households with modest incomes and for developers of housing for low-income tenants (in place until 1974). More funds were provided for the public housing program, and required that housing constructed in urban renewal projects must provide units for lower-income households. The act also permitted the FHA to insure mortgages in older, declining areas in an attempt to attack the practice of "red lining" of inner-city neighborhoods by lenders. And the act created the Government National Mortgage Association (GNMA), which was set up as part of the Department of Housing and Urban Development to issue mortgage securities created from loans under various government programs. Both GNMA and the Federal National Mortgage Association (FNMA) later were made government-sponsored private corporations in the business of issuing mortgage-backed securities.

In addition to these programs undertaken at the initiative of President Johnson, a major expansion of the nation's basic welfare system took place. In 1963 there were 3.08 million recipients of the Aid to Dependent Children (ADC) program. The program expanded to 10.8 million in 1973 even as the economy grew and the poverty rate reached its all-time low of 11.1 percent. The program expanded as a result of a series of administrative and legal decisions. Much of the expansion of the program took place in the large urban areas. The number of recipients in Illinois increased by five times from 154,000 in 1960 to 773,000 in 1973, and the average monthly benefit increased from $168 to $262, a real increase of about 10 percent. See McDonald (2008) for more details.

With the exception of the Voting Rights Act, all of these programs had an impact on Illinois and Chicago. Indeed, these programs changed the nature of government at all levels and in the longer run have had an impact on societal attitudes toward race. The idea of equal opportunity seems to be met with general agreement.

How does Chicago compare to other urban areas?

One might wish to ask some basic questions about how metropolitan Chicago performed relative to other urban areas. What about overall growth? How rapidly did suburbanization take place? How much did the central city decline? McDonald (2008) provides some answers.

The comparisons from McDonald (2008) for 1950 to 1970 are with averages for the 17 largest urban areas in the North.[3] Growth in metropolitan Chicago was near the middle of the pack of 17 in population, employment, and median family income. It placed tenth in population growth (36.8 percent versus an average of 46 percent for the 17) and in employment growth (31.6 percent compared to an average of 43 percent). Pittsburgh and Buffalo were the slowest population and employment growers (at or just over 20 percent on both), and the really fast growers were the smaller urban areas of Minneapolis-St. Paul, Kansas City, Indianapolis, and Columbus. Washington, DC beat everyone with 93 percent population growth and 98 percent employment growth. Median family income growth in real terms was 92 percent in metropolitan Chicago compared to an average of 89 percent for the 17 metropolitan areas. Chicago placed eighth on this measure. Another way to look at it—metropolitan areas in the North did pretty well overall in the 1950s and 1960s.

The population of the city of Chicago fell by 7.1 percent in these 20 years. Thirteen of the 17 central cities did not annex territory, and their average population decline was 13 percent.[4] Chicago came in fifth place behind New York, Philadelphia, Washington DC, and Baltimore. Among these 13, only the city of New York did not lose population (zero change, as it happened). Double-digit losers of at least 18 percent up to 27 percent were Detroit, Boston, Pittsburgh, St. Louis, Cleveland, and Buffalo. The other four central cities (Milwaukee, Kansas City, Indianapolis, and Columbus) did annex large amounts of territory and their populations increased by an average of 302 percent! This includes the city of Indianapolis, which expanded to include its county, and increased its population by 587 percent!

McDonald (2008) followed R.D. Norton (1979) in estimating a simple equation to explain the change in the central city population as it depended on population growth in the metropolitan area and any annexation of territory undertaken by the central city. The estimate equation for 1950 to 1970 is:

$$CCPOPGRO = -23.35 + 0.41 \, METPOPGRO + 5.21 \, AREAUP$$

The variables are:

CCPOPGRO is percentage change in central city population,
METPOPGRO is percentage change in metropolitan area population, and
AREAUP is percentage change in the area of the central city.

The equation says that if the metropolitan population did not grow (which did not happen during this period) and the central city did not annex any territory, then the central city would have declined by 23 percent. From this starting point, the central city grows at 41 percent of the rate of metropolitan population growth. If there is no annexation, then the central city population remains constant if metropolitan population growth is 57 percent. Note that metropolitan Chicago grew by 37 percent and the city declined by 7 percent. The equation predicts a decline of 8 percent in the city with no annexation. The model works for Chicago.

The city of Chicago can be compared to the other 16 major central cities of the North on a variety of economic and social indicators as listed in Table 6.9. Poverty refers to the percentage of the population under the federal poverty level for 1970. Murder is the rate per 100,000 population as reported to the FBI crime statistics. HS Dropouts is the percentage of the adult population (aged 25 and over) that had not graduated from high school. Single-parent families is the percentage of families with children in which only one parent is present. Population in high poverty areas is the Jargowsky (1997) definition—the population in poverty in a census tract is 40 percent or greater. We see that the city of Chicago is pretty much average for the 17 central cities. Increases in poverty, murders, single-parent families, and population in high-poverty areas in the coming decades will serve as measures of the degree of urban distress.

Table 6.9 Economic and social indicators, 1970

Indicator	City of Chicago	Mean of 17 northern cities	Chicago rank
African-American population	32.8%	28.7%	11
Poverty	14.4%	14.7%	7
Murder	24 per 100K	20 per 100K	6
HS Dropouts	56%	54%	7
Single-parent families	22%	22%	7
Population in high poverty areas	4.3%	5.6%	8

Source: McDonald (2015).

Alonso, Muth, Kain, and early urban economics

Urban economics was developing as a field in the 1950s. Notable studies in the New York Metropolitan Study initiated in 1956 and were led by Edgar Hoover and Raymond Vernon (1959). This study produced nine published volumes that examined virtually all aspects of the nation's largest metropolitan area. The Chicago Area Transportation Study that was begun in 1955 also is worthy of mention and was discussed above. And Charles Tiebout (1956) published his vote-with-the-feet theory of local government expenditures at that time. But it was Alonso (1960 and 1964) and Muth (1961 and 1969) who developed a theory of urban spatial patterns based on the old von Thünen concentric zones model. Until this was done urban economics really did not have its own theoretical framework that makes it into a separate field in economics. Alonso's publications grew directly out of his PhD dissertation, the first one written in the new Department of Regional Science at the University of Pennsylvania. A fundamental result in that model is that households trade off land rent and transportation costs to find their optimal location within an urban area. What is now known as the Muth equation states that household equilibrium location is determined where:

Marginal cost of distance minus Marginal benefit of distance = Zero

or,

Travel cost per mile plus Change in price of housing per mile = Zero.

Muth broke the price of housing into two parts: the "price" of a standard unit of housing and the number of units of housing—the quantity. One immediate implication is that a reduction in travel cost per mile puts the household out of equilibrium and induces it to move to a location where the change in the price of a unit of housing per mile is lower, i.e. farther from the center of the urban area. This idea has been used repeatedly so far in this study, and will continue to be used.

It turned out that Chicago became the main source of data for empirical studies in the "new" urban economics. In addition to his theoretical work, Muth is notable for his pursuit of topics related to urban housing problems in the 1960s in his classic book *Cities and Housing* (1969). Most of the empirical work in the book is based on Chicago, and some of his results and views have been mentioned in previous chapters. However, Muth's work fell short of providing a more comprehensive picture of the urban problems that had emerged in the 1950s and 1960s. Other urban economists began to look at the bigger picture.

A major contribution along these lines is the book *The Urban Transportation Problem* by Meyer, Kain, and Wohl (1965). This volume contains a great deal of data from Chicago, and began by examining the decentralizing trends in population and employment location after 1948. Then they presented information on trends in the supply of urban transit and travel patterns in major urban areas. In a nutshell, the basic conclusion is that urban decentralization trends make for more dispersed travel patterns, but that existing transit systems work efficiently (or at all) only for trips taken to downtown locations from relatively dense residential corridors. The authors call for a very different approach to providing urban transportation systems that are based on internal combustion vehicles. Autos and buses are very flexible in terms of trip origins and destinations. One recommendation was bus rapid transit.

Meyer, Kain, and Wohl (1965) included some discussion of race, housing, employment, and transportation, but it was Kain (1968) who wrote the most influential study that succeeds in bringing together all of these topics that are part of the overall urban problem. Kain (1968, p. 175) introduced his study as follows:

> This paper investigates the relationship between metropolitan housing market segregation and the distribution and level of nonwhite employment. Numerous researchers have evaluated the effects of racial discrimination in the housing market. Others have investigated discrimination in employment and have attempted to determine the extent to which the higher unemployment rates among Negroes are attributable to causes other than racial discrimination, such as lower levels of educational attainment. However, possible interactions between housing segregation and nonwhite employment and unemployment have been all but ignored. To the author's knowledge, the research reported here is the first to link discrimination in the housing market to the distribution and level of nonwhite employment in urban areas. Hypotheses evaluated in this paper are that racial discrimination in housing markets (1) affects the distribution of Negro employment and (2) reduces Negro job opportunities, and that (3) postwar suburbanization of employment has seriously aggravated the problem.

The empirical test of these hypotheses made use of data on Chicago as of 1956 provided by CATS. Kain estimated an equation using data on the 98 CATS zones. The variables are:

AAW = percentage of workers employed in a zone who were African-American
AAR = percentage of resident workers in a zone who were African-American
D = distance (miles) to nearest African-American residential zone.

The estimated equation is:

$$AAW = 9.18 + 0.46\,AAR - 0.52\,D,$$

with all coefficients statistically significant. In short, the percentage of workers employed in a zone who were African-American was positively related to the percentage of employed people who live in the zone and who were African-American, and negatively related to the distance that the employment zone is from the nearest African-American residential zone. These results are not surprising, of course. Next, Kain computed what the number of employed African-Americans would be if all zones had the same percentage of employed African-American residents, which was 14.6 percent. Inserting 14.6 into the above equation (and setting D at zero) results in an African-American employment percentage of 15.9 percent for all zones, which translates into a gain of 22,000 jobs for African-Americans added to their actual employment level of 257,000.

Kain estimated the same equation for major industry categories, and found that the effect of the residential percentage variable was stronger in the industries in which there is direct contact with customers (retail trade, services, and public administration) and less strong in other industries (manufacturing, transportation, communication and utilities, and wholesale trade). Kain ended his study by noting the decentralization of manufacturing jobs relative to the residential decentralization of the African-American population.

Here comes an example of how economists argue with each other. Paul Offner and Daniel Saks (1971) obtained the data from Kain, and estimated the same equation—except they included a quadratic term for AAR. The result is:

$$AAW = 10.84 + 0.049\,AAR + 0.005\,(AAR)^2 - 0.67\,D.$$

Now the AAR variable is not statistically significant, but the $(AAR)^2$ variable is. The computation of job gain by perfect residential integration of African-American workers results in an average employment percentage of 12.6 percent, and a job loss of 34,000. This result crops up because of the non-linear tendency of employers in African-American residential areas to hire African-American workers. Donald Steinnes (1980) repeated the exercise using the CATS survey data for 1970, and found a result similar to Offner and Saks using a linear equation. Do these empirical tests mean anything? Yes, all three studies show that employers tend to hire people who match the race of the residents in the immediate area. So that means if jobs exit the African-American residential areas and African-Americans are unable to move to the places where the jobs are going, then their employment opportunities have been reduced.

McDonald (1984a, p. 108) dubbed the two effects tested in Kain's equation as the direct effect and the indirect effect of segregation on employment opportunities:

> The direct effect is simply the notion that the constraint on residential loca-
> tion choice resulting from housing segregation makes some jobs physically
> inaccessible to black workers. The indirect effect is a more complex hypoth-
> esis in which the racial composition of a small area influences, ceteris paribus,
> the racial composition of workers hired by employers in that area. The exist-
> ence of this effect means that the movement of Blacks into formerly all-white
> areas (with a corresponding movement of whites into houses formerly occu-
> pied by Blacks) has an impact on the employment opportunities for the
> Blacks who do not move.

Empirical tests using data from the Journey to Work survey for 1970 showed that the number of African-American workers who commute to a work zone was smaller the greater was the distance from their residential zone to the work zone, and was greater the larger was the percentage of African-American residents of the work zone. In short, a model of work trip distribution for African-American workers needs to include the racial composition of the work zone. The model should not be based only on distance.

An important study by David Bradford and Harry Kelejian (1973) estimated "an econometric model of flight to the suburbs." Using data from 87 large metropolitan areas for 1960, they found that a middle-class family was more likely to live in the suburbs (rather than the central city) the higher was the poverty rate in the central city in 1950, the higher was the median income level in the metropolitan area, and the lower was the net fiscal surplus in the central city. The net fiscal surplus is local government expenditures per capita minus an estimate of the taxes paid to local government per capita by a middle-class family. The model is called a model of flight to the suburbs because, if the poverty rate increases and the net fiscal surplus decreases in the central city, middle-class families will exit the central city. Also, flight to the suburbs results simply from real income growth.

Conclusion

This long chapter has come to an end. The basic message is that, like nearly all of the northern urban areas, over the two decades metropolitan Chicago experienced growth and increasing prosperity, but ended the period of 1950 to 1970 with its central city in some trouble. Employment was suburbanizing, and so was the white population. The African-American population had grown rapidly as a result of the Great Migration. Manufacturing employment had only begun to decline. A major riot had occurred on the west side of the city. Much more trouble was coming.

Notes

1   CATS was merged with the Northeastern Illinois Planning Commission to form the Metropolitan Agency for Planning in 2004.
2   The Midway Line (or Orange Line) opened in 1993. McMillen and McDonald (2004) found that prices of single-family homes near the stations increased over time in anticipation of the opening of the line.
3   New York, Chicago, Philadelphia, Detroit, Boston, Pittsburgh, St. Louis, Cleveland, Washington DC, Baltimore, Minneapolis-St. Paul, Buffalo, Cincinnati, Milwaukee, Kansas City, Indianapolis, and Columbus.
4   Actually, the City of Chicago annexed the O'Hare Airport area, which added 7 percent of the land area of the city. However, few people live there. Should the city have annexed more? Yes!

7 The decades of urban crisis

Introduction

Glena McDonald and I moved from New Haven, Connecticut, to the near west side of Chicago in August 1971, and we became bit players in the Chicago drama. The period of urban crisis had begun with a bang in 1968, and we arrived just in time to watch it unfold over the following 20 years. Glena was a public school teacher in some of the worst Chicago neighborhoods, and I taught urban economics and did studies of Chicago. To reiterate from Chapter 6, the signs of trouble in the late 1960s included:

- rapid growth in the African-American population with continued housing segregation;
- segregated schools;
- large losses of jobs located in the city of Chicago;
- employment discrimination;
- discrimination in mortgage lending;
- inadequate retail and financial services in the African-American community; and
- increasing social problems in the inner city—concentrations of poverty, high homicide rates, low educational attainment, increasing rates of single-parent families.

Over 20 years the population of the city of Chicago was to fall to 2.784 million, a decline of 17.2 percent from 1970 to 1990. The population of the metropolitan area (2000 definition) increased by only 3.8 percent (compared to national population growth of 22.2 percent), so it is not surprising that the central city suffered a very large population loss. The gross population density gradient flattened from −14 percent per mile in 1970 to −12 percent in 1980 and −11 percent per mile in 1990. The African-American population of the metropolitan area continued to increase from 1970 to 1980 from 1.346 million to 1.547 million (14.8 percent), but then actually declined in the 1980s to 1.521 million in 1990. The African-American population in the city of Chicago increased by 86,000 in the 1970s to 1.188 million in 1980, and then fell by 112,000 to 1.076 million in

1990. In net migration terms African-Americans in the 1980s exited the Chicago metropolitan area at a rate that exceeded the natural rate of population growth. The overall growth of the African-American population in the metropolitan area of 13.8 percent from 1970 to 1990 falls well short of their national population growth of 32.7 percent. People were voting with their feet—and automobiles and buses and moving vans. The task of this chapter is to answer the question, "Why?"

The two decades roughly from 1970 to 1990 are labeled a time of urban crisis, so what is meant by urban crisis must be explained carefully. First, the urban crisis was visited primarily on the big central city (although Gary, Indiana, had its share too). McDonald (2008) assembled a set of economic and social indicators for the central city to measure the degree to which a central city is in crisis. These indicators are:

- Population loss, because loss of population means loss of middle-class residents, businesses, and tax base.
- Increase in the poverty rate.
- Decrease in median family real income. The poverty rate and median family income measure two aspects of income in the city.
- Increase in the population living in high-poverty areas, because the concentration of poverty creates a negative environment that leads to many social problems.
- Increase in the murder rate (the crime that is almost always reported).
- Change in the number of adults (aged 25 and over) who are not high-school graduates.
- Increase in the percentage of single-parent families (with children).

If most of these indicators are moving in the wrong direction, in my judgment a city is in crisis. And movement in the wrong direction in one indicator is likely to cause others to get worse as well.

The Great Migration ends

The Great Migration from the South to the North came to an end during the 1970s. Data in Table 5.5 can be used to show the net outcomes of the end of what has been called the southern diaspora. From 1950 to 1970 the African-American population in the nation grew from 15 million to 22.6 million (50.7 percent), but the growth of this group in the North was from 4.96 million to 10.23 million (106.2 percent). From 1970 to 1980 the growth of the African-American population was 17.3 percent in the nation and 14.3 percent in the North. The decade of the 1980s had an increase in the African-American population of 12.8 percent in the nation and 11.5 percent in the North. The states of the Old Northwest had African-American population growth of 107.5 percent from 1950 to 1970, 16.7 percent from 1970 to 1980, and just 6.8 percent from 1980 to 1990. In short, the rate of African-American population growth in the North went from double the national growth to figures that were below the national growth rates.

The figures for the African-American population of the South are opposite those for the North. From 1950 to 1970 southern African-Americans increased from 9.52 million to 10.65 million (11.9 percent increase, compared to the 50.7 percent increase for the nation as a whole). The increase for the 1970s was 21.4 percent, and this was followed by an increase of 32.7 percent in the 1980s. The percentage increase of African-Americans in the South from 1970 to 1980 was only 4.1 percent greater than the national increase, and this difference in growth rates widened to 19.9 percent for 1980 to 1990. The African-American population of the West grew rapidly in all decades but at 2.78 million still was only 9.3 percent of the national total in 1990 (up from 3.8 percent in 1950).

The Chicago metropolitan area had gained more than its share of African-Americans during the Great Migration. From 1950 to 1970 the increase was 130.1 percent (from 585,000 to 1.346 million) compared to 106.2 percent for the entire northern region. The growth from 1970 to 1980 was 14.9 percent, slightly above the national growth rate. But from 1980 to 1990 the African-American population actually declined from 1.547 million to 1.532 million (down 1 percent). The African-American population figures for the city of Chicago show an increase of 124 percent from 1950 to 1970, an increase of 7.8 percent for 1970 to 1980, and a decline of 9.4 percent from 1980 to 1990.

A friend and colleague in Chicago, H. Woods Bowman, offered a simple explanation for the dramatic change. Everyone could see the urban riots of the 1960s on television. Of course, as he recognized, there was much more to it than that, but his notion has a ring of truth to it, does it not?

As for migration patterns, a new trend was to emerge in the 1980s that has continued. Population growth in many metropolitan areas, including Chicago, has depended to a sizable degree upon the migration of the Hispanic population.

Population changes: Central city and suburbs

Population changes were summarized earlier, so now let us look at more of the details as in Table 7.1. Metropolitan population growth was 2.2 percent in the 1970s and 1.6 percent in the 1980s, for a grand total of 3.8 percent over two decades. Given that the expressway system had just opened in the 1960s (with one important link opened in 1971—the extension of the Eisenhower Expressway to the West and Northwest), it should come as no surprise that the population of the city of Chicago plummeted by 579,000 (17.2 percent) over 20 years. Population decline in the city was dominated by the areas that had completed racial transition to African-American occupancy by 1970 (60.3 percent of the decline). The population of the inner suburban ring increased by 719,000, and the outer suburban ring added 159,000 residents. The African-American population of the inner suburban ring increased by 208,000 as the city of Chicago began to lose African-Americans after 1980.

Figures for the Hispanic population are added in Table 7.1. The Hispanic population of the nation grew rapidly during these decades—from 9.6 million in 1970 to 14.6 million in 1980 and 22.4 million in 1990. This ethnic group had established a significant presence in the metropolitan area by 1980 with a

Table 7.1 Population of metropolitan Chicago: 1970–1990 (1000s)

Area	1970	1980	1990
Metro area			
Total	7,883	8,053	8,182
African-American	1,346	1,547	1,532
Hispanic		634	896
City of Chicago			
Total	3,363	3,005	2,784
African-American	1,102	1,188	1,076
Hispanic		422	535
Inner suburban ring			
Total	4,050	4,478	4,769
African-American	241	355	449
Hispanic		201	340
Outer suburban ring			
Total	470	569	629
African-American	3	4	7
Hispanic		11	21

Source: U.S. Bureau of the Census.

population of 634,000, most of which (66.6 percent) was located in the city of Chicago. Over the next ten years the Hispanic population grew to 896,000 (up 41.3 percent), and this growth of 262,000 was greater in the inner ring of suburbs (139,000) than in the central city (113,000). One way to look at it is that, if the Hispanic population of the city of Chicago had not grown during the 1980s, the population of the city would have declined from 1980 to 1990 by 334,000 rather than 221,000. In the coming years the Hispanic population would outnumber the African-American population in the metropolitan area.

The African-American population of the city of Chicago did not change much from 1970 to 1990, but population location patterns underwent significant change. Community areas of the city were put into the following categories for 1950 to 1970. The total population changes from 1970 to 1990 are listed here:

Community area type	Total population change, 1970–1990	Number of community areas
Completed racial transition, 1950	−95,800	5
In racial transition in 1950, completed in 1970	−70,000	6
Began racial transition 1950–1970, completed in 1970	−177,800	9
Began racial transition 1950–1970, not fully in process of racial transition, 1970	6,800	5
Began racial transition 1950–1970, in transition in 1970	−76,800	9
Began racial transition after 1970	−66,000	8

As shown above, the community areas that had completed racial transition as of 1970 lost total population of 344,000. The areas that were in racial transition in 1970 experienced a loss of total population of 76,800. Together these 29 community areas (out of 77) account for 71.5 percent of the total population loss of the city of Chicago of 587,000. The remaining population loss is scattered around the city. The six areas that were not fully in the process of racial transition in 1970 gained 6,800 in population. Of these, only one (CA53 on the south side) had completed racial transition in 1990. The other five were still in the process of transition, with African-American populations no more than 62 percent. During these two decades only eight community areas gained population. One of those is the downtown area (the Loop, CA33), which gained population of 7,000 and had an African-American population of 21 percent in 1990. Four of the other seven are community areas that attracted Hispanic population. One of these (Pilsen, CA30, on the near southwest side) gained 18,000 in population because it was a primary location for Hispanic population growth.

In addition, the last line of the above list has eight community areas that had little or no African-American population in 1970 and had African-American of 10 percent or more as of 1990. Only one of these community areas underwent full racial transition (a very small community area on the south side, CA47, with a population of only 3,400). The other seven had no more than 42 percent African-American population, and three had just 10 percent to 13 percent. One of the community areas is on the north side (CA77), one on the west side (CA24), four on the southwest side (CA56, CA66, CA70, CA72), and two one the south side (CA47, CA61). These eight community areas had population loss of 66,000 from 1970 to 1990.

If the inner suburbs gained 208,000 African-Americans, where did the increases occur? A tabulation for the 16 major suburbs shows the following:

Type of suburbs	African-American population gain
Old satellite cities	20,600
South suburbs	28,900
West suburbs	23,900
North suburbs	11,200

The old satellite cities are Kenosha, Wisconsin, Waukegan, Elgin, Aurora, Joliet, and Gary, Indiana. The major suburbs included in this tabulation account for 84,600 on the African-American population increase—only 40.8 percent of the total increase. The largest increases were in south-suburban Harvey (13,100) and in Oak Park (10,200) adjacent to the city on the west side. The remaining increase was located in small suburbs and/or scattered around the metropolitan area. Only three of these suburbs had a majority of African-Americans (Harvey and Gary, Indiana, on the south side, and Maywood on the west side). African-Americans in the remaining 13 suburbs were no greater than 34 percent.

Now let us turn to poverty and how it correlated with race. The poverty rate for the city of Chicago was 14.4 percent in 1970, 20.3 percent in 1980, and

21.6 percent in 1990. The sociologist William J. Wilson studied the concentration of poverty in Chicago in his 1987 book *The Truly Disadvantaged: The Inner City, the Underclass, and Public Policy*, and McDonald (2004a) updated the study to 2000, tabulating families in poverty. A summary of the results of this study is:

Number of community areas with family poverty rate of:

	30% and over	40% and over	50% and over
1970	8	1	0
1980	13	9	2
1990	17	11	6

The overwhelming fact is that the number of high-poverty community areas doubled from 1970 to 1990, and that the number with poverty of 40 percent or higher went from one to 11. Indeed, in 1990 there were six community areas in which a majority of the families was in poverty. This is a living, breathing urban crisis.

Now make sure you are seated. All eight of the high-poverty community areas in 1970 were African-American areas. The lowest percentage African-American among the eight is 72 percent (CA28, on the near west side). The other seven were at least 85 percent African-American. Likewise, all 13 high-poverty areas in 1980 were African-American areas. This time Community Area 28 was 75 percent African-American, and all the other 12 were 79 percent or higher. Six of these community areas were 99 percent African-American. Not all African-American community areas were high-poverty areas, but all of the high-poverty areas were African-American. In 1990 four community areas joined the high-poverty club. These were communities of mixed races or ethnicities. Three of these had mixed African-American and Hispanic populations (CA23, CA24, and CA61 on the near northwest and southwest sides). The fourth one (CA34) includes Chinatown. Each of these four community areas had a poverty rate of 31 percent or 32 percent in 1990. All 11 of the community areas with a poverty rate of at least 40 percent were African-American areas. This group includes Community Area 28, which had slipped to 67 percent African-American. Community Area 36 (Douglas, on the near south side) had a poverty rate of 70 percent in 1990, and Community Area 38 (Grand Boulevard, next door to Douglas) came in second with a poverty rate of 64 percent. These were areas with large public housing developments. It was almost correct to say that high-poverty concentration means African-American (but the reverse statement is not correct). In 1990 there were 25 African-American community areas (67 percent or greater), and 13 of them were high-poverty areas. No high-poverty community area was a white area.

There is a simple explanation for the increase in the number of high-poverty areas and the increase in the poverty rates in those areas. People who could move out, i.e. people not in poverty, did so. This idea can be tested easily. There were 17 high-poverty areas in 1990, 13 were African-American areas and four were of mixed ethnicity. The 13 African-American community areas had an average increase in the family poverty rate of 19 percent from 1970 to 1990, and those community areas lost an average of 44.3 percent of their population. The four community areas of mixed ethnicity had an average increase in the poverty rate of 16 percent, but lost only 16.4 percent of their population—about the average for the entire city. In short, the simple explanation works for the African-American high-poverty areas. Here is an example. The population of North Lawndale on the west side (CA29) fell from 94,800 in 1970 to 47,300 in 1990, and its family poverty rate increased from 30 percent to 44 percent.[1] Here is an even more extreme example. Washington Park on the south side (CA40) had its population fall from 46,000 in 1970 to 19,400 in 1990, and its family poverty rate increased from 28 percent to 57 percent. Where did the people who moved out go? We have already seen that mainly they moved to other areas in the city, and some moved to suburbs.

Employment changes: Central city and suburbs

Metropolitan Chicago experienced substantial employment growth during the two decades from 1970 to 1990 even as population growth was minimal. Employment data by place of residence for the major industry categories are shown in Table 7.2. Total employment increased from 3.23 million to 3.80 million, and the population-employment ratio increased from 41 percent to 48.6 percent as the baby boomers, both female and male, grew up and joined the work force. The table shows very large increases in professional services, business and repair services, and finance, insurance, and real estate—the service economy. These three industry groups added 707,000 jobs. In addition, employment in wholesale and retail trade increased by 38.3 percent, adding 237,000 jobs. Now look at manufacturing. Jobs in manufacturing actually increased by 124,000 from 1970 to 1980, but then fell by 316,000 in the next decade. Manufacturing was 30.3 percent of employment in 1970, but just 19.8 percent in 1990. Manufacturing employment

Table 7.2 Employment in metropolitan Chicago (data by place of residence, in 1000s)

Industry	Metro area 1970	Metro area 1980	Metro area 1990	City of Chicago 1970	City of Chicago 1980	City of Chicago 1990
Total	3,231	3,665	3,979	1,264	1,237	1,209
Construction	141	159	208	44	38	45
Manufacturing	978	1,102	786	404	329	225
TCU*	232	301	321	103	111	103
Whls., ret. trade	618	758	855	255	230	235
Fin., ins., real est.	172	267	344	81	100	111
Bus. and repair serv.	110	174	213	51	58	74
Personal services	120	114	159	58	44	58
Professional services	462	691	894	192	249	288
Public admin.	131	144	136	73	72	61

Source: U.S. Bureau of the Census.

Note
*Transportation, communication, and utilities.

in the nation declined by 5.5 percent from 1980 to 1990, so the share of manufacturing jobs in the metropolitan area dropped rather drastically from 5.88 percent to 4.44 percent in just ten years.

Employment of residents of the city of Chicago actually held up reasonably well given that the population fell by 17.2 percent. The total number of employed residents declined by just 55,000 (4.4 percent). However, the industry composition changed. The number of city residents employed in manufacturing fell from 404,000 in 1970 to 329,000 in 1980 even as manufacturing in the metropolitan area was increasing. And then city residents working in manufacturing fell by another 104,000 as of 1990. Employment in manufacturing for city residents fell by 44.3 percent in 20 years. What happened? Among other things, some major employers abandoned the city, or went out of business completely. In the early 1980s most of the South Chicago Works of US Steel were closed, as was Wisconsin Steel.[2] These sites are still vacant. The Union Stockyards closed for good in 1971, and the associated meat packers and other food manufacturers had already moved elsewhere. The Hawthorne Works of Western Electric in Cicero had employed many city residents since the early years of the twentieth century. This giant facility closed in 1983— eventually to be replaced by a shopping center. The tractor works of International Harvester closed in 1969. The giant Brach candy plant complex on the west side closed, and remains an eyesore. Its only use in recent years has been for movie producers who wish to blow up a building. Most of the printing and apparel firms located near downtown either moved or went out of business. Hart, Schaffner, and Marx moved, as did Formfit. Donnelly Printing and Lakeside Press on the near south side are not there anymore. Employment for city residents was buoyed up by professional services, business and repair services, and finance, insurance, and real estate. These three sectors added 139,000 jobs for city residents, with 96,000 coming in professional services. However, the education and skills needed for the new service economy and the old manufacturing economy are not the same.

What about jobs located in the city of Chicago? The main source of data is a publication of the Illinois Department of Employment Security called *Where Workers Work*. This publication includes jobs that were covered by the unemployment compensation system, so it does not cover all employment— especially public employment. Nevertheless, looking at the data over time gives us a pretty good idea of the changes that took place. Table 7.3 shows the figures by major employment sector, and includes special tabulations for the city of Chicago from County Business Patterns, a source that includes workers who are members of the Social Security System.

According to Table 7.3, the city of Chicago lost 47,000 jobs covered by unemployment insurance from 1970 to 1980, and manufacturing employment fell by 162,000. Manufacturing jobs continued in sharp decline to 1990, losing another 98,000 jobs. The city gained non-manufacturing jobs, mainly in services and finance, insurance, and real estate (FIRE). In Table 7.3 services include a long list of types of services, including business services, health services, and engineering, management, and related services. But the largest category (43 percent of services in 1990) is called "miscellaneous other services," which includes repair services,

Table 7.3 Private employment in the city of Chicago covered by the unemployment compensation system (data by place of work, in 1000s)

Industry	1970	1980	1983*	1987*	1990
Total private	1,297	1,250	1,137	1,218	1,201
Manufacturing	476	314	250	227	216
Non-manufacturing	821	906	887	991	984
Construction	43	42	33	35	35
TCU**	108	122	84	90	103
Wholesale trade	103	98	78	77	88
Retail trade	183	176	168	181	176
Fin., ins., real est.	100	132	152	177	174
Services	285	336	364	407	408

Sources: Illinois Department of Employment Security (1970, 1980, 1990), *Where Workers Work*, and special tabulations of County Business Patterns (1983, 1987).

Notes
* Employment covered by Social Security, special tabulations of County Business Patterns (1983, 1987)
** Transportation, communication, and utilities.

educational services, and personal services. Employment in wholesale and retail trade fell too, by a total of 22,000 jobs from 1970 to 1990. County Business Patterns appears to undercount TCU and wholesale trade, although 1983 was just one year after a deep recession in 1982. In all the loss of employment from 1970 to 1990 was 7.4 percent, which is less than the population decline of 17.2 percent. However, the industry mix had changed markedly. Manufacturing jobs fell from 36.7 percent to 18 percent of the private sector jobs reported in Table 7.3. Recall that the city contained 668,000 manufacturing jobs in 1947, and that number was down by 67.7 percent as of 1990. From that point jobs in manufacturing in the city would go lower, much lower. In addition to private sector employment, the Northeastern Illinois Planning Commission estimated that 231,000 public sector jobs were located in Chicago in 1980.

The city of Chicago still had 216,000 manufacturing jobs in 1990. The leading manufacturing industries in the city are familiar. The top industries and their employment levels in the city as of 1990 are:

Printing and publishing	34,254
Machinery	33,121
Food and allied products	31,893
Fabricated metals	23,890
Chemicals	13,749
Paper and paper products	10,731
Primary metals	9,548
Transportation equipment	8,092
Apparel and textiles	7,877

Source: Illinois Department of Employment Security (1990).

Note the diminished presence of the apparel industry, which had been one of the city's leading industries.

A comparison of data in Tables 7.2 and 7.3 reveals some interesting outcomes. First of all, the total number of jobs for the city in the two tables is not comparable because public employment is included in Table 7.2, but not in Table 7.3 for 1970 and 1990. But look at the figures for employment in manufacturing and FIRE. The number of city residents employed in manufacturing in 1980 and 1990 was roughly equal to the number of manufacturing jobs located in the city in those years. However, the number of city residents employed in FIRE was less than the number of jobs in this sector located in the city—substantially less in 1990 by 63,000. Here is indirect evidence of what has been called the mismatch hypothesis, the idea that the skills demanded for workers in the city do not match the skills of the workers who live in the city.

Table 7.4 shows more details of the composition of employment in the central city as of 1987. Air transportation is the largest employer in the TCU sector, and eating and drinking places employs the most people in the retail trade sector. The largest components of the FIRE sector are, in order of employment level,

Table 7.4 Employment in the city of Chicago: 1987 workers covered by social security (data by place of work)

Industry code	Industry name	Employment 1987 (1000s)	Percentage change, 1983–1987
15	Construction	35.0	6.20%
20–39	Manufacturing	226.6	−9.40%
	Food	31.7	−2.06%
	Printing and publishing	36.8	−0.63%
	Fabricated metals	24.7	−16.94%
	Nonelectrical machinery	15.1	−6.19%
	Electrical machinery	16.7	−25.92%
	Primary metals	7.5	−40.67%
40	TCU*	89.7	7.36%
	Air transportation	30.9	35.18%
	Communication	19.0	−21.35%
	Trucking and warehousing	15.4	0.93%
50	Wholesale trade	76.7	−1.20%
52	Retail trade	181.0	7.42%
	Eating and drinking places	62.3	19.77%
	Food stores	24.1	0.24%
	General merchandise	14.9	−12.81%
	Apparel	12.4	6.82%
60	Finance, insurance and real estate	177.4	16.98%
	Insurance carriers	37.2	24.84%
	Banking	37.1	−19.36%
	Real estate	32.7	29.03%
	Security, commodity brokers and services	26.8	24.63%
	Insurance agents and services	16.7	54.71%

(Continued)

Table 7.4 (Contiunued)

Industry code	Industry name	Employment 1987 (1000s)	Percentage change, 1983–1987
70–89	Services	406.7	11.62%
	Business services**	105.0	10.42%
	Health services	99.6	9.69%
	Educational services	35.4	1.73%
	Membership organizations	29.6	14.69%
	Legal services	28.2	27.88%
	Social services	18.4	21.08%
	Hotels and other lodging	16.5	–0.67%

Source: Special tabulation of County Business Patterns.

Notes
* Transportation, communication, and utilities
** The main components of business services are computer and data processing, management and public relations, personnel supply (e.g. temporary help), advertising, services to buildings, detective and protective services, and reproduction and stenographic services.

insurance carriers, banking, real estate, and security, commodity brokers and services. The huge service sector includes, in order of employment level, business services, health services, educational services, membership organizations, and legal services. Table 7.4 also shows sizable employment growth in the city in the FIRE and services sectors in just four years from 1983 to 1987 of 17 percent and 11.6 percent, respectively. And note the huge decline in employment in primary metals of 40.7 percent. This was the time of the closing of major steel plants as noted earlier.

The principle center of employment in the metropolitan area was still the CBD. The CBD was home to 490,000 jobs in the private sector in 1979 and this number grew to 533,000 jobs in 1990, according to *Where Workers Work*, which does not include government employment. In 1990 the inner CBD contained 250,000 jobs, and the outer downtown ring added 282,000 more. CBD employment was dominated by services and FIRE. Increases in these two sectors more than offset the declines in manufacturing and wholesale and retail trade. Indeed, one of the major innovations in finance was made in Chicago with the creation of markets for many types of futures and option contracts. The Chicago exchanges had offered contracts only in agricultural commodities. The Chicago Mercantile Exchange, which began in 1898 as the Chicago Butter and Egg Board, made the big conceptual leap in 1972 by offering futures contracts in foreign currencies, and then added stock index futures in 1982. The Chicago Board of Trade expanded into the markets for financial futures and options as well. Overall the FIRE sector contributed 137,000 jobs to the downtown job market in 1990. Table 7.5 shows the industrial breakdown of downtown employment for 1979 and 1990. In addition, the Northeastern Illinois Planning Commission estimated that there were 78,600 public sector jobs in downtown Chicago in 1980 and 62,900 in 1990, a decline which offsets much of the gain in private sector employment.

Table 7.5 Private employment in downtown Chicago: 1979 and 1990 (data by place of work, in 1000s)

Industry	1979	1990
Total private	490.4	532.8
Construction	10.6	10.1
Manufacturing	73.0	49.3
TCU	32.3	46.6
Wholesale	47.8	33.8
Retail	54.8	50.8
FIRE	103.0	137.0
Services	152.7	211.3

Source: Illinois Department of Employment Security, *Where Workers Work.*

One feature of the suburbanization of employment is the growth of suburban employment centers. Actually, this is not such a new phenomenon. The opening of the Union Stockyards in 1865 represented a major move of jobs to the accessible urban periphery. So did the building of the South Chicago Works, Pullman, Gary, the Cicero Industrial District (with the Hawthorne Works), and others. All of these early examples were based on the availability of rail transportation and, in some cases, water transportation. If employment centers are important, then there should be some impact on population location and land value patterns. Clearly these industrial developments drew population. Indeed, George Pullman built his own town. Using data from Hoyt (1933), McDonald and McMillen (1990) tested whether the South Chicago Works, the Union Stockyards, or Pullman had any impact on surrounding land values in 1928. They controlled for distance to downtown and Lake Michigan, and found that the South Chicago Works had no discernable impact on land values, probably because land adjacent to Lake Michigan had a strong positive effect. It was not possible to find a separate impact of proximity to the South Chicago Works, located on Lake Michigan. The study did find that land values declined by 15 percent per mile of distance from the Pullman factory. And land values within two miles of the stockyards were an estimated 100 percent lower than land values outside this area. Why? Well, you would not notice it now, but in those days your nose could tell that there was something in the air around the stockyards.

McDonald and McMillen (1990) used data from CATS in an effort to find employment centers other than downtown in 1956 and 1970. They defined an employment center as a CATS zone with gross employment density greater than in the adjacent zones. A CATS zone typically has four adjacent zones: one nearer to downtown, one farther away from downtown, and two at the same distance to downtown. So a zone cannot be an employment center if employment density declines with distance to downtown. For 1956 no zone (other than the downtown zone) qualified as an employment center based on the density of total employment, but three zones were found to be centers of manufacturing employment. These include the Cicero Industrial District just to the west of the city of

Chicago (with the Hawthorne Works of Western Electric), the Clearing Industrial District adjacent to Midway Airport in the near southwest suburb of Clearing, and the zone that contained the US Steel South Chicago Works. In 1970 the zone that included the Cicero Industrial District qualified as an employment center based on the density of total employment as well as manufacturing employment. Manufacturing employment centers in 1970 were located near the US Steel South Chicago Works and a zone located on the northwest side of the city about seven miles to the east of O'Hare Airport. Note that all of the employment zones discussed so far were manufacturing zones. As of 1970 the Cicero and Clearing zones had lost their earlier prominence.

A newer type of employment center began to emerge in the 1970s. This newer type is an agglomeration based to some degree on office employment, and relies on highways for transportation. Joel Garreau (1991) popularized this new type in his book *Edge City*. Research on these centers has been underway since the 1980s to identify centers, to explain their existence and growth, and to study their impacts on the surrounding area. The basic idea is that both accessibility and positive external effects exist for the various firms that cluster in the suburban centers. John McDonald and Paul Prather (1994) identified three suburban employment centers for metropolitan Chicago in 1980. They defined their search to exclude the old satellite cities in order to concentrate on the new phenomenon of suburban centers. The zones are the O'Hare Airport area, Schaumburg to the west-northwest of O'Hare Airport, and central DuPage County, just west of Cook County. The O'Hare center is located 18 miles northwest of downtown, and contains employment in transportation, wholesale trade, and manufacturing (and some government employment too). Schaumburg is located 26 miles from downtown to the northwest, and is home to the largest shopping center in the metropolitan area (Woodfield Mall) and Motorola and other manufacturers. The area also includes some employment in financial and other services. Central DuPage County, located 26 miles west of downtown, had an employment base consisting of financial and other services and hi-tech manufacturing (known as "Silicon Prairie").

McDonald and Prather (1994) found that these three employment centers captured a significant share of employment growth in the metropolitan area from 1979 to 1989. Most of the employment growth in the metropolitan area during those years took place in the northwest suburbs and DuPage County. An area defined by six counties in Illinois (Cook, DuPage, Kane, Lake, McHenry, and Will) added 394,000 private sector jobs over that decade, and 65 percent of that growth took place in northwest Cook County and DuPage County. Of those 257,000 jobs, 106,000 of the increase took place in the O'Hare, Schaumburg, and Central DuPage employment centers. Employment growth within five miles of O'Hare was 59,000 (from 248,000 to 307,000), 21,000 in Schaumburg, and 26,000 in the two major towns in central DuPage (Naperville and Wheaton). The three centers captured 27 percent of total employment growth in the six-county area, indicating the benefits of clustering.

The much more comprehensive study was done by McMillen and McDonald (1998). This study investigated suburban employment centers in the Illinois portion of metropolitan Chicago for 1980 and 1990, and included a wider area than examined by McDonald and Prather (1994). Using data on quarter sections, they identified centers as groups of quarter sections with at least ten employees per acre and at least 10,000 employed in either 1980 or 1990. The 20 centers are listed in Table 7.6, and the employment subcenters map (Figure I.2) shows the municipalities in which the centers are located. Gary, Indiana, would have been on the list of subcenters if the data source had included the Indiana portion of the metropolitan area.

The centers are grouped into six types:

- Old satellite cities (3)
- Old industrial suburbs (3)
- Post-World War II industrial suburbs (6)
- New industrial/retail suburbs (2)
- Edge cities (3)
- Service and retail centers (3)

Table 7.6 also includes the breakdown of employment in each center by major industry category for 1990.

In addition to the three satellite cities on the list, three industrial suburbs reached prominence shortly after 1900. Manufacturing still dominated these six centers in 1990. Six industrial centers emerged after World War II and after the opening of O'Hare Airport to all of the passenger flights in 1962. Two centers emerged since 1970 that combine industry with retail trade. The three edge cities come next, followed by three centers that combine service and retailing. Burbank and Maywood specialize in health care services, and of course Evanston is the location of Northwestern University.

The five centers with the most rapid growth in employment from 1980 to 1990 are the three edge cities and the two newer industrial/retail centers. Indeed, these five centers added 131,000 jobs from 1980 to 1990 (with 57,000 added in the Oak Brook edge city). Two centers near O'Hare Airport also grew (Addison and O'Hare), as did seven of the others. However, six of the centers declined in employment. Five out of these six had concentrations in manufacturing (and the sixth is Evanston, with Northwestern University and retailing). Additional research by McDonald and McMillen (2000) found that subsequent industrial and commercial real estate development in the suburbs during 1990 to 1996 was attracted to locations near O'Hare Airport and highway interchanges. Residential development was attracted to the O'Hare area as well, but also formed clusters of its own in between major highways.

Measuring the urban crisis

In the introduction to this chapter I proposed a set of indicators to measure the extent to which the central city was experiencing what can be called a crisis. The outcomes for the city of Chicago for 1970, 1980, and 1990 are given in Table 7.7.

Table 7.6 Suburban employment centers in metropolitan Chicago: 1980 and 1990

Subcenter municipality	1980 Empl.	1990 Empl.	Govt. %	Mfg. %	Retail %	Serv. %	TCUW* %	Other %
Old satellite city								
Aurora	13,766	10,689	3.5	58.9	8.3	14.6	8.0	6.6
Elgin	10,198	13,095	6.6	35.9	11.4	37.7	2.3	6.1
Waukegan	10,562	11,506	28.4	64.4	0.2	1.3	0.0	5.8
Old industrial suburbs								
Chicago Hts.	10,516	10,862	4.1	62.2	1.8	21.7	4.5	5.6
Harvey	11,755	9,880	6.7	42.6	4.5	25.2	14.5	6.6
McCook	45,002	31,109	1.1	64.3	3.6	4.9	19.9	6.2
Post-WWII industrial suburbs								
Addison	15,641	23,409	1.8	61.8	4.3	5.2	15.3	11.6
DesPlaines	22,633	27,653	0.00	30.9	3.4	3.8	51.1	10.8
Franklin Pk.	28,155	27,462	10.0	55.8	17.7	1.1	8.2	7.1
Niles	44,152	40,040	0.7	65.4	3.7	5.7	15.5	8.9
Norridge	9,565	10,457	5.9	43.2	17.3	20.9	6.3	6.4
O'Hare	23,270	32,681	4.8	21.4	5.5	27.2	30.7	10.4
New industrial/retail suburbs								
Northbrook	28,451	43,030	2.0	30.6	21.4	22.9	10.5	12.7
Palatine	3,514	19,385	0.0	18.7	45.3	9.0	8.2	18.8
Edge cities								
Naperville	9,001	35,168	7.3	19.9	12.2	51.6	1.9	7.1
Oak Brook	54,196	111.5K	1.2	12.5	22.0	36.5	19.4	8.4
Schaumburg	23,640	40,295	4.8	13.1	36.0	26.2	12.2	7.7
Service and retail								
Burbank	10,783	14,028	2.8	0.9	23.0	65.2	2.0	6.1
Evanston	20,491	19,551	4.3	4.1	13.4	69.4	2.6	6.1
Maywood	23,873	26,749	25.5	6.8	10.6	39.2	11.8	6.2

Source: McMillen and McDonald (1998).

Note
* TCUW is transportation, communication, utilities, and wholesale trade.

Table 7.7 Social and economic indicators, 1970–1990

Indicator	1970	1980	1990
Population	3,363,000	3,005,000	2,784,000
		−10.6%	−7.4%
Poverty rate	14.4%	20.3%	21.6%
Med. family income ($2,009)	$59,600	$55,500	$53,100
		−6.9%	−4.3%
Population in high-poverty areas			
Family poverty			
30% and higher	389,000	515,000	553,000
40% and higher	18,000	309,000	282,000
50% and higher	0	70,000	127,000
Poverty population in			
Census tract > 40%	144,000	323,000	328,000
Murder rate/100K	24	29	31
High-school dropout	56%	44%	34%
Single-parent family	22%	44%	41%

The table leads off with population loss, which was 17.2 percent over the two decades. The poverty rate (persons in poverty) increased from 14.4 percent in 1970 to 20.3 percent in 1980, and then increased a smaller amount from 1980 to 1990. The increase in the 1970s meant that the number of people in poverty increased from 484,000 to 610,000 from 1970 to 1980, and then the number actually fell slightly to 601,000 in 1990. Median family income in real terms fell by 6.9 percent and 4.3 percent in the two decades.

The population in high-poverty community areas from McDonald (2004a) shows a big jump of 291,000 in the number of people in areas with a family poverty rate of 40 percent or greater from 1970 to 1980. Recall that there was only one community area with a family poverty rate in excess of 40 percent in 1970. However, Jargowsky (1997) computed the population poverty rates by census tract (average population of about 5,000) for these years, and his data show that 144,000 people were in census tracts with 40 percent poverty or higher in 1970. At the census tract level, the jump from 1970 to 1980 of 179,000 is smaller. By either method, the data show a very large increase in the number of people in high-poverty areas from 1970 to 1980. The figures for 1990 actually show very little change from the 1980 figures, with the exception of the number of people who lived in community areas with a majority of the families in poverty. By this last measure the situation was getting worse.

The murder rate is used to stand for the crime rate because murders are almost always reported. The national murder rate had increased sharply during 1960 to 1970, from 5 to 7.8 per 100,000 population. Murders in the nation reached a peak of 10.2 per 100,000 in 1980 and declined slightly to 9.4 per 100,000 in 1990. The murder rate for the city of Chicago stood at 10 per 100,000 in 1960, and increased to 24 per 100,000 in 1970. The 1970s and 1980s brought further increases in this rate as street gangs in the drug business fought over "turf." In other words, the murder rate in the city of Chicago was double the national rate in 1960 and about triple the national rate in 1970, 1980, and 1990. The one positive note in the indicators is the sharp reduction in the number of adults who had not graduated from high school. High-school graduation rates had increased rapidly, and the replacement of the older generation by a newer generation of adults brought high-school dropouts down in both decades. The last indicator may be one of the most important. The percentage of families with children that had only one parent present increased from 22 percent in 1970 to 40 percent in 1980. The percentage did not change much for 1990, but this jump in single-parent families in just one decade reflects a major change in the nature of the society. How can this not be harmful for children?

The bottom line here is that the city of Chicago scored a big negative on six out of seven of the indicators for 1970 to 1980. The changes from 1980 to 1990 are not as negative. The murder rate and the single-parent family percentage did not increase much, and the population loss, increase in the poverty rate, and median income decline were smaller. However, six out of seven indicators still were negative. Could some of these negatives turn positive in the next decade? Yes, as it turned out.

Local public finance: Central city fiscal problems

The decline of a central city means that fiscal problems are likely. The tax base shrinks and businesses and middle-class taxpayers leave. They vote with their feet in favor of suburban schools, less crime, and other features. Expenditures exceed revenues, and cities turn to borrowing. But lenders eventually discover that lending to cities to cover deficits is risky. Cities sell off assets to cover deficits. Cities raise tax rates too, but mainly cities cut back on services. Raising tax rates and cutting back on services serve to stimulate further decline. The City of Chicago has been under this pressure since the 1960s. One method for reducing the pressure is for the State of Illinois to make a substantial payment in support of the Chicago public schools. The state law requires that the state shall provide 50 percent of the funding for the public schools in Chicago, although this requirement sometimes has not been met. Other school districts are not so supported.

The list of problems that create the stress on the finances of the central city, including Chicago, is long:

- Loss of commercial and industrial tax base.
- Retention of low-income households with heavy demands for public services such as education and health care.
- High crime rates, which require more police and criminal justice expenditure.
- Aging infrastructure that requires expensive maintenance.
- Population loss, meaning that fixed costs are spread over a smaller population.
- Old buildings, which create fire hazards and demolition expenses.
- Inability to annex territory.

The City of Chicago and Cook County have a particularly unusual device for attempting to deal with the fiscal problem. The property tax rate applied to business property is much higher than the rate applied to residential property, and much higher than business faces in the adjacent counties. Briefly, here is how it works. Cook County has a classification system for the property tax which places a higher assessment ratio on business property (ratio of assessed value to estimated market value). The Cook County statutory rate was 16 percent on residential property and 40 percent on business property. However, the State of Illinois requires that the property tax base in a county must be equal to 33 percent of the total value of taxable property in the county. Because Cook County does not come close to that ratio because of the low assessment on residential property, the State of Illinois "multiplies" the assessed values to make the total assessed value for Cook County equal to 33 percent of total property value. There is more. The actual assessment ratios for property in Cook County fell well short of the 16 percent and 40 percent required by law, so the State of Illinois multiplier applied was large, almost 2 in most years. The actual assessment ratios in the City of Chicago in 1990 were 8.7 percent for small residential buildings (six units or fewer), 16.7 percent for large residential buildings (more than six units), and 20.5 percent for commercial and industrial property. With these actual assessment ratios, with a multiplier of 2, the adjusted assessment ratios would be about 17 percent for small residential property, 33 percent for large residential property, and 41 percent for commercial and industrial property. However, the assessment of business property was highly variable. McDonald (1993a) showed that the lowest 25 percent of assessment ratios for business property were 14.5 percent or less, while the highest 25 percent of assessment ratios were greater than 31 percent. This means that 25 percent of business property in Cook County faced an "equalized" assessment ratio of greater than 60 percent.

This system created sharply different property tax rates for business property in Cook County compared to the adjacent counties. In the other counties all property is assessed at 33 percent of market value. The assessment system, combined with higher demands for public services in Cook County compared to the adjacent counties, as shown by McDonald (1993b), resulted in the following property tax rates as a percentage of market value in 1985 and 1988:

	Commercial property		Industrial property	
	1985	1988	1985	1988
Cook	4.01%	4.63%	4.23%	5.19%
DuPage	2.19%	1.83%	2.26%	1.91%
Kane	2.32%	1.98%	2.22%	1.99%
Lake	2.30%	1.95%	2.33%	2.05%
Will	2.67%	2.31%	1.26%	0.92%

Do these differences matter? Empirical studies reviewed by Robert Newman and Dennis Sullivan (1988) showed that differences in local tax rates can influence location decisions within a metropolitan area. The empirical study by McDonald (1993b) showed that the changes in property tax rates shown above were associated with changes in the market values of commercial and industrial property. Note that Cook County increased the tax rates on business property from 1985 to 1988, while the other counties reduced these tax rates. Both the level and the increase in the property tax rate relative to other counties were associated with lower growth in the commercial and industrial tax base.[3] A study by Richard Dye, Therese McGuire, and David Merriman (2001) found that higher property tax rates led to significantly slower growth rates for employment, commercial property values, and industrial property values in suburban municipalities during 1990–1996. (The city of Chicago is not included in the study.) The across-county differences are particularly strong for commercial property value growth. Within-county differences are more important for industrial property value growth, and both across-county and within-county differences are implicated for employment growth.

Public housing disaster

When last we visited the public housing in the late 1960s, we found a system that seemed to be operating fairly well. The vacancy rate was minimal, and there was a long waiting list of households hoping to live in public housing. The main problem seemed to be a shortage of public housing, but the Gautreaux decision had halted construction. Federal policy was shifting to housing vouchers. What could go wrong? Just about everything.

Hunt (2009) has provided the definitive history of the public housing program in Chicago. This book is highly recommended, and the details need not be discussed at length here. Hunt points to the following problems:

• Many of the "projects," including high-rise projects, had high ratios of youths to adults. As Hunt (2009, p. 179) puts it, "No one had ever constructed a community with two youths for every adult in vertical space, and no one . . . had the social resources to confront the problems caused by overwhelming populations of youths."
• A series of administrative decisions resulted in the loss of working-class tenants. The median income for CHA families with children was about $12,400 in 1968 (1984 dollars), and the median fell to about $4,400 in 1984. About 51 percent of these tenants had income from employment in 1968, but only 11 percent did in 1984. The percentage of tenants who received public assistance (AFDC) increased from 22 percent in 1968 to 66 percent in 1984. CHA had been turned into developments for people on welfare.
• The management by CHA was grossly incompetent.

Hunt (2009, p. 259) summarizes the situation in the 1980s:

By the early 1980s the Chicago Housing Authority, in a deep irony, had become a slumlord, with tenants at its large-scale projects enduring hostile surroundings. Inoperable elevators, erratic heat, leaky roofs, uncollected garbage, infested apartments, darkened hallways, and unrepaired playground equipment were norms, not aberrations. As a community builder, the CHA could not provide basic security, especially in its elevator buildings, leading to gang control of public spaces, routine gunfire, widespread drug dealing, debilitating addictions, and sexual violence against women. Not every project or even every building in the worst projects was chaotic . . .

As a Chicago resident, this author was aware that the emergency medical technicians (EMTs) would not enter certain CHA buildings, and police officers were wary of entering some of them as well. Other than that, Ms. Gautreaux, how do you like public housing? There is more to the story. Most of the worst projects were torn down in the "plan for transformation" as implemented in the new century. More on that in the final chapter.

Responses to industrial decline

The term "rust belt" had entered the dictionaries by the late 1980s. The Collins English Dictionary defines the term as "an area where heavy industry is in decline, especially in the Midwest of the U.S." The American Heritage Dictionary states: "A heavily industrialized area containing older factories, particularly those that are marginally profitable or that have been closed." Webster's College Dictionary is more elaborate: "the Great Lakes states and adjacent areas of the eastern U.S. in which much of the work force has traditionally been employed in manufacturing and metals production." Chicago is always included in discussions of the rust belt.

But let us back up a bit. Richard J. Daley took office as mayor of the City of Chicago in 1955. The latest data for 1954 showed that manufacturing employment in the city was 615,000—down a bit from 1947, but still dominant in the economy of the city. Not only that, Mayor Daley looked out his window in city hall and saw a downtown that was run-down and had not seen much development in years. Just one million square feet of rentable office space was built from 1947 to 1962. The only sizable office building that had been built since World War II was the Prudential Building (completed in 1955). Mayor Daley resolved to do something about downtown, and by the time of his death in 1976 he had succeeded in bringing development to the Loop. The zoning ordinance was changed to favor large-scale developments, and the Mayor centralized urban planning work for the city in his Department of City Planning. This new department in 1958 produced a plan for the central area that was, in the words of D. Bradford Hunt and Jon DeVries (2013, p. 29), "focused on protecting, strengthening, and strategically expanding the downtown core with a mix of office, residential, and institutional development." The projects that followed over the next 15 years included the Sears Tower (with four million square feet of office space), the Standard Oil Building, the First National Bank Building, the Inland Steel Building, the Chicago Civic Center, the Federal Center, Water Tower Place, Illinois Center, and other major projects. Dearborn Street was the Mayor's project. Large residential properties such as Marina City and Outer Drive East began to be built in the downtown area as well.

Mayor Daley also was the force behind the decision to build the Chicago campus of the University of Illinois near downtown. His favored site was the abandoned rail yards to the south of downtown to provide an institutional barrier that would force office development to the compact core, but the railroads refused to sell these properties at that time. Instead the decision to build the campus on the near west side was set in 1961. The City controlled the site as it had been designated an urban renewal zone. The site that had to be cleared was a viable ethnic neighborhood, and the residents mounted vocal protests. George Rosen (1980) provides a detailed history of this decision, and estimates that clearance for the campus displaced about 8,000 people (1,900 households) and 650 establishments. Among those displaced were Hull House (founded by Jane Addams), John M. Smyth Furniture, and the recently rebuilt Holy Guardian Angel Church and school. The University of Illinois at Chicago became one of the largest employers in Chicago, with 12,700 employees in 2002.

In the early 1960s it became clear that industrial Chicago was having trouble. Manufacturing employment in the city had dropped to 509,000 in 1963—down 106,000 jobs in less than a decade. Studies of industrial relocation were being done, and the largest one by the Northeastern Illinois Planning Commission was described in Chapter 6. The City had organized the Mayor's Committee for Economic and Cultural Development in 1961, and this group turned its attention to Chicago's industry in 1964. The executive board consisted of Chicago business leaders (and one labor leader). The Committee included the top men in the two major banks (Continental and First National), Illinois Bell, Hallicrafters, Chicago and Northwestern Railway, Standard Oil of Indiana, U.S. Steel, Commonwealth Edison, and the Janitors Union.

The Mayor's Committee undertook a major study (1966), with policy recommendations, of the near west and near south sides. The area included the massive Union Stockyards, which were in steep decline. The Mid-Chicago Economic Development Study (1966) made several recommendations to:

- create industrial incubator facilities,
- conserve existing industry by providing assistance with site clearance and security,
- assist with the development of in-city industrial parks,
- establish new industrial zoned areas accompanied by incentive programs,
- take advantage of the Chicago Medical District and the three universities located in the area,
- organize industrialists by geographic area, and
- make infrastructure repairs and change street patterns to facilitate industrial development.

The Committee had undertaken a major study and made policy recommendations that it felt would be effective. It was not true that the City administration was ignoring Chicago industry and focused only on downtown development, but implementation of the recommendations of the Committee fell short.

Economic development policy focused on the Stockyards area during the time after the Mid-Chicago report, but by the 1970s it was clear that the problems were city wide. Manufacturing employment in the city had dropped to 430,000 in 1972 after a small recovery during 1963–1967. It turned out that the increase in manufacturing jobs in the city during the Vietnam War buildup was a misleading signal in that many thought it was possible to expand manufacturing employment in the city in the longer run. In 1972 the Committee was reorganized as the Mayor's Council of Manpower and Economic Advisors, and convened with a much broader membership that included business leaders, public officials from the City and other agencies, members of the academic community, and labor leaders. This author assisted the Council with its research work, and joined as the Chair of the Committee on Urban Economic Analysis and Reporting in 1975.

The Council produced a major study in 1974, and specified a set of goals and policies for economic development, workforce development, and equal opportunity. The Council recommended a more aggressive approach to economic development that went beyond the coordination of city functions such as public works programs with private investment projects, as was being done in the Stockyards area. There should be an agency with the power to assemble land, prepare the site, and provide it for industry at reduced cost. This agency should also have the power to formulate special tax incentives and financing (which would require approval by the City Council, of course). Firms that participate should meet performance goals, and it was hoped that the program could be self-supporting by the increases in tax revenue that would accrue. The Council also recommended expansion of public transit in order to improve access to employment, and supported development of the Crosstown Expressway. This highway project was mentioned in the previous chapter as a plan for something akin to the world's largest industrial park.

The City followed up with the creation of the Economic Development Commission, and this agency undertook a major survey of Chicago's manufacturing firms during 1975–1976. The survey of 1,012 firms was intended to establish relationships with companies, find out the attitudes of manufacturers toward their locations, identify firms that were most likely to relocate, and identify problems for which assistance could be offered. The survey is described in detail in McDonald (1984a). The main finding of the econometric study of the data showed that a firm that considered its site inadequate for its needs had a 25 percent greater chance of intending to relocate than a firm with an adequate site. A firm that leased rather than owned its plant had a 10 percent greater chance of intending to relocate. Many other variables were found not to be related to the intention to relocate, including crime, property taxes, problems recruiting skilled workers, age of building, and condition of the neighborhood. This absence of results flies in the face of conventional wisdom.

The Economic Development Commission also initiated a program of industrial revenue bonds in 1977. Bonds are issued with the approval and in the name of a local government and are used to finance private industrial or commercial investment. The bond yields are exempt from federal income taxation, and the savings in interest is passed on to the firm for which the bond has been issued. This type of program has been popular at the state and local level (but not so much among officials at the U.S. Department of the Treasury). The City of Chicago began issuing the bonds in 1977, and by 1981 a total of 85 bonds had been issued, 63 to manufacturing firms (and 22 to non-manufacturing firms). Firms that apply for such a program have intentions to expand. Firms in fabricated metals were 17 of the participants. McDonald (1984b) conducted an empirical evaluation of the program. The bonds provided an average of $1.53 million in funding for the firms. Average initial employment for all 85 firms was 210, and on average the firms planned to hire an additional 67 workers (a 34 percent increase in employment). The program provided a substantial reduction in the cost of capital. These years were a time of very high interest rates; the prime interest rate faced by the firms at the time of bond issue averaged 15.9 percent, and the interest rates on the industrial revenue bonds were 8.6 percent on average. A reduction in the cost of capital means that the firm expands, but also has an incentive to substitute capital equipment for labor. According to the proposals from the firms, the expansion effect was to outweigh the substitution effect. So, for a reduction in the cost of capital of 46 percent, the firms planned to expand employment by 34 percent. The employment figures are estimates of planned employment expansions provided by the firms. These figures may have been exaggerated, of course, but the proposals from the firms were reviewed by industry experts and had to be approved by the City Council twice. It is likely that gross exaggerations would have been noticed.

A report by the Illinois Advisory Committee to the U.S. Commission on Civil Rights (1986) reported that the 91 industrial revenue bonds closed from 1977 to 1983 had plans for 6,900 new jobs, an increase of 49 percent over the existing levels of employment in the participating firms. However, the Committee noted a lack of minority firm participation in the program. A tentative conclusion is that the industrial revenue bond program can assist a firm that has the potential to expand. However, the studies do not indicate how much the firms would have expanded in the absence of the program. Nor does the program help a company that is just trying to survive in the city. The Industrial Revenue Bond program is now called the Industrial Development Bond program, and is limited to manufacturers. Both the State of Illinois and Cook County also have similar programs.

Mayor Daley died in November 1976, and he was followed in office by Michael Bilandic and Jane Byrne. Mayor Bilandic continued to follow the Daley program, but Mayor Byrne abolished the Mayor's Council of Manpower and Economic Advisors in 1979 for reasons that were unexplained to its members.

Congressman Harold Washington became the city's first African-American mayor in 1983. He had run partly on a platform of a new economic development policy that would pay more attention to the neighborhoods and not concentrate so much on downtown. He was influenced by people who believed that downtown development had come at the expense of industry and the neighborhoods. This school of thought decried what is termed the "growth machine" of property interests by Harvey Molatch (1976). In this notion, pro-growth advocates are pitted against residents who suffer displacement, rising rents, and environmental deterioration. One specific item in the indictment of previous city administrations was the decline of light manufacturing around the downtown area. These industries included printing, apparel, and food processing. For example, Joel Rast is a member of the growth machine school, and he wrote a book (1999) about the "political origins of industrial decline" in Chicago. For example, he found that the number of apparel firms just to the west of the Loop declined from 183 in 1951, to 116 in 1960, to 57 in 1970, and to 26 in 1980. Rast's basic point is that public policy destroyed the localization economies that existed for the printing and apparel industries near the downtown area. That may be, but computers in the case of printing and old buildings and foreign competition in the case of apparel may have been more important. Development of the west Loop for office space and residential use was encouraged by the City and proceeded during these years. For example, Rast (1999, p. 68) discussed the Sears Tower, completed in 1972. This building with four million square feet of office space that at the time was the world's tallest building replaced two buildings housing garment factories. This was a problem?

Mayor Washington created the Department of Economic Development, and appointed as Commissioner Robert Mier, a professor of urban planning at the University of Illinois at Chicago. The new policies put in place by Mayor Washington's administration were:

- Creation of planned manufacturing districts, in which industrial zoning could not be changed. Previously zoning changes could be made by the alderman of the ward, who would come under pressure from developers of residential or commercial property.
- Provision of funding for neighborhood industry groups and other community action organizations.
- Formulation of agreements with downtown developers to participate in some form of neighborhood development as well.

Mayor Washington died in 1987, shortly after being reelected. His policies largely were followed by those who succeeded him, including Mayor Richard M. Daley, who took office in 1989.

Cook County recognized that its property tax system was a problem for business, and in 1984 instituted property tax incentives for industry that apply to manufacturers anywhere in the county. This incentive lowers the property tax by about half for a period of eight years, and applies to new, substantially rehabilitated, or formerly abandoned property. This program has never undergone empirical evaluation, other than as part of the enterprise zone study discussed later.

The State of Illinois added to economic development efforts in the city by creating an enterprise zone program in 1982. The purpose of the program is to stimulate business and industrial growth and retention in depressed areas of the state using relaxed government controls and tax incentives in those areas. Each enterprise zone is limited to ten square miles and is authorized for a life of

20 years. An enterprise zone is designated on the basis of high unemployment, low income, poverty, or population loss. The program incentives are:

- exemption of the 7 percent sales tax on building materials used by business in a zone,
- state income tax credit of 0.5 percent for investment in the zone,
- state income tax credit of $500 for each job created if at least five jobs are created and dislocated or disadvantaged workers are hired,
- exemption of state utility taxes and state sales taxes on materials and machinery used by certain large businesses, and
- property tax incentives at the discretion of the local municipality. In Cook County the property tax incentive for eight years included industrial property not engaged in manufacturing production located in an enterprise zone, i.e. firms engaged in the distribution of industrial products—transportation and wholesale trade.

By 1986 there were 12 enterprise zones that had been certified in Cook County, including six in the city of Chicago. An evaluation of the impact of the program for 1985 to 1989 by McDonald (1993c) showed that the program had no effect on total employment, but that employment growth in the distribution sector (transportation and wholesale trade) was much higher in the Cook County enterprise zones than in other areas of the county. Employment growth in this sector averaged 32 percent over the four years compared to 5.4 percent in similar areas of the county. The reason cited by firms that were surveyed indicated that the property tax incentive was the most important factor in the decision to invest in an enterprise zone. The distribution sector was one sector that was growing at the metropolitan level and willing to consider locating in a depressed area. In effect, the enterprise zone program with its county property tax incentive moved employment in the distribution sector around within the urban area in favor of the enterprise zone locations. This outcome is consistent with the goals of the program even if total employment in very large Cook County is not enhanced. The enterprise zone program was found to have had no effect on employment in manufacturing or other sectors. Employment change in the entire sample of areas in the study was negatively related to the size of the manufacturing base in 1985. The enterprise zone program has little or nothing to offer firms that are experiencing decline and trying to survive. The stated goals of the program include retention of business, but the program has no feature that promotes simple retention. It is basically a "bricks and mortar" program.

What are we to make of these efforts? Development in the downtown area boomed, and by 1989 there was a serious oversupply of office space that curtailed further downtown office development for a decade. As reported by McDonald (1987), the supply of office space in the downtown area increased from 65 million square feet to 72 million square feet in 1980, and then boomed to 101 million square feet in 1987. The addition of 8.6 million square feet in the next two years brought the total to 110 million square feet in 1989. The vacancy rate was only

13.8 percent in 1989, but then it jumped to 16.7 percent in the recession year of 1991 and 21.6 percent in 1993. As reported by McDonald (1999), in 1993 effective rent (after expenses and tenant incentives) had dropped to just $0.55 per square foot. Downtown development had gone too far. And manufacturing employment in the city continued to decline. Manufacturing employment in the city tracked over time is:

1970	476,000
1972	430,000
1977	366,000
1980	314,000
1990	216,000
2000	123,000
2010	65,000

One might conclude that the effort to preserve and expand manufacturing employment in the city of Chicago, despite a small victory here and there, has not been successful. Indeed, this may be an example of one of the least effective programs ever. As shown in Tables 7.2 and 7.3, the city was able to hang on to almost all of its employment in wholesale trade and transportation, at least up through 1990. Economic development programs, including the property tax incentive that was part of the enterprise zone program, appear to have helped in this sector.

Myrdal's vicious circle in central cities

Myrdal's vicious circle was introduced in Chapter 1, and there is evidence that northern central cities, including Chicago, were in its grip during the 1970–1990 period. Here is how the vicious circle works for a central city. As proposed in McDonald (2008), the idea is that, once a central city or a portion of it starts downhill, the negative features of that downhill slide reinforce each other. The slide downhill can begin for a variety of reasons external to the city such as industrial decline, construction of an expressway system leading to movement of population and employment to the suburbs, and rising incomes for the middle class leading to its move to the suburbs. As it happened, all of these forces occurred in the late 1960s or early 1970s. Typically the worst outcomes for the central city are concentrated in particular parts of town that contain minority populations and/or housing that is vulnerable to deterioration. Households that have the means to move out do so. The negative external effects of neighborhood decline hasten the decline of the housing stock, and large-scale abandonment takes place. Crime is perhaps the most important negative external effect, but declining quality of public schools also plays an important role as schools become dominated by children with disadvantaged backgrounds. Negative economic and social behaviors seem to be contagious.

Seven indicators of economic and social decline were introduced in the "Measuring the urban crisis" section earlier in this chapter, and six out of the seven moved in the "wrong" direction in the city of Chicago during 1970 to 1990. McDonald (2008) examined these same indicators for the 16 other major central cities of the North for each of the two decades, 1970 to 1980 and 1980 to 1990. Chicago was awarded a net score of –5 for the 1970–1980 decade because only one indicator (high-school dropouts) moved in the "right" direction. The net score for the 1980–1990 decade is –3 because the population in high-poverty census tracts and single-parent families barely increased. Net scores were worse in the 1970–1980 decade for New York City, Philadelphia, Detroit, Cleveland, and Buffalo. All five had net scores of –6. Two other cities had net scores of –5 (Baltimore and Indianapolis), and four had net scores of –4 (St. Louis, Minneapolis, Milwaukee, and Columbus). In other words, 12 of the 17 central cities had most of the indicators moving in the wrong direction. Of the other five, only Boston had a positive net score (+1) because four positive outcomes for median family income, murder, concentrated poverty, and high-school dropouts outnumbered the negatives of population loss, increase in poverty, and increase in single-parent families. The net scores for the 1980–1990 decade are better, except for Detroit. Detroit had a decline in median family income of 21.5 percent, and the number of people living in high-poverty census tracts increased from 120,000 to 419,000. The other five indicators moved in the wrong direction too, so Detroit was assigned a score of –9 for 1980–1990 (double points for median income decline and people living in areas of high poverty). However, no other central city among the 17 had a score of –6 (or worse). Milwaukee got a score of –5, and three were given –4 (Cleveland, Minneapolis, and Cincinnati). Chicago and three others (Pittsburgh, Buffalo, and Kansas City) scored –3. The other eight had a better score, and Boston was joined by New York, Washington DC, and Baltimore as cities with positive net scores. The turnaround in the city of New York is quite notable. Population increased and median family increased by 19.7 percent (2 points), and the poverty rate and adult high-school dropouts declined. The population in high-poverty census tracts and the percentage of single-parent families did not increase. The murder rate increased from 26 to 31 per 100,000, so New York City got a net score of +4. Median family income in the city of Boston increased by 36.6 percent (two points), population increased, and the poverty rate declined (along with adult high-school dropouts), so Boston's net score is +2. But that still leaves 15 out of 17 northern central cities with negative scores— negative indicators outnumber the positive indicators. The bottom line for Chicago is that it was a little worse than the average for northern central cities on the seven economic and social indicators.

One telling result from McDonald (2008, p. 230) is an examination of the simple correlations among five of the economic and social indicators for the 17 cities. The five indicators are the central city poverty rate, the percentage of population living in high-poverty census tracts, the murder rate, adult high-school dropout percentage, and the percentage of single-parent families. There are 11 correlations among five variables, and these correlations were computed for 1970, 1980, and 1990. All 11 correlations are positive and statistically significantly different from zero for both 1970 and 1980. In 1990 eight of the correlations are positive and statistically significant, and the other three are positive but not statistically significant. These three are the correlations of the murder rate with high-school dropouts, the poverty rate, and the percentage of people living in high-poverty areas. In other words, all five of these indicators were highly positively correlated. For example, a central city with a relatively high percentage of single-parent families also had a relatively high murder rate, high-school dropout rate, poverty rate, and percentage of the population living in high-poverty census tracts. The other four versions of this sentence could be stated, but will not in the interest of brevity. These results suggest that, as Myrdal (1944) believed, if one aspect of the economy or the society gets worse, others do too. And, if improvement in one aspect can occur, then maybe others will improve too. As we shall see, something resembling a virtuous circle happened in the 1990s in many of these same central cities.

Conclusion

The two decades from 1970 to 1990 were a time of urban crisis for the city of Chicago and most of the other major central cities of the North. Only Boston and then New York in the 1980s seem to have escaped the crisis as defined in this chapter. Population growth in the metropolitan area was quite small, and the forces of suburbanization were in full force. The city lost 17.2 percent of its population, and much of that decline was concentrated in lower-income African-American neighborhoods, which resulted in a dramatic increase in the number of people living in areas of concentrated poverty. Administrative decisions regarding public housing tenants aggravated the problem by eliminating working-class households from the projects. Manufacturing jobs in the metropolitan area had held up pretty well through 1980, but the 1980s brought a drastic decline from 1.1 million to 786,000. Employment opportunities for city residents declined as the city's old manufacturing base dwindled from 476,000 jobs located in the city in 1970 to 216,000 in 1990. The number of city residents employed in manufacturing fell from 404,000 to 225,000 over these years. Employment opportunities were growing in the service economy, especially in finance and business and health services. Employment in the new service sector calls for a different set of skills and typically more formal education than did a job in manufacturing.

After taking office in 1955, Mayor Richard J. Daley, with good reason initially, had focused on downtown development. His efforts met with success, likely in part because the overall economy was shifting in the direction of service sector office employment of various types. Aligning city economic development policy with positive trends in the economy is a good idea, not a bad idea. By the early 1960s it had become clear that the city was losing some of its manufacturing base. The Mayor, who died in 1976, responded with a series of committees, studies, and policies. These efforts did little to stem the tide. Indeed, community activists and others began to complain that downtown development was leaving the neighborhoods behind and not addressing the economic problems of city residents (and voters). Congressman Harold Washington responded to these concerns, was elected mayor in 1983, and added to city economic development efforts by focusing on manufacturing and industrial districts. However, these efforts also have proved to be ineffective.

The decade of the 1980s ended with Richard M. Daley in the mayor's office, population in decline, public housing in a mess, 17 community areas with high concentrations of poverty, manufacturing employment in the city at a level not seen since very early in the twentieth century, and many other problems. . . . Could the city dig itself out of this hole?

Notes

1   The story of North Lawndale is tragic. The Chicago Fact Book Consortium (1995, p. 107) states the following:

> First were the riots which came after the King assassination in 1968, during which substantial parts of the Roosevelt Road shopping strip were destroyed by fire. After that storeowners moved when insurance companies either canceled their policies or prohibitively increased their premiums. Another severe blow fell when the International Harvester Company's tractor works closed in 1969, with the loss of an estimated 3.400 jobs.
>
> [. . .]
>
> In 1974 Sears, Roebuck moved its headquarters to Sears Tower downtown, leaving behind a reduced facility employing 3,000. During the 1970s, 80 percent of the area manufacturing jobs disappeared, as Zenith and Sunbeam electronics factories shut down, and a Copenhagen snuff plant was closed. The closing of Alden's catalogue store was a signal event in a sequence that wiped out 44 percent of the retail and service jobs in North Lawndale. The downturn continued through the 1980s, when Western Electric started closing down, to disappear completely by 1985. Two years later, without warning, Sears, Roebuck closed the Homan Avenue complex, resulting in the dismissal of 1,800 employees.

2   David Bensman and Roberta Lynch (1987) provided a detailed history of the steel industry in Chicago, including the failed battle waged by the unions and local politicians to keep these plants open. The South Chicago Works had employed 10,000 workers, and 3,400 worked for Wisconsin Steel.

3   A later study of the selling prices of industrial real estate in the O'Hare Airport area for 2001–2004 by John McDonald and Yuliya Yurova (2006) found that properties in Cook County sold for 16 percent less than comparable properties located in DuPage County because the property tax rate in Cook County was higher by 2.63 percent of market value (4.32 percent versus 1.69 percent of market value), which implied that 83 percent of the difference in property taxes was capitalized into property value rather than passed forward to rents paid by tenants. Lower value means less development.

8 The old century ends on a high note, and a new century begins

Introduction

The city of Chicago staged a comeback in the 1990s. Population growth at the metropolitan level resumed, and the city experienced its first population increase since the 1940s. The crime rate, the poverty rate, and concentrated poverty all declined. Median family income increased, single-parent families did not increase, and the high-school dropout percentage continued to fall. That adds up to a net score of +6 on urban crisis indicators, compared to –5 for the 1970s and –3 for the 1980s. The city still faced serious problems, but things were looking up.

The comeback of Chicago and several other major cities in the 1990s was unexpected and, at first, difficult to discern. The urban crisis began in the late 1960s literally with a "bang," but the turnaround experienced in Chicago and elsewhere began quietly. Many of the urban problems started to get better. And some journalists, scholars, and advocates who were invested in the theme of urban decline were reluctant to see the change in trends. Some eventually did realize what was happening in the 1990s. For example, the distinguished urban sociologist William J. Wilson (2009, p. 59) discussed the trends in the 1990s and the first years of the new century in some depth and concluded: "Thus, the notable reduction in the number of high-poverty neighborhoods and the substantial decrease in the population of such neighborhoods may simply be blips of economic booms rather than permanent trends." Were the 1990s a one-time "blip," or are there aspects of the 1990s that are permanent? The task in this chapter is to look back over the previous 24 years in an effort to answer this question.

A good way to set the stage is to do a quick survey of the macro economy for the two decades. Some annual macroeconomic data for 1990 to 2013 are provided in the appendix to this chapter. After the shallow recession of 1991, the growth rate of GDP averaged 3.8 percent from 1992 to 2000. Another recession took place in 2001 (although the GDP actually increased by 1 percent in the annual data). Average GDP growth from 2002 to 2007 was 2.7 percent, more than a percentage point below average growth in the 1992–2000 years. Real investment growth was 8.3 percent per year and investment in residential construction was up 6 percent per year during 1992 to 2000. In other words, residential construction did not run hotter than investment as a whole in the 1990s. In fact, firms were investing in equipment, intellectual property, and non-residential structures at a growth rate of 8.6 percent per year. The computer and information technology revolution was in effect, and the productivity data bear this out. Real investment ran at 5.4 percent growth per year during 2002–2006, and residential construction averaged 8 percent growth, so the building of houses was leading total investment during these years prior to the big recession and financial crisis. Investment in equipment, intellectual property, and non-residential structures grew by only 1.8 percent per year from 2002 to 2006 (with a big negative 6.9 percent in 2002). The Federal Reserve Bank was concerned that the economy was not snapping back from the 2001 recession, and made the decision to lower interest rates and to take other administrative actions to stimulate investment in houses. These efforts succeeded.

Employment data reflect the GDP and investment data. Total non-agricultural employment increased from 108.8 million in 1992 to 132 million in 2000, and the unemployment rate dropped from 7.5 percent to 4 percent. Manufacturing employment actually increased from 16.8 million in 1992 to 17.6 million in 1998 and 17.3 million in 2000 as people were hired to make technology gear. The ratio of employment to adult population increased from 61.5 percent to 64.4 percent. Total non-agricultural employment fell to 130.3 million in 2003, and then increased to 137.9 million in 2007 (the peak year for this figure). However, manufacturing employment, which had declined to 15.3 million in 2002, kept on falling to 13.9 million in 2007. Manufacturing jobs did not recover from the recession of 2001. The unemployment rate was 6 percent in 2003 and fell to 4.6 percent in 2007, but the employment-population ratio, which had dropped to 62.3 percent in 2003, came back only to 63 percent in 2007. The basic point is that, during the recovery years of 2002–2006/7, the economy was doing OK, but was relying on housing construction for part of that OK-ness. And manufacturing was not helping on the jobs front at all.

Now comes the big recession. The bubble in housing prices ended and residential investment led the economy into the recession by declining 7.6 percent in 2006. Then house building fell by 21.3 percent per year for the next three years! Total investment actually was up by 2.1 percent in 2006, but then declined in 2007–2009 by an average of 11.4 percent (with a big drop in 2009 of 21.6 percent). Total non-agricultural employment fell from 137.2 million in 2008 to 131.2 million in 2009, and reached bottom in 2010 at 130.3 million. From 2007 to 2010 there were 7.6 million jobs lost. Manufacturing employment fell to 11.5 million in 2010. The annual figure for unemployment jumped from 4.6 percent in 2007 to 9.6 percent in 2010, and the employment-population ratio fell from 63 percent to 58.5 percent. The recession, which officially had begun in the last quarter of 2007, was magnified when the financial system melted down in the second half of 2008. The impacts of the unsound lending practices on Chicago will be examined later in this chapter.

The economy began to recover, but more slowly than the nation needed. GDP growth had been 2.3 percent per year from 2010 to 2013, and real investment was up 8.2 percent over these years. Housing investment had been up just 5.8 percent on average from a very low point. Employment had increased from 130.3 million in 2010 to 136.4 million in 2013, and the unemployment rate was down to 7.4 percent as of 2013 (and 5.9 percent in early 2015). Manufacturing has helped some by adding about 475,000 jobs from 2010 to 2013. However, the creation of jobs had not yet produced an increase in the ratio of population to employment, which remained at 58.6 percent in 2013.

Another trend at the national level is the increasingly unequal distribution of income. Average hourly earnings in real terms are actually lower today than in the early 1970s. Real average hourly earnings (1982–1984 dollars) were $9.26 in 1973, fell to $7.78 in 1993, and then increased somewhat to $8.30 in 2000 during the good economic times of the 1990s. Since then average hourly earnings increased to $8.90 in 2010 and declined only slightly in the wake of the deep recession to $8.73 in 2012. Real average weekly earnings fell from $342 in the 1970s to $291 in 1980. Average weekly earnings fluctuated slightly over the next 30 years, but stood at $291 in 2007. A recent figure is $295 for 2013. The failure of the average worker to receive an increase in earnings has meant that the distribution of income has moved sharply in favor of the higher-income groups. Numerous reports have documented this trend that has been operating since the 1970s. The most recent figures provided by DeNavas-Walt and Proctor of the Census Bureau (2014) show the mean household incomes in 2013 dollars for each quintile, and a few figures are displayed in Table 8.1. The mean household income for the top 20 percent increased rapidly from $108,669 in 1967 to $190,420 in 2005, and dropped slightly to $185,206 in 2013. The mean for the top 5 percent doubled from $171,414 in 1967 to $335,484 in 2005 (and $322,434 in 2013). Mean household income for the third quintile (40th percentile to 60th percentile) stood at $43,158 in 1967, increased to $55,248 in 2005, and pulled back to $52,332 in 2013. The mean for the bottom 20 percent of households increased from $9,755 in 1967 to $11,899 in 1973, hit $12,714 in 2005, and then fell to $11,651 in 2013, which is less than the mean for this group in 1973.

So there we have it. During the 1990s the economy was led by the technology revolution and grew briskly. The tech boom came to an end with the stock market crash in 2001 and the resulting shallow recession, from which recovery was difficult and skewed toward housing investment. The recovery during 2002 to 2006 was fueled by housing, which was fueled by low interest rates and outlandish lending practices, and led to the deep recession and the financial crisis. The financial crisis made the recession much worse, and recovery has been rather slow.

Population growth in the nation was 13.2 percent during the 1990s, an increase over the 9.7 percent growth in the 1980s. Then it slowed back to 9.7 percent for 2000 to 2010. The African-American population grew by 15.7 percent and then by 12.4 percent over the two decades. The Hispanic population grew by 57.1 percent from 1990 to 2000 and by a still strong, but diminished, 43.5 percent in the first decade of the new century. The regional population growth figures are in Table 8.2.

Table 8.1 Mean incomes for quintiles, the top 5 percent, and median household income in the U.S.

Group	1967	1973	1985	1995	2005	2013
Quintile 1*	9,755	11,899	11,591	12,666	12,714	11,651
Quintile 2	27,031	29,917	29,372	30,958	32,694	30,509
Quintile 3	43,158	49,072	48,755	51,764	55,248	52,322
Quintile 4	60,384	70,592	73,337	70,574	86,898	83,519
Quintile 5	108,669	128,309	136,992	166,058	190,420	185,206
Top 5%	171,414	194,555	211,317	286,593	335,484	322,343
Median	43,453	49,282	48,761	52,471	55,278	51,939
Poverty rate	14.2%	11.1%	14.0%	13.8%	12.6%	14.5%

Source: DeNavas-Walt and Proctor (2014) of the U.S. Bureau of the Census.

Note
* Quintile 1 is the lowest 20 percent of households; Quintile 2 includes households from the 20th percentile to the 40th percentile, and so on.

Table 8.2 Regional population growth, 1990–2010

	1990–2000	*2000–2010*
North total	7.0%	3.9%
North African-American	12.0%	7.5%
North Hispanic	42.1%	51.1%
South total	17.9%	14.6%
South African-American	20.4%	16.3%
South Hispanic	81.4%	47.4%
West total	20.2%	13.8%
West African-American	9.0%	11.6%
West Hispanic	51.9%	35.1%
Old Northwest total	7.9%	3.9%
Old Northwest African-American	13.8%	6.5%
Old Northwest Hispanic	84.1%	51.3%

Source: U.S. Bureau of the Census.

The regional growth figures show that population growth in the North (7 percent) and in the states of the Old Northwest (7.9 percent) increased in the 1990s in comparison to the very slow growth in the 1970s and 1980s of 5 percent for these two decades combined. Population growth in the North and the Old Northwest fell back to 3.9 percent for 2000 to 2010. Hispanic population growth was rapid in all regions in both decades. The growth in the states of the Old Northwest of 84.1 percent in the 1990s was from a small base of 1.49 million. The leading states for Hispanic population in 2010 are, in order:

California	14.01 million
Texas	9.46 million
Florida	4.22 million
New York	3.42 million
Illinois	2.03 million
Arizona	1.90 million
New Jersey	1.56 million

It may come as a surprise that Illinois ranks fifth. Illinois had 48.8 percent of the Hispanic population of the states of the Old Northwest in 2010.

While all of this was happening, what was going on in Chicago?

A catalog of reasons for a comeback

Reasons for the comeback of an urban area or a central city fall into three categories:

- forces that are exogenous to the urban area,
- forces that are part of the evolution of the urban area, and
- actions taken in response to urban problems.

This is a catalog, not a theory. The hypothesis that these factors "caused" an urban comeback cannot be rejected with evidence. The issue is to place the various real causes of a comeback into one of these three categories, and then to try to explain how each one happened and to document its impacts.

What are the likely candidates for positive exogenous forces that acted on cities during the 1990s? First among them is the strong macro economy of the 1990s. Productivity growth had a strong resurgence in the 1990s thanks to the use of new information technology. Two other factors seem to be at least partly exogenous. Crime rates declined markedly across the nation, and migration to urban areas from abroad increased substantially. The decline in crime was partly caused by policies adopted in response to crime such as increased use of prisons, tougher gun laws, larger police forces, and longer sentences, but the drop in profits from dealing crack cocaine (which occurred roughly in 1991) and aging of the population are exogenous factors. While this notion is controversial, John Donohue and Steven Levitt (2001) provided statistical evidence that another exogenous factor is the Supreme Court decision in 1973 to legalize abortion in the first two trimesters. It so happened that 18 years later crime rates began to fall. Migration to urban areas such as Chicago increased dramatically after 1990. Migrants were responding in part to economic opportunity that was created by the strong economy, but they were also responding to "push" factors in their home counties.

Federal policy can be exogenous to an individual urban area. Two major cases in point are the Earned Income Tax Credit and the end of welfare as we knew it. Anti-poverty policy had been on the federal agenda since the Roosevelt Administration, and very big changes were made in the Johnson Administration, which were discussed in Chapter 6. The idea of a guaranteed income for families had been proposed by Milton Friedman, of all people, in *Capitalism and Freedom* in 1962. His idea of a negative income tax was brought up in the Nixon Administration, and field tests of the program were conducted in the early 1970s. President Nixon actually proposed a negative income tax. However, concern that a guaranteed floor to income for all families would reduce the incentive to work tabled the idea. Instead the first Earned Income Tax Credit (EITC) was enacted in 1975 and expanded in 1986, 1990, 1993, and 2001. The EITC supplements earnings (rather than taxing them) up to a cut-off point. The program is, in effect, a wage subsidy for low-wage workers. Note that the EITC was expanded three times in the 1990–2001 period. Were these expansions exogenous to metropolitan Chicago? Largely, but not entirely, because poverty in Chicago was part of the bigger picture.

The end of welfare as we knew it came in 1996. The Personal Responsibility and Work Opportunity Reconciliation Act requires that welfare recipients have a lifetime limit of 60 months on what is now Temporary Assistance to Needy Families (TANF), and must be employed or engaged in job search or education or training. The program is a result of a political compromise between President Clinton and Republicans in Congress. In my view the timing of this major change in policy, which had been brewing for years, can be considered exogenous to metropolitan Chicago. Clearly the new program had strong incentives to work. Its impacts on Chicago are discussed below.

How about forces that are part of the evolution on an urban area? This book has repeatedly emphasized the importance of the construction of urban highway systems that took place mainly in the 1960s. Urban areas spread out a great deal as a result. But expressway construction ceased. The details for Chicago have been covered at length. The expressways were basically a one-time thing, and adjustment to a finite change in the transportation system does not go on forever. As economist Herbert Stein (the father of Ben Stein) said on many occasions, "Something that can't go on forever, won't." In fact, increases in demand, coupled with no increase in supply, add up to worsening traffic congestion—an increase in the cost of commuting by auto. Has suburbanization reversed? This idea will be checked out.

The transition of the economy from goods production to the production of services has been cited many times in this book. This major transition to services is exogenous to an urban area, but the manner in which the transition works out locally is part of the evolution of the urban area. Some of the services tend to cluster in the downtown areas of major cities. As we have seen, manufacturing tended to spread out even as its total employment level declined. The economy is now driven by industries, some of which need to be located in big central places. Health care is a very big and growing portion of the service economy. The delivery of health care tends to cluster in major medical centers; many small hospitals have closed down. Health care is a major driver of several central city economies, including Chicago. Higher education is another sector that often clusters in major cities. The economic development watchwords in my new home city of Philadelphia are "eds and meds." Migration to an urban area also is determined partly by its evolution. A city with more Hispanic population tends to draw more Hispanic migrants. And more Hispanic migrants created greater demand for more workers who speak Spanish, and so on. As we saw in Chapter 7, the growth of the Hispanic population had saved some Chicago neighborhoods from abandonment even before 1990. Another factor that is part of the evolution of an urban area is the existence of a graceful older housing stock that was ripe for renovation and "gentrification." These structures became popular among people who work downtown in the new service economy. The conversion of this housing stock began to pick up in the 1960s, and continued into the new century.

As for policy to address urban problems, a leading example is the federal government response to the crisis in public housing. Congress created a program in 1992 that was intended to fund major overhauls of the public housing projects. This program has led to the demolition of many of the worst public housing projects in the nation. Chicago is a major participant in the program, which will be discussed below. Funding for housing vouchers was expanded.

Cities and their citizens responded to the urban crisis. Efforts to control crime are noted above. Indeed, it is fair to say that many urban governments became more effective by improving fiscal management and becoming more adept at economic development policy. At first cities attempted to do (and still do) what is called "smokestack chasing." This effort proved to be ineffective for places like Chicago, in part because there were few smokestacks to chase. The next strategy was to focus on the retention of existing firms to prevent the loss of jobs. However, this sort of effort often involved city officials in responding to emergency situations at the last moment—when little could be done to prevent a firm from moving. Finally, cities realized that they needed to pursue a more comprehensive strategy that built on the existing strengths of the local economy. The idea is to build on the successful parts of the city's economy by supplying through public policy what those industries need to become even more successful. The strategy involves providing education and training programs targeted toward those industries, supplying public amenities for the people who work in those industries, assisting with land assembly, promotion of tourism and marketing the city's convention facilities, and so on. Not-so-trivial examples are that the City of Chicago sponsors some sort of downtown parade on nearly every summer weekend, and built Millennium Park at great expense (including funds from private donors). Most importantly, infrastructure investments can be made. Chicago did some big ones in the first decade of the new century, the transformation of public housing and the expansion of O'Hare Airport.

Others get credit for responding to urban problems. Community-based organizations sprang up, including many in Chicago. They fixed up old houses, built some new ones, pressured city government for better services, organized crime watches, and sponsored day care and drug rehabilitation programs. Many of these organizations did not come out of thin air, but were funded by private foundations. For example, the Ford Foundation established the Local Initiative Support Corporation (LISC) in 1980. LISC raises funds from a variety of sources and funds hundreds of community organizations. These organizations also worked to get more home loans into the inner city. The Community Reinvestment Act of 1977 requires banks to report on lending patterns, and this information is taken into account by bank regulators. A Chicago community organization, led by a woman named Gail Cincotta, was behind the passage of the Community Reinvestment Act. The effectiveness of this act can be questioned in light of subsequent events, but community organizations have had an impact along several dimensions of urban policy.

So here we have a panoply of forces acting to revitalize troubled central cities. Some, such as the economic boom of the 1990s, were temporary blips (maybe). Others are permanent. Migration from abroad continues (at a diminished pace), crime rates remain lower, the EITC and the new welfare system are in place, community organizations continue their efforts, cities continue to work on their economic development strategies, public housing is being transformed and housing vouchers are being issued, and expressways are not being built. However, at this point the nation is not even able to maintain its highways and especially its bridges. Before we jump to conclusions, we need to get back into the weeds of the data on Chicago and its metropolitan area.

Population

The contrast between the two decades can be seen in the basic population data shown in Table 8.3. The population of the metropolitan area increased 11.2 percent

Table 8.3 Population of metropolitan Chicago: 1990–2010 (1000s)

Area	1990	2000	2010
Metropolitan area			
Total	8,182	9,098	9,461
African-American	1,532	1,675	1,626
Hispanic	896	1,495	1,869
City of Chicago			
Total	2,784	2,896	2,696
African-American	1,076	1,054	888
Hispanic	535	754	779
Suburban Cook County			
Total	2,321	2,481	2,499
African-American	225	336	378
Hispanic	159	318	378
Rest of inner suburban ring			
Total	2,448	2,939	3,309
African-American	224	270	326
Hispanic	181	375	608
Outer suburban ring			
Total	629	782	957
African-American	7	15	34
Hispanic	21	48	104

Source: U.S. Bureau of the Census.

in the 1990s, and just 4 percent from 2000 to 2010. Population growth in metropolitan Chicago grew more rapidly in the 1990s than did population in the North and the Old Northwest, and is in stark contrast to the weak growth of the metropolitan area in the 1970s and 1980s. One result of this stronger population growth is that the population of the city of Chicago increased by 4 percent, the first increase for the city since the 1940s. Strong metropolitan area population growth meant rapid suburban population growth of 13.7 percent in the inner ring of suburbs and 24.3 percent in the outer ring. The population of the inner suburban ring in 2000 was 5.42 million. Separate figures for suburban Cook County and the other counties of the inner suburban ring are included because suburban Cook was a mature suburban area with a different property tax system that levies a higher property tax rate on businesses than do the other counties. In 2000 the inner ring population was 46.1 percent located in suburban Cook County, with 53.9 percent in the other counties. Table 8.2 is gross evidence that there was a lot of voting with the feet going on as people continued to seek suburban jurisdictions.

Metropolitan Chicago had become a sprawling urban area of 9.5 million people that spreads from southeast Wisconsin to northwest Indiana to counties that are as much as 70 miles to the west of downtown Chicago. The suburbs provide many options for households and businesses. At this point virtually all suburbs had adopted at least a rudimentary form of zoning, but they vary widely in their use of other development controls. In a study of 198 suburbs as of 1995, McDonald and McMillen (2004) showed that the nature of these other suburban regulations can be grouped roughly into three types. These are quality development regulations (such as architectural review and appearance regulations), regulation of lower-class development (for example, regulations for group homes, mobile homes, and adult uses), and growth controls (e.g. adoption of a comprehensive plan, use of development impact fees, and failure to have an enterprise zone or a tax-increment financing district). The propensity of a suburb to use quality development regulations is positively related to median household income, and the adoption of lower-class regulations is negatively related to income. Growth controls are positively related to the propensity of the suburbs to grow and negatively related to crime, poverty, and minority populations (African-American and Hispanic). The basic conclusion is that suburbs adopt development regulations in the interest of the home owners. Suburbs with lower incomes and larger minority populations have an interest in promoting growth by using enterprise zones and do not have development impact fees. Numerous older suburbs and satellite cities fall into this category. Also, some of these suburbs regulate lower-class development. Higher-income suburbs use a variety of development controls to regulate quality and restrict growth.

Growth of the African-American population resumed in the 1990s after the decline in the 1980s. The growth at the metropolitan level from 1990 to 2000 was 9.1 percent, which is less than the national growth of 15.7 percent. The African-American population of the city of Chicago declined by 2 percent, as the decline in the 1980s of 8.9 percent slowed down appreciably. African-Americans in the inner ring of suburbs increased by 157,000 (35 percent) to 606,000, with most of that growth taking place in suburban Cook County. The largest growth occurred from 1990 to 2000 among the Hispanic population. At the metropolitan level the population increased from 896,000 to 1.495 million, which almost equals the African-American population of 1.672 million in 2000. The city of Chicago added 221,000 Hispanic residents, an increase of 40.9 percent. The growth of the population of the city can be attributed to the growth of the Hispanic population. Hispanic population growth was even greater in the inner suburban ring with an increase of 353,000 (103.8 percent). The outer ring of suburbs recorded strong population growth as noted, but still contained very few African-American or Hispanic residents.

Now we come to the first decade of the new century. Population growth at the metropolitan level of just 4 percent resulted in the resumption of population decline in the city of Chicago. This time the decline in the city was 200,000 (6.9 percent), which is very close to the 7.4 percent decline of the 1980s. By this measure the old problems had returned. The African-American population in the metropolitan area resumed its decline too, from 1.672 million to 1.626 million (down 2.8 percent). Decline at the metropolitan level was coupled with a large decline in the city of 166,000 (15.7 percent drop), which was 83 percent of the total population decline in the city. Decline of African-Americans in the city was partly offset by increases in the inner suburban ring of 98,000 and a smaller increase in the outer suburban ring of 19,000. Movement of the African-American population to the suburbs was less than in the 1990s, but still ongoing. The growth of the Hispanic population remained strong, but diminished. The growth from 2000 to 2010 at the metropolitan level was 374,000 (25 percent, which is less than the national growth of 43 percent). The Hispanic population growth was largely in the inner ring of suburbs; by 2010 the Hispanic population in the inner suburban ring exceeded this group's population in the city of Chicago by 295,000. The Hispanic population must be thought of as both a city and a suburban population. The part of the metropolitan area that grew most rapidly was the outer suburban ring. Its growth in total population in the 2000–2010 decade of 22.4 percent almost was as rapid as the growth in the 1990s of 24.3 percent. And by 2010 10.9 percent of that population of 957,000 was Hispanic.

The population of the downtown area had increased strongly in the 1980s from 6,462 to 11,954. New condominiums and apartments had begun to spring up, led by the Dearborn Park development to the south of the Loop. Then the population grew to 16,388 in 2000 and 29,283 in 2010. In 30 years downtown had become a place of residence, primarily for those who could afford rather up-scale apartments or condos. The population of downtown was only 11 percent African-American and 7 percent Hispanic in 2010. The majority (63 percent) was white, and 16 percent were Asian.

A more detailed look at population in high-poverty areas in the two decades is provided below.

Employment

This section presents the basic employment data much in the same manner as in the earlier chapters, with one difference. The discussion primarily uses employment by place of work rather than place of residence because the census data for the latter are up through 2006, and not available for 2010. The place-of-work data are sufficient to paint the picture.

Employment figures for the metropolitan area by place of work are displayed in Table 8.4. The data are provided by the Bureau of Labor Statistics, and are organized into the new major industry categories. Total employment in the metropolitan area grew by 13.4 percent from 1990 to 2001 (as population grew by 11.2 percent from 1990 to 2000). Employment growth was led by the service sector, professional and business services and education and health services, to be more specific. These two sectors together added 324,000 jobs. Employment gains occurred in all other sectors, save one. Manufacturing employment actually fell by 13.6 percent as manufacturing in the nation decreased by 7.1 percent. The manufacturing industry mix was not favorable. Chicago did not have a concentration of the hi-tech industries that were growing rapidly. Recession and recovery brought the metropolitan area to its peak year of employment in 2007. Total employment had barely returned to its 2001 level (up just 9,000 jobs). The chief reason for the weak job recovery is, once again, to be found in manufacturing. Jobs in the manufacturing sector fell by 113,000 (19 percent). Manufacturing employment had dropped by 30 percent since 1990.[1] Gains in the service sectors of 137,000 jobs offset the losses in manufacturing. Information was the other sector that lost an

Table 8.4 Employment in metropolitan Chicago (data by place of work in 1000s)

Industry	1990	2001	2007	2010	2013
Total	4,011	4,548	4,557	4,247	4,439
Construction	n.a.	n.a.	215	146	149
Manufacturing*	690	596	483	404	410
Transp. and utilities	183	213	204	190	204
Wholesale trade	243	258	251	229	241
Retail trade	455	470	476	437	452
Information	101	117	91	80	80
Finance, ins., real est.	299	325	328	288	289
Prof. and bus. services	512	707	743	685	766
Educ. and health serv.	388	517	571	637	677
Leisure and hospitality	297	368	407	396	426
Other services	162	191	199	189	191
Government	498	558	566	566	550

Source: U.S. Bureau of Labor Statistics.

Note
* BLS data are corrected for the reclassification of publishing from manufacturing to information between 1990 and 2001.

appreciable number of jobs. This is the sector that includes computer information specialists, which lost jobs after the tech stock bust.

The low point for employment in the new century was 2010. Total employment declined by 6.8 percent from 2007 to 2010, which is comparable to the national job loss of 5.5 percent. Employment losses were recorded in all sectors except for two—education and health services, and government. Jobs in education and health services (mainly health services) increased by 66,000, and government employment held steady as the federal economic stimulus package of 2009 provided funds to local governments to avoid laying off their workers as their tax revenues fell. The financial sector lost 40,000 jobs during its meltdown, and the manufacturing sector lost another 79,000 jobs. Employment began to recover after 2010, and by 2013 the metropolitan area had regained 192,000 of the 310,000 jobs that had been lost from 2007 to 2010. The comeback was across the board, but the biggest gain was in professional and business services (81,000 jobs). Manufacturing added 6,000 jobs. However, the notion that manufacturing could even go back to the 2007 level seems to be out of reach. So total employment had its ups and downs, but through it all the industry proportions kept changing away from manufacturing toward services.

As shown in Chapter 7, the metropolitan area suffered a large decline in manufacturing employment of 28.7 percent from 1980 to 1990 while manufacturing jobs in the nation fell by only 5.5 percent. An important question is whether the metropolitan area has continued to lose its share of manufacturing jobs as the nation's manufacturing sector has continued to shed jobs. The answer is "yes," but the loss in share has slowed down. Data from Table 8.4 and the table of macroeconomic data in the appendix (Table A.8.1) show that the metropolitan area had

3.90 percent of the nation's manufacturing employment in 1990, and this share fell continuously to 3.48 percent in 2007 as local employment fell from 690,000 to 483,000. Since that time the share has remained at or above 3.4 percent. The loss of share is attributable to a declining share of jobs in durable goods manufacturing, which fell from 3.98 percent in 1990 to 3.27 percent in 2007 and 3.18 percent in 2013. The share of employment in nondurable goods manufacturing has remained stable since 1990 at roughly 3.8 percent even as local employment fell from 263,000 in 1990 to 196,000 in 2007 and 170,000 in 2013.[2]

Employment located in the city of Chicago covered by unemployment insurance is displayed in Table 8.5. The table includes data from 1990 based on the old industry categories, and the data for the later years use the new industry categories. Nevertheless, most of the industry definitions remained the same, so comparisons over time can be made. The main changes are that communication was renamed information with publishing moved from manufacturing to the information category, and more details are provided for the service sector.

Total employment in the city declined during the 1990s because manufacturing employment fell by 93,000 (partly because publishing was reclassified from manufacturing to the newly defined information sector) and wholesale and retail trade declined by 128,000. These massive losses were partly offset by growth in the service sector of 161,000 jobs. Health services added 38,000 workers. The wholesale and retail trade sectors displayed weak growth at the metropolitan level in Table 8.3. Suburban growth was almost entirely offset by declines in the city. Chicago residents increasingly had to seek work in the suburbs. The record for jobs located in the city is disappointing given that the decade of the 1990s was one of a strong economy at both the national and metropolitan levels.

Table 8.5 Employment in the city of Chicago: 1990–2013 (data by place work in 1000s)

Industry	1990	2001	2007	2010	2013
Total	1,201	1,142	1,095	1,011	1,089
Construction	35	28	30	19	19
Manufacturing*	216	123	82	65	63
TIC**	103	127	103	91	99
Wholesale trade	88	46	40	34	37
Retail trade	176	90	91	86	90
Fin., ins., real est.	174	156	148	131	129
Services	408	569	599	583	649
Prof. and bus. services	n.a.	243	240	222	244
Education services	n.a.	40	47	53	59
Health services	n.a.	126	140	141	164
Leisure and hospitality	n.a.	105	119	114	127
Other services	n.a.	54	53	53	54

Source: Illinois Department of Employment Security, *Where Workers Work*.

Notes
* Publishing was reclassified from manufacturing to information between 1990 and 2001.
** Transportation, information, and utilities (transportation, communication, and utilities in 1990).

Recall that the peak year for employment in the metropolitan area was 2007, but that the employment gain from 2001 was very small. The small increase at the metropolitan level meant decline in the central city once again. The decline in jobs in the city covered by unemployment insurance was 4.1 percent (47,000 jobs), which actually was smaller than the decline of 59,000 jobs from 1990 to 2001. Manufacturing jobs declined again, this time by 41,000, and the service sector gained 30,000 jobs. Then the recession and financial crisis hit, and the city reached its low point in 2010. Total covered employment was down by 84,000 with job losses across the board, including declines in manufacturing of 23,000 and in the financial sector of 17,000. The recovery as of 2013 has brought total covered employment almost back to its 2007 level. The main employment changes for 2007 to 2013 are the decline in manufacturing of 21,000 and in the financial sector of 19,000, and the increase of 50,000 in the service sector. The mix of jobs in the city changed as the economy went into the deep recession and made a recovery.

The data on employment by place of residence for the Census shows somewhat different patterns. Table 8.5 shows a decline of private employment in the city from 1990 to 2000 to 2007, but the data by place of residence show that employment of city residents in the private sector increased slightly from 1990 to 2000 (by 10,000), and then had another increase of 25,000 as of 2006. This divergence in trends suggests that city residents increasingly held jobs in the suburbs. Table 8.5 indicates a drastic decline in manufacturing jobs located in the city from 216,000 to 82,000 between 1990 and 2007.[3] However, the Census shows that the number of city residents employed in manufacturing was 225,000 in 1990, but fell to 173,000 in 2000 and 143,000 in 2006. The place-of-residence data tell of a large decline, but the jobs located in the city fell even more rapidly. Similarly, jobs in wholesale and retail trade located in the city fell by a large amount from 1990 to 2000, and then declined by small numbers after 2000. City residents employed in wholesale and retail trade jobs declined by only 20,000 from 1990 to 2006. Jobs in FIRE located in the city fell after 1990, but residents employed in this sector did not (holding steady at approximately 110,000). Service sector jobs located in the city increased rapidly after 1990 from 408,000 to 599,000 in 2007. Service sector jobs held by city residents were 301,000 in 1990 and 420,000 in 2006, also a big increase. However, the increase in service jobs located in the city far exceeded the number of jobs held by city residents. In short, the place-of-work data compared to the place-of-residence data tell us that more city residents found work in the suburbs in manufacturing and wholesale and retail trade because of the declines in jobs located in the city in these sectors. In contrast, while the number of city residents employed in service sector jobs increased, the increase in the service sector jobs located in the city increased even more rapidly—meaning that suburban residents were finding more service jobs in the city.

The record of the leading manufacturing industries in the city of Chicago is dismal. The main exception is the boost to employment in transportation equipment from 2010 to 2013, probably primarily from the recovery of the auto industry, which includes a major Ford Motor Company plant in south Chicago.

Table 8.6 Manufacturing industries in the city of Chicago

Industry	Employment				
	1990	2001	2007	2010	2013
Machinery	33,121	15,409	8,975	7,618	7,469
Food and kindred products	31,893	25,520	20,843	17,640	15,522
Fabricated metals	23,890	21,799	12,842	9,207	9,002
Printing	n.a.	8,557	5,659	3,834	3,211
Chemicals	13,749	6,533	3,638	3,156	2,850
Paper and allied products	10,731	7,127	4,439	3,595	3,829
Primary metals	9,548	4,094	2,290	1,808	1,910
Transportation equipment	10,882	6,056	4,721	3,584	5,645
Rubber and plastics	8,017	3,644	1,837	1,769	1,628
Apparel and textiles	7,877	7,184	4,700	3,284	3,026
Furniture	5,975	5,842	3,978	3,226	3,017
Total manufacturing*	216,190	122,623	81,624	64,727	63,074

Source: Illinois Department of Employment Security, *Where Workers Work.*

Note
* Publishing was reclassified from manufacturing to information between 1990 and 2001.

The list of the top industries in employment as of 1990, with subsequent employment levels, is shown in Table 8.6. There is no obvious explanation for the precipitous decline in these industries. What is clear is that the economics of industrial location had turned against the city. Perhaps any favorable external effects of industrial clusters in the city disappeared as employment fell. Much has been written about localization economies and how they may be created, but I know of no research on the reversal of the effect that was suggested in Chapter 1.

The employment record for manufacturing in the suburbs is not as stark. The data from Tables 8.4 and 8.5 provide the following estimates for manufacturing employment in the metropolitan area outside the city of Chicago (1000s):

	Metro area	City	Suburbs
1990	690	216	474
2001	596	123	473
2007	483	82	401
2010	404	65	337
2013	410	63	347

These figures suggest that most of the decline in manufacturing employment of 94,000 in the metropolitan area from 1990 to 2001 took place in the city (but recall that publishing has been reclassified from manufacturing to information in the city data, but not in the metropolitan-level data). But the even larger decline in the metropolitan area of 103,000 from 2001 to 2007 largely took place in the suburbs—a decline of 62,000 jobs. The deep recession brought another decline at the metropolitan level of 79,000 jobs, and 64,000 of that drop occurred in the suburbs. The modest recovery of jobs from 2010 to 2013 took place in the suburbs. During these years the job losses first took place in the city, but as the city reached something approaching rock bottom, further job losses took place mainly in the suburbs. Overall the metropolitan area lost 280,000 manufacturing jobs from 1990 to 2013; the city lost 153,000 (70.8 percent of the 1990 figure); and the suburbs lost 127,000 jobs (26.8 percent of the 1990 number).

Employment in downtown Chicago declined by 4 percent from 2001 to 2007, and then declined another 5.4 percent from 2007 to 2010. But then downtown came back. In 2013 employment had returned almost to the 2001 level by increasing 9.9 percent from the low point in 2010. Downtown was back. A detailed breakdown of private employment in downtown covered by unemployment insurance is provided in Table 8.7.

Total employment in the downtown area has been remarkably stable for decades, but the industry mix has changed. Since 1990 jobs in manufacturing, wholesale trade, and retail trade have dropped by 70.4 percent and employment in the service sector has grown by 61.7 percent. After large declines from 1990 to 2001, jobs in wholesale trade and retail trade have been pretty stable. The largest sectors within the huge downtown service sector are broken out in the data beginning in 2001. Employment in health services increased 19,500 from 2001 to 2013 (with a small dip in 2010). Employment in accommodation and food service increased over those 12 years as well by 15,000. Unfortunately the data for 1990 do not provide the same breakdown of the service sector, so the particular sources of the increase of 90,700 jobs from 1990 to 2001 cannot be determined.

The recovery of downtown jobs from 2010 to 2013, with the exceptions of manufacturing and FIRE, was across the board. The largest increases came in

Table 8.7 Employment in downtown Chicago (1000s)

Industry	1990	2001	2007	2010	2013
Total	532.8	528.2	506.8	479.2	526.8
Construction	10.1	7.2	7.7	5.2	5.6
Manufacturing*	45.3	14.9	7.6	6.4	6.1
TIC**	46.6	42.5	33.2	27.8	32.9
Wholesale trade	33.8	12.8	10.6	9.2	11.1
Retail trade	50.8	27.9	24.5	23.9	27.4
FIRE	137.0	120.9	112.5	102.7	102.1
Services	211.3	302.0	310.4	304.0	341.6
Professional and technical	n.a.	118.0	109.2	108.3	119.2
Health services	n.a.	29.0	35.5	33.2	48.5
Accommodation and food serv.	n.a.	41.1	53.3	48.7	56.1
Admin. support and waste mgmt.	n.a.	48.5	43.7	41.4	45.6

Source: Illinois Department of Employment Security, *Where Workers Work*.

Notes

* Publishing was reclassified from manufacturing to information between 1990 and 2001.

** Transportation, information, and utilities (transportation, communication, and utilities in 1990).

professional and technical services, health services, and accommodation and food services. It seems that more workers in accommodation and food service are needed to serve the professional and health care employees (and the tourists, of course). Note that almost half of private-sector jobs located in the city of Chicago is located downtown (48.4 percent as of 2013).

A perusal of lists produced by publications such as Crain's Chicago Business indicates that the largest employers of local residents that produce at least some goods or services for export outside the metropolitan area include a wide variety of organizations in education, health care, transportation, finance and insurance, and manufacturing. The major universities (University of Illinois at Chicago, Northwestern University, and University of Chicago—all of which have major hospitals and medical research centers) and other health care providers (Advocate Health Care, Rush University Medical Center) are on the lists. Two major airlines (United and American) are among the top employers, and Chicago is a major hub for both the United States Postal Service and United Parcel Service. Metropolitan Chicago is home to major insurance companies Allstate and Aon's North American operations, and CNA has a large office in downtown Chicago. Chicago remains a major banking center with Bank One, ABN AMRO, JP Morgan Chase, and Northern Trust. However, Northern Trust is the only one of these major banks that retains Chicago ownership. And CME Group resulted from a merger of the Chicago Mercantile Exchange and the Chicago Board of Trade. Major manufacturers include two top drug firms (Abbott Laboratories and Baxter International). Motorola was divided into two companies, but each is a major employer. US Steel and Arcelor Mittal (which includes the former Inland Steel plant) in Indiana are still large employers in the much-diminished steel industry. The corporate headquarters of Boeing (but only a few jobs) are located in downtown Chicago. In retailing the corporate headquarters of Sears, McDonald's and Walgreen's, and the Walmart Midwest division headquarters are located in the suburbs. AT&T provides service to local customers, but also includes research facilities in the western suburbs. This recitation illustrates the idea of a hierarchy of urban areas in the cases of higher education, medical research and health care, banking and financial services, transportation services, and retailing. The appendix to this chapter includes an example of the list of largest employers from Crain's Chicago Business for 2002 (that does not include the Indiana portion of the metropolitan area). Note that, with five of the top nine, federal, state, and local government dominates the top of the list—an outcome that is typical of such lists for any large metropolitan area.

Concentrated poverty in the city of Chicago

In Chapter 7 we saw that in 1990 there were 17 community areas in the city of Chicago with a rate of family poverty of 30 percent or more. Table 8.8 lists the community areas with poverty rates in excess of 30 percent in 1990, 2000, and 2010. In 1990 there were 11 of these areas with family poverty of 40 percent or higher, and six with a majority of families in poverty. Three community areas had

Table 8.8 High poverty community areas: city of Chicago (percentage of families in poverty)

Community Area	1990	2000	2010
23 West side	32%	29%	32%
24 West side	31%	18%	14%
26 West side	36%	31%	42%
27 West side	46%	29%	42%
28 West side	52%	30%	15%
29 West side	44%	42%	42%
33 South side	61%	30%	8%
34 South side	32%	28%	34%
35 South side	49%	36%	25%
36 South side	70%	45%	39%
37 South side	41%	32%	31%
38 South side	64%	44%	28%
40 South side	57%	49%	44%
42 South side	32%	35%	27%
54 Far south	63%	54%	55%
61 South side	32%	30%	28%
68 South side	40%	40%	42%
30 West side	22%	26%	31%
47 Far south	13%	29%	33%
67 South side	28%	29%	34%
69 South side	23%	28%	31%
Number > 30%	17	13	14
Number > 40%	11	6	6
Number > 50%	6	1	1

Source: Chicago Fact Book Consortium (1995) and U.S. Bureau of the Census.

family poverty in excess of 60 percent. McDonald (2004a) showed that the 1990s brought a reduction in concentrated poverty in Chicago. The poverty rates in four of those 17 community areas were below 30 percent in 2000, and only six of them had poverty levels of 40 percent or higher. Only one community area had a poverty rate in excess of 50 percent (Riverdale on the far south side, CA54, with the huge public housing project that dates back to the 1940s). Fifteen of the 17 had reductions in the family poverty rate. The percentage of families in poverty residing in the 17 community areas fell from 41 percent in 1990 to 32 percent in 2000. The number of families in poverty in the 17 areas fell from 49,500 in 1990 to 35,200 in 2000. The reductions in the poverty rate were accompanied by relative population stability. The population of the 17 areas in 1990 was 553,000 and 514,000 in 2000—a reduction of 7.1 percent. McDonald (2004a, p. 2136) examined the reduction in the family poverty rate in these community areas as a function of changes in the percentage receiving public assistance and the changes in the percentages of males and females who were employed. The decline in the family poverty rate was strongly associated with the increase in the percentage of females who were employed (but not with the other variables). The percentage of females employed increased in 13 of the 17 areas. Recall that welfare reform requires recipients to work, search for work, or undertake education or training. The number of households in the 17 areas receiving public assistance fell by 56.5 percent (from 60,200 to 26,200). McDonald (2004a) also found some evidence that the family poverty rate declined less in those community areas with smaller declines in the percentage receiving public assistance. So, in spite of the fact that employment opportunities in the city of Chicago were declining, more females in the high-poverty areas found work and apparently reduced the rate of poverty in their neighborhoods.

You the careful reader may be apprehensive about what comes next. See Table 8.8. There were 14 community areas with a family poverty rate in excess of 30 percent in 2010, compared to 13 in 2000. As in 2000, six community areas had a family poverty rate of 40 percent or higher, and one (Riverdale, again) had a poverty rate above 50 percent. Three of the four community areas that had dropped below 30 percent in 2000 went back above 30 percent in 2010, and four were new to the list with poverty in excess of 30 percent. Six community areas that had a poverty rate greater than 30 percent in 2000 had reductions in poverty to less than 30 percent in 2010, so the net increase in high-poverty areas is one. The population of the 17 high-poverty community areas in 1990 declined to 470,000 in 2010 (down 8.5 percent from 2000). Recall that the 13 African-American community areas with high concentrations of family poverty in 1990 had declined by 44.3 percent in population from 1970 to 1990, and the other four declined by 16.4 percent. So the 17 community areas present a mixed picture. One's reaction might be, "It could have been worse." The not-so-good news is the four community areas that were added to the group with family poverty of 30 percent or higher. That brought the total of high-poverty community areas to 14. Three of the four are African-American areas on the south side, and one is a Hispanic area on the west side. The family poverty rates were in the low 30s—from 31 percent to 34 percent, and had been in the high 20s in 2000 (from 26 percent to 29 percent). These new members of the high-poverty group had total population decline from 178,000 to 150,000 (down 15.7 percent), so the increase in the poverty rate seems to be a result of people moving out.

Jargowsky updated his earlier study of concentrated poverty at the census tract level in a 2003 report titled "Stunning Progress, Hidden Problems: The Dramatic Decline of Concentrated Poverty in the 1990s," and came up with somewhat different numbers. His calculations show that the number of people in Chicago living in areas of 40 percent or higher poverty fell from 413,000 to 235,000 in the decade. Stunning progress indeed. A recent report by Elizabeth Kneebone, et al. (2011) finds, using a slightly different method, that the population in Chicago in census tracts with 40 percent poverty or greater increased from 210,000 in 2000 to 304,000 over the 2005–2009 period. The number of high-poverty census tracts increased from 96 to 124.

Administrative decisions had turned the projects into concentrations of poverty, and grossly incompetent management by the Chicago Housing Authority had created a disaster. By the early 1990s the crack epidemic, coupled with vacant CHA units and street gangs, turned some of the projects into centers of the drug trade. Spending on security was increased many fold, but gains were temporary. The election of 1994 produced a Congress dominated by the Republicans, who demanded a viability test for public housing projects with high vacancy rates to determine whether the residents instead should be given housing vouchers for use in the private market. The Department of Housing and Urban Development (HUD) investigated CHA's performance, and found it to be failing. The CHA Director offered to turn the entire agency over to the federal government, so HUD began to run CHA in 1995. HUD ran the CHA for three years until the agency was back on its feet, but it was clear that many of the projects were not viable and needed to be torn down. Recall that public housing projects built up through the 1960s contributed to the creation of high-poverty community areas. Of the total of 38,776 CHA units standing in 2000, 20,669 were located in high-poverty community areas. Only 9,478 of the 20,669 units were occupied. Three community areas (CA28 on the near west side, and CA33 and CA38 on the south side) contained 17,149 CHA units, of which 6,639 were occupied.

Mayor Richard M. Daley assembled a team that formulated the "Plan for Transformation" that would constitute a complete overhaul of the mission of the CHA. The plan privatized the management of all CHA properties. CHA itself would become the agent for demolition and renovation of the projects. The plan called for the demolition of 18,500 of the 29,300 family units and the renovation of the remaining 9,700 family and senior citizen units. The plan was to last for ten years, at the end of which time CHA would have a total of 24,500 new and renovated units. This number was slightly above the number of occupied units in 2000 of 23,162, but far short of the 38,776 total standing. The plan was based on a steady stream of federal funding. Residents who had leases and were paying rent on time would be permitted to return to a CHA unit, and in the meantime were given housing vouchers. The new projects are built to blend into the neighborhood as "mixed income" developments, and so typically include units rented on the open market. The new projects are built by non-profit and for-profit developers under CHA and HUD supervision using a combination of funding sources, including the Low Income Housing Tax Credit program. The plan began in 2000, and the development of the new units was still underway 14 years later.

Given that the new developments contain "market rate" units, and that public housing units are supposed to be indistinguishable from the other units, the per-unit cost of the developments is very high. Indeed, housing economists have repeatedly demonstrated that housing vouchers are a much cheaper method than public housing projects for providing decent housing to low-income households. The implementation of the Plan for Transformation is proving this to be true once again.

The Plan for Transformation created a great deal of controversy. Who is eligible to return? Why the tough rules, including drug tests, for tenants? Why are there not more housing vouchers so that more non-CHA families can rent decent housing? What about services for the CHA households which move away? Why cannot those new units be built faster? Or, why are we building new units at all and not just using housing vouchers? All good issues, to be sure. But the transformation of CHA was necessary. This author says, "Two cheers for the new CHA."

Rebirth of the central city in the 1990s?

We have seen that population growth returned to the city of Chicago for a brief time in the 1990s, and that concentrated poverty declined. How about the other economic and social indicators that were used in Chapter 7? Was the virtuous circle at work? (See Table 8.9 for the figures.)

As shown in Table 8.9 Seven indicators, and six moved in the right direction and one was unchanged, a score of +6. The decline in the number of people living in the areas with family poverty of 40 percent or higher and the drop in the murder rate are particularly notable.

Chicago is a leading example of what I called (2008) central city rebirth. Eight of the other 16 major central cities of the North improved on these indicators, four did not get better or worse, and three had lower scores. These last three are Philadelphia, Washington DC, and Buffalo. The cities with the best net scores of +5 or better, in addition to Chicago, are Detroit (believe it or not), Minneapolis-St. Paul, Kansas City, and Indianapolis. Chicago and Minneapolis-St. Paul had the best net scores with +6. Median family income in the city of Detroit increased by 17.1 percent to $29,500, to earn double points. The poverty rate in Detroit fell from 32.6 percent to 26.1 percent. The murder rate had been a truly disastrous 57 per 100,000, and it fell to 41. That is still pretty awful, but it is progress. Jargowsky's computation of the population in high-poverty areas in Detroit showed a huge drop from 421,000 to 108,000. It was not so long ago that progress was being made in Detroit.

Computations show that the same five variables discussed in Chapter 7 were still positively correlated for the 17 central cities of the North. The variables are:

- central city poverty rate,
- percentage of population living in high-poverty census tracts,
- murder rate,

Table 8.9 Social and economic indicators: 1990–2000

Indicator	1990	2000
Population	2,784	2,896
		+4.0%
Poverty rate	21.6%	19.3%
Med. family income ($1999)	$41,300	$42,700
		+3.4%
Population in high-poverty areas		
Family poverty		
30% or higher	553,000	514,000
40% or higher	282,000	140,000
50% or higher	127,000	10,000
Poverty population in		
Census tract > 40%	413,000	235,000
Murder rate/100K	31	22
High-school dropout	34%	28%
Single-parent families	41%	41%

- adult high-school dropout percentage, and
- percentage of single-parent families.

Eight of the ten correlations are positive and statistically significant, and two are positive and not quite statistically significant at the 95 percent level. These two are the correlations of high-school dropouts with the murder rate and single-parent families. It was still true that, if your city has a relatively bad score on one indictor, chances are your city has a relatively bad score on the other four.

Housing market bubble and financial crisis

The facts of the financial crisis are well known, and this study will not include a detailed account of the strange doings in the mortgage market. The reader is referred to the excellent books by Mark Zandi (2009) and Alan Blinder (2013), as well as the final report of the Financial Crisis Inquiry Commission (2011). Here in a nutshell is how the mortgage market worked in the five years or so up to the financial crisis of 2008. Mortgage brokers prepared mortgage loan applications for households who had no business applying for loans. The applications left off critical pieces of information such as income and other debts. Applicants were persuaded to apply for what was called a 2-28 loan in which the initial interest rate was relatively low, given the risk. Then the interest rate would adjust upward after two years. Applicants also were persuaded to borrow very high percentages of the purchase price of a house (up to 95 percent or more if a second loan is added). They were told not to worry about any of this because house prices were rising rapidly. When two years had passed the borrower could obtain a new loan at a lower interest rate because the loan would now just repay the first loan, and the house would be worth much more so the loan-to-value ratio would be reduced to normal levels.

What happened next? Mortgage brokers succeeded in getting their applicants approved by a small lender (with a line of credit from a large lender) because the small lender could sell the loan to the large lender and roll over its line of credit to make more loans. The large lender could then turn around and sell the loan to a large institution in the business of creating mortgage-backed securities, which were then sold to investors such as insurance companies, pension funds, and so on. As the loan was passed along in this process, less and less information about the loan was transmitted. Indeed, at each step the seller of the loan had an incentive to hide information from the buyer. This is what economists (and others) call moral hazard. The bond rating companies that rated the mortgage-backed securities were complicit in the game. Creators of mortgage-backed securities shopped around for (and paid) the rating company that would give them the best rating. The rating companies coached the creators of the securities in how to achieve a good rating. The worst creators of mortgage-backed securities were private firms such as Bear Stearns, Citigroup, Morgan Stanley, Goldman Sachs, and Lehman Brothers. Investors relied on the rating companies in choosing their investments. Not only that, some insurance companies—the largest participant was AIG—insured the securities against negative news. The government-sponsored companies Fannie Mae and Freddie Mac participated in the process too. But in their case they guaranteed the mortgage-backed securities, to their eventual dismay.

Federal policy had played a supporting role. First, the law that had separated investment banking from regular banking was repealed in 1999 so that banks could make a wide variety of investments. Second, the Federal Reserve had the authority to supervise much of the activity described in the previous two paragraphs, but chose not to do so. One governor of the Federal Reserve, the late Edward Gramlich, warned of the problems that were brewing, but his views were not influential. Then the Federal Reserve Bank decided to lower short-term interest rates to very low levels. The interest rate on federal funds was 6.25 percent in 2000, and it was cut to 1.25 percent in 2004. As noted in the introduction to this chapter, the Federal Reserve Bank intended to stimulate housing construction to help the economy out of the recession. Very low short-term interest rates enabled lenders to offer 2-28 loans with relatively low initial interest rates.

Loose lending standards, coupled with low interest rates, fueled a housing price bubble. The exact date for the beginning of the housing price bubble is not clear, but it happened. Zandi (2009, pp. 163–164) thinks that the bubble began in 2003. For him:

> The bubble was born out of the boom. The boom had been based on solid demand and supply fundamentals, such as affordable loans, strong incomes, and ample household savings. The bubble developed when Americans started buying not simply because they needed someplace to live, but because they thought that housing was a great investment. Prices had risen; therefore, they would continue to rise. This is speculation. A bubble develops when an asset's price becomes disconnected from its fundamental value.

One piece of evidence for Zandi (2009, p. 166) is the ratio of housing prices to rents, which increased from about 16 prior to 2002 to 25 at the end of 2005.

One popular index of housing prices, the S&P/Case-Shiller 20-city index, increased from 100 in January 2000 to 206.52 in July 2006. Housing prices had more than doubled in nominal terms in a little over six years. The index for metropolitan Chicago did not increase as much—from 100 in January 2000 to 168.59 in October 2006. The index for the Minneapolis-St. Paul metropolitan area increased from the same base to 170.97 in August 2006, but the index for metropolitan Cleveland increased only to 123.17 in September 2005. The housing price bubble was much more pronounced in the West and in Florida. The index for Los Angeles reached 273.85 in July 2006, and the Las Vegas index was 234.78 in August 2006. But bubbles always burst. The 20-city index fell to 139.26 in April 2009, a drop of 32.6 percent. The metropolitan Chicago index fell to 122.50 in March 2009 and then to 102.75 in March 2012. The March 2012 index says that housing prices in nominal terms had returned to their January 2000 level, which means a decline in real housing prices. The Minneapolis and Cleveland indexes came back to earth at 109.58 in March 2009 and 98.07 in April 2009, respectively. The Los Angeles index fell to 159.37 in April 2009, and the Las Vegas index collapsed to 90.24 in January 2012.

What does the bursting of the bubble, which began in mid-2006, mean for home buyers? Those who bought a house during the bubble period on the 2-28 adjustable rate loans found that they were unable to refinance at favorable terms because their house was now worth less than the outstanding balance on the loan. Indeed, many of the loans required monthly payments that only covered the interest, and did not reduce the principal. These buyers had to stay with the loan as the interest rate adjusted upward, or default. Many defaulted on their loans, and foreclosures increased dramatically. Mortgage-backed securities lost much of their value. Those who were holding these securities, and those who were backing them, were now in deep financial trouble. The value of assets fell, so many institutions were bankrupt (debts far in excess of assets). Some major institutions such as Bear Stearns had financed their operations with overnight loans, so if lenders refused to roll over the loans the next day, the institution is bankrupt immediately. Bear Stearns was purchased by JP Morgan Chase in March 2008, but Lehman Brothers went bankrupt in September. The bankruptcy of Lehman set off the financial crisis.

As we have seen, the housing price bubble was smaller in metropolitan Chicago than in other urban areas, but housing prices fell by 27.3 percent between October 2006 and March 2009—and by 39.1 percent if we extend the date to January 2012. Declines on this order of magnitude are quite enough to put a lot of borrowers far "under water," i.e. the house is worth less than the out-standing balance on the loan. If you borrowed 90 percent of the original house value, a 10 percent drop in value wipes out your equity, and any further drop puts you under water.

The decline in housing prices was far greater in some areas of the inner city. Only two of the high-poverty community areas as of 2000 had at least 100 sales of single-family houses in the second half of 2006 and first half of 2007 according to Midwest Real Estate Data (based on the Multiple Listing Service records). These two are New City (CA61) and Englewood (CA68), two community areas located just to the west of the original Black Belt. New City is a mixed Hispanic and African-American neighborhood, and Englewood is 99 percent African-American. The median housing price data for these two community areas are:

	New City	Englewood
Median price 2006–2007	$173,000	$94,000
Number of sales	117	117
Median price 2010	$42,000	$26,000
Number of sales	95	119
Median price 2013	$30,000	$9,000
Number of sales	83	59

These price figures do not control for the type and quality of the house, but the drops in prices are breathtaking none the less.

A study of mortgages in Cook County by McDonald (2010) established the following link. Census tracts with a large volume of high-cost lending in 2006 had a large volume of foreclosure filings in 2007 and 2008. Foreclosure filings lead to foreclosure auctions, in which the lender takes ownership of the property. High-cost loans are loans with an interest rate figured over a ten-year period that exceeds the ten-year Treasury bond rate by 3 percent. The actual ten-year Treasury bond rate in 2006 was 4.80 percent, and the median interest rate for high-cost loans in Cook County for that year was 5 percent over the Treasury bond rate. This means that the median interest rate on these loans was 9.80 percent. This compares to 6.63 percent for the standard 30-year mortgage (figured for ten years), so the high-cost loans were 48 percent more expensive than the standard mortgage. Most of the high-cost loans had lower rates for the first two years and higher rates for the following years, which bumps up the ten-year interest rate.

The number of high-cost loans awarded in 2006 in a census tract in Cook County was strongly positively related to two control variables—the total number of households and the number of mortgageable properties in the census tract. The number of these loans was unrelated to the median family income in the tract, but was strongly positively related to the percentages of African-American and Hispanic population. On the other hand, the number of standard loans awarded in a census tract was positively related to the two control variables and median family income (as one would expect), but negatively related to the percentage African-American population. In short, there is evidence that African-American borrowers in Cook County in 2006 were being steered into high-cost loans in a discriminatory manner. The effect of percentage African-American population on the number of high-cost loans is large. The mean number of high-cost loans in a census tract was 72.5. A tract with the mean value for percentage African-American population of 33.4 percent had, on average, 24.4 more high-cost loans and a tract that was 100 percent African-American had 73 more high-cost loans compared to a tract with no African-American or Hispanic population. At the mean value for percentage Hispanic population of 21.3 percent the census tract had 12.1 more high-cost loans than the tract with no Hispanic or African-American population.

Foreclosure filings in a census tract for 2007 and 2008 are so strongly related to the number of high-cost loans in 2006 that basically nothing else matters very much. The simple correlations between the number of high-cost loans in 2006 and the number of foreclosure filings in 2007 and 2008 are 0.90 and 0.94, respectively. The mean value for foreclosure filings was 19.16 in 2007 and 29.01 in 2008. An increase in the number of high-cost loans in 2006 increased foreclosure filings in 2007 by 0.28 per high-cost loan and in 2008 by 0.37 per high-cost loan. This means that a census tract with 24 more high-cost loans in 2006 had 6.7 more foreclosure filings in 2007 *and* 8.9 more foreclosure filings in 2008. Over two years that adds up to 15.6 more foreclosure filings. This does not mean that the actual loans awarded in 2006 are being foreclosed upon in 2007 or 2008. It does mean that a census tract with a pattern of high-cost loans had a lot of foreclosures. And it all means that, since high-cost loans were being generated in the African-American and Hispanic areas, the foreclosures were concentrated in these same areas. Numerous studies have demonstrated that foreclosures in a neighborhood have a negative impact on the prices of nearby houses. The decline in prices puts more borrowers under water and leads to more foreclosures. The two variables interact in a downward spiral.[4]

Data compiled by the Woodstock Institute of Chicago show that foreclosure filings in Cook County peaked in 2010, but did not decline by a large amount until 2013. Foreclosure filings in suburban Cook County were as great as (or greater than) filings in the city of Chicago, but most heavily concentrated in the African-American and Hispanic areas in both city and suburban Cook. There were 241,000 foreclosure filings in Cook County from 2008 to 2013, and 204,000 of those were on single-family houses or condos. There were 3.92 million mortgageable properties in Cook County in 2007, which means that 6.2 percent of them enter foreclosure during the six years from 2008 to 2013. Foreclosure filings for the county and the city of Chicago by year are:

Year	Cook County	Chicago	Rest of Cook
2008	39,000	21,000	18,000
2009	45,000	23,000	22,000
2010	50,000	23,000	27,000
2011	41,000	19,000	23,000
2012	42,000	18,000	24,000
2013	24,000	11,000	13,000
Total	241,000	115,000	126,000

The Attorney General of Illinois has been active in filing lawsuits against lenders who acted in an apparently predatory and discriminatory fashion during the housing bubble. For example, in 2009 a lawsuit was filed against Wells Fargo and Company alleging that the lender illegally discriminated against African-American and Hispanic mortgage borrowers in Cook County by selling them high-cost subprime loans while white borrowers with similar incomes were granted standard mortgages with lower terms. Data provided by Wells Fargo under the Home Mortgage Disclosure Act show the following percentages of high-cost loans out of all home loans:

	2005	2006	2007
African-American	43%	58%	49%
Hispanic	23%	35%	25%
White	11%	16%	15%

These raw percentages do not prove discrimination, of course, but are suggestive.

Return of the vicious circle?

Let us return to the taxonomy of forces that act on an urban area and its central city. Exogenous factors, forces that grow out of the evolution of the urban area, and local policy actions, can be negative as well as positive. When it comes to the first decade of the twenty-first century, clearly one might hypothesize that exogenous factors hurt the metropolitan area and the city. Weak economic and job growth occurred at the national level. Migration to the nation and the urban area slowed down, largely because job opportunities had declined. Loose lending standards were fomented by the "innovations" in the financial system, and brought bad lenders to most towns. Federal Reserve policy to "bet on housing" to stimulate the economy was exogenous to an individual city. The bubble in housing prices got started. Buyers in the urban area kept the bubble going, of course. The inevitable happened; the bubble burst and the foreclosure crisis hit Cook County and the city. Maybe Herb Stein's comment that something that cannot go on forever, won't should be supplemented with "and something that is inevitable will happen." Another exogenous factor is the financial crisis and the subsequent low interest rate environment. Cities can borrow at low rates of interest (as long as they keep their fiscal affairs in order), but low interest rates mean that public employee pension funds earn less money than had been anticipated. Low returns put pressure on state and municipal budgets in paying pensions and other expenses that rely on invested funds.

Then there is the next phase of the evolution of the urban area and the city. The massive change in the mix of employment away from goods production toward services is national in scope, but Chicago had been one place that relied on goods production to make a living. There was a decline in the demand to hire people for this purpose. Where would the remaining goods production jobs be located? Clearly not in the city of Chicago for a variety of reasons. Chicago workers and facilities evidently were not well suited to the new demands of the manufacturing sector. Economies of agglomeration for manufacturing in the city seem to have collapsed over time. Manufacturing survives in a diminished state in the suburbs, but 63,000 manufacturing jobs in the city in 2013 are less than 10 percent of the number for 1947. Another aspect of the evolution of the city is the aging housing stock. A relatively small percentage of that stock was being renovated, but most of it just got older, and many neighborhoods suffered from the abandonment of large numbers of houses. The old smaller apartment buildings were particularly vulnerable. Abandonment breeds more abandonment. A lot of abandonment accompanied the population declines of the 1970s and 1980s. The remaining structures were much older in 2007, and their potential for refurbishing that much diminished.

What about actions of local government? It is fair to say that local government had a mixed decade. Mayor Richard M. Daley, like his predecessors, was critically aware that he must try to retain the middle class in the city, and increase its numbers if possible. But how do you do that? He supported the building of Millennium Park, planted trees and shrubs in median strips of streets, and encouraged downtown housing developers with a new zoning ordinance. Perhaps most importantly, he continued to push for the transformation of public housing into mixed-income developments and he orchestrated a major expansion of O'Hare Airport (and renovated Midway Airport as well). The new mayor, Rahm Emanuel, is moving to have the city colleges specialize in programs that train students for the top industry sectors in the metropolitan area. These policies are all based on reasonable presumptions about the factors that promote growth.

Mayor Daley avoided raising property taxes and instead used a variety of other means to balance the budget of the city. Hunt and DeVries (2013, p. 248) show that debt per capita for the City of Chicago increased during the younger Mayor Daley's term from $700 in 1990 to $2,600 in 2010. One popular idea that has been used around the nation is to under-fund the public employee pension systems. Chicago and the State of Illinois are the national leaders in this movement, which inhibits the ability of a government to borrow and in the longer run is self-defeating. The pension fund for public school employees had been well funded (90 percent in 2001), but then the decision was made to under-fund the pension system to pay other expenses. The funding level stands at 51 percent in 2014. Other pension funds for public employees in Illinois are similarly under-funded because required contributions by the employers were not made. Another tactic is to sell public assets. The Chicago Skyway, the tollway that runs to Indiana, was sold (leased for 99 years actually) to a private firm in 2005 and provided the City with an infusion of $1.83 billion in cash. The notorious case is the selling in 2008 of the parking meters in the city to a private firm for $1.16 billion in cash. These funds have largely been used to plug gaps in the city budget. Hunt and DeVries (2013, p. 249) note that as of 2010 $973 million of the parking meter money had been spent, and only 27 percent of the Skyway money remained. Once the money is spent, it is gone (another Herb Stein-like statement). The City also has attempted to sell Midway Airport, but so far there have been no buyers acceptable to the City. What else can be sold? Public school quality and funding have been big issues in Chicago and in most other center cities as well. The loss of middle-class kids hurts the performance of a school, so what do you do when you lose them? The Chicago public schools have tried a variety of measures, but they have not found the formula that will work in general. Budget pressures do not help.

Somewhat strangely the City is still trying to figure out how to attract manufacturing jobs to the city. Hello 1970s? Such efforts have their place, one supposes. Cook County continues to offer a variety of property tax incentives for commerce and industry, and the State of Illinois, Cook County, and the City of Chicago offer Industrial Development Bond programs and small business loan programs. The state program was used to finance a new "vertical campus" building for Roosevelt University in the downtown area. The state enterprise zone program continues. The main tool that has been used by the City in recent years is the tax increment financing district (TIF district). Illinois passed enabling legislation in 1983. This policy involves selling bonds on the basis of future tax revenues expected in a small area, and using the proceeds to invest in infrastructure in support of private development. As reported by Hunt and DeVries (2013, pp. 250–253), as of 2011 Chicago had formed 163 TIF districts covering 30 percent of the area of the city (but only 10 percent of the property tax base). These districts produce about $500 million in revenue each year, and since 1983 some $3.7 billion has been spent on projects in the TIF districts. According to Hunt and DeVries (2013, p. 252) about half of the money has gone on public projects, and half has been used to support private development. TIF districts are popular among Chicago aldermen because, in effect, funds can be used at the alderman's discretion to support favored local projects. Hunt and DeVries (2013, p. 252) reach the conclusion that:

> TIFs now amount to an "off-budget" pool of funds, resulting in a perception of corruption and widespread cynicism about the tool. This outcome is unfortunate because in the right circumstances and with careful planning TIF can be a powerful tool.

Careful research by Rachel Weber, Saurav Bhatta, and David Merriman (2003) from the inception of the TIF program in 1977 to 2001 shows that industrial property values were not increased in Chicago TIF districts that were restricted to industrial use. However, industrial property values did increase in those TIF districts that were designated mixed-use areas. These outcomes indicate that industrial property owners likely wished to convert their parcels to non-industrial use. It is evident that whatever localization economies may have existed in the industrial areas of Chicago had vanished. Brent Smith (2006) studied multi-family housing property values from 1992 to 2000 in the Chicago TIF districts, and found a positive impact. In effect, both studies indicate that uses other than industry were preferred in Chicago. Chicago has a couple of highly successful TIF districts in the downtown area (a location with little manufacturing).

Another policy that has been used is the federal empowerment zone that was created in 1995. Chicago was among the first recipients of a zone. The main incentive in this zone is a wage subsidy paid to firms located in the zone that hire zone residents. The subsidy is in the form of a tax credit up to $3,000 for each person hired. Originally the tax credit could be claimed up through 2001, to be phased out by 2004. But the tax credit was extended, and still could be claimed for 2013. Research by Deirdre Oakley and Hui-shien Tsao (2007) and Matias Busso, Jesse Gregory, and Patrick Kline (2010) used census data to show that residents of empowerment zone census tracts gained in employment in relation to comparison areas. Oakley and Tsao (2007) found that unemployment in the empowerment zone census tracts fell by 3.75 percent compared to other similar census tracts. In addition, Busso, et al. (2010) found that employment located in the empowerment zone census tracts increased by 13 percent in relation to comparison areas from 1992 to 2000.[5]

One question is whether the positive effect of the empowerment zone lasted beyond 2000. A preliminary answer to this question can be provided by examining the employment data by postal zone from *Where Workers Work*. The five postal zones that have the largest shares of their areas included in the empowerment zone are compared to five nearby postal zones. The five empowerment zone zip codes have an average of 57 percent of their areas included in the empowerment zone. Total employment changes are as follows.

	Five empowerment zone zip codes	Five nearby zip codes
1993–2001	6.2%	–7.0%
1993–2007	2.8%	–12.9%
1993–2010	–1.0%	–21.4%
1993–2013	–3.5%	–24.3%

We see that the early employment gain in the empowerment zone areas does not last, but that employment in the comparison areas declined sharply. It seems that the empowerment zone is able to hold on to employment far better than nearby comparison areas. The composition of employment in the empowerment zone changed along with the rest of the city. The five zip codes contained 24,315 manufacturing jobs in 1993, but this total fell to 23,888 in 2001, 13,664 in 2007, and 12,764 in 2013. Manufacturing employment in these areas fell by 47.5 percent in the 20 years from 1993 to 2013. Other sectors showed employment gains, particularly health care. The five empowerment zone zip codes gained 6,400 jobs in health care from1993 to 2007.

So we have a variety of negative forces at work, along with some positive factors that survive from the 1990s. Among the positive factors is the transformation of the public housing system. The main negative forces are exogenous. What were the net outcomes for the city? The rundown for the seven economic and social indicators is given in Table 8.10.

Population is down, the poverty rate is up, and median household income is down. But the data for the population in high-poverty areas shows a mixed picture.

Table 8.10 Social and economic indicators: 2000–2010

Indicator	2000	2010
Population	2,896	2,696
		–6.9%
Poverty rate	19.6%	21.4%
Median household income ($2009)	$49,700	$45,900
		–7.94%
Population in high-poverty areas		
Family poverty		
30% and higher	514,000	352,000
40% and higher	140,000	123,000
50% and higher	10,000	6,500
Poverty population of		
Census tract > 40%	210,000	304,000
Murder rate/100K	21.8	16.0
High-school dropout	28%	20%
Single-parent family	41.5%	42.8%

Based on community areas, there was a drop in the population located in areas with high concentrations of families in poverty. However, at the census tract level the population in high-poverty areas has increased. The murder rate declined, as did the percentage of adults who had not graduated from high school. Single-parent families increased marginally. The net score might be –1 or –3. This scoring assigns a –1 to single-parent families and either +1 or –1 to population in high-poverty areas. The clear positive is the decline in the murder rate, even though Chicago makes the headlines every time there is a rash of shootings.

If we go by the score of –3, the 2000–2010 decade gets the same score as did the 1980s. Not good. But the data on concentrations of family poverty at the community area level show much smaller populations in these areas. In 2000 514,000 people lived in community areas with 30 percent or more of families in poverty, but the number for 2010 is 352,000. The figures for 40 percent or more are 140,000 in 2000 and 123,000 in 2010, and 10,000 in 2000 for areas with a majority of the families in poverty compared to just 6,500 in 2010. Thanks mainly to the demolition of the worst public housing projects, the number of community areas with a majority of families in poverty had been reduced to one small area. So this author might be inclined to go with a score of –1 on this group of indicators because of the major reform of the Chicago Housing Authority. But then there is the wave of foreclosures that only began to subside in 2013.

Chicago, Detroit, and other cities of the North

What about our group of 17 major central cities in the North? McDonald (2015) presents the details of the study of the seven indicators. One of those indicators is concentrated poverty based on census tract data (not community areas). The bottom line is that the city of Detroit did horribly and was forced into bankruptcy, and the others managed. The city of Detroit lost 24.9 percent of its population in just the ten years from 2000 to 2010. Seven of the remaining 16 gained population, population in two was unchanged, and seven lost population. The average population loss for those seven that lost population was 8 percent. Among this group the largest population loss of 10.9 percent occurred in Buffalo. Eleven of the 17 central cities did better than Chicago on this measure. Given that the economy was in deep recession in 2010, it is not surprising that the poverty rate increased in 14 of the 17 cities and real median household income declined in those same 14. The poverty rate declined and median household income increased only in New York City, Washington DC, and Baltimore. The mean poverty percentage for the 17 cities was 24.5 percent compared to 21.4 percent for Chicago. Median household income fell by 29.2 percent in Detroit. Cleveland came next with a decline of 20.5 percent. Nine of the cities had median household income declines greater than the 7.9 percent decline in Chicago. Ten of the 17 (including Chicago) had increases in the number of people living in high-poverty census tracts (40 percent or higher). In Detroit the number increased from 94,000 to 265,000, meaning that 37 percent of the population of the city of Detroit lived in a high-poverty census tract in 2010. The mean for this measure was 13.3 percent. The figure for Chicago was 11.3 percent.

Eight cities had an increase in the murder rate. The murder rate in Detroit was 43 per 100,000 in 2010. St. Louis actually had a higher murder rate of 45. Compare these to the murder rate in New York City of 6.6 and 7.9 in Minneapolis-St. Paul. The mean murder rate for the 17 cities was 21.3 per 100,000 compared to 16 for Chicago. All 17 had a decline in the percentage of adult high-school dropouts (mean percentage 18 percent). Thirteen had increases in the percentage of single-parent families, one had a decline (Washington DC), and two were unchanged (with one city not reporting). In Detroit 69 percent of families with children had only a single parent. It was 68 percent in Cleveland. The average for the 16 cities on this indicator is 55 percent, and the lowest ones are 42 percent in Minneapolis-St. Paul and 43 percent in Chicago. Single-parent family data such as these cannot spell good things for children.

The net scores on the seven indicators were demonstrably worse for 13 of the central cities in 2010 compared to 2000. New York City and Washington DC improved greatly on the net index (up five points and nine points, respectively) and Philadelphia and Baltimore improved slightly (by one point). As we have seen, Chicago went from +6 to –3 on the net index, which was one of the two worst reversals in the group. Cleveland had the same net outcome. These bad results stem primarily from the deep recession that was in full force in 2010.

The correlations among five indicators show that, once again, the poverty rate, the percentage of the population living in high-poverty census tracts, the murder rate, the high-school dropout percentage, and the single-parent family percentage are all highly correlated. In fact, for 2010 all the simple correlations are highly statistically significant.

So Chicago did not do well compared to the other 15 central cities (omitting Detroit). Only Detroit, Cleveland, and Cincinnati had lower scores than the –3 for Chicago on the net index. Chicago was tied with St. Louis, Buffalo, and Columbus. But the index result for the 1990s shows that Chicago has been able to bounce back in the recent past.

Infrastructure and innovation

One proposition in this book is that the economic future of a metropolitan area depends critically upon two major factors—the state of the urban infrastructure and the ability to innovate. Indeed, one emphasis in this book is that Chicago has relied on infrastructure and innovation from the very beginning. Two reports prepared for the Chicago Metropolitan Agency for Planning (CMAP), McDonald (2009a, 2009b), are used here to provide a brief account of the state of these two systems for metropolitan Chicago.

Infrastructure

Urban areas rely on a long list of infrastructure systems. Some of those systems are provided by the public sector, and other systems are the province of private enterprise. The purposes of this discussion are to assess the ability of each infrastructure system to function and support additional economic growth and development for the metropolitan area. Urban infrastructure systems include the following:

- Transportation

  o   Roads, highways, bridges
  o   Freight rail, inside the metropolitan area and intercity
  o   Mass transit, commuter rail
  o   Airports
  o   Waterways

- Utilities

  o   Water
  o   Electricity
  o   Natural gas

- Telecommunications
- Waste disposal

  o   Sewers
  o   Waste treatment
  o   Landfills

- Stormwater management
- Public buildings
- Convention facilities

McDonald (2009a) shows that there are issues that need to be addressed in several of these categories. The following discussion highlights these issues.

The transportation system of the metropolitan area suffers from traffic congestion on the highways and major arterial streets. The Texas Transportation Institute (2012) estimated that, in the recession year of 2011, commuters in metropolitan Chicago lost 2.7 million hours in travel delay—behind only much larger New York (5.4 million hours) and Los Angeles (5 million hours) in total hours lost. However, the metropolitan area ranked eighth in travel delay per auto commuter among the 15 largest metropolitan areas with 51 hours per year. Travel delay per auto commuter was only 13 hours per year in 1982, 39 hours in 2000, and 55 hours in 2005. The lack of sufficient circumferential highways means that too much traffic is funneled downtown. Major highway construction projects are not in the cards, but other efforts to mitigate traffic congestion are needed. Transportation economists favor imposing congestion tolls on major highways, but drivers generally are not in favor of tolls unless tied to access to additional road capacity. The Illinois Tollway System has the open-road tolling system in place that could be used to charge tolls that vary by time of day, but so far has not experimented with the idea. It is not clear whether the metropolitan area will be able to implement a program to reduce congestion.

The Chicago metropolitan area is the hub—and the bottleneck—of the freight rail system in the U.S. The problems in the system also affect Amtrak and Metra commuter services. The bottleneck problem has been examined carefully and solutions have been proposed by the Chicago Region Environmental and Transportation Efficiency Program (CREATE). Projections cited by CREATE indicate that the demand for freight rail service in the Chicago area is expected to double over the next 20 years. CREATE is a partnership among U.S. DOT, the State of Illinois, City of Chicago, Metra, Amtrak, and six of the seven nation's freight railroads (BNSF Railway, Canadian National, Canadian Pacific Railway, CSX Transportation, Norfolk Southern Corp., and Union Pacific Railroad). These are the railroads that converge on Chicago. Selection of capital projects was a collaborative effort, with research assistance provided by CMAP. Those projects include extensive improvements to tracks, switches, and signal systems as well as roadway and rail overpasses and underpasses and other projects that improve the flow of traffic. There are 78 projects in all with an expected cost of $1.5 billion, and 32 projects were in design or construction by 2009. Metra and the six railroads are committed to providing $232 million, and the remainder of the funds will come from federal, state, and local governments. CMAP has a "freight snapshot" report that is a comprehensive review of freight facilities, conditions, and operations—and will identify best practices. This work is critical to the future of the metropolitan area.

The major airports—Midway and O'Hare International—have been and are undergoing major upgrades. The Chicago Department of Aviation has a 20-year master plan for O'Hare International Airport that includes the O'Hare Modernization Program (OMP), which includes construction of a new runway, relocation and extension of existing runways, and terminal and gate facilities on the west side of the airport. OMP costs $6.6 billion, which is provided by the sale of General Airport Revenue Bonds, passenger facility charges, and federal Airport Improvement Funds. OMP reduces delays and expands capacity so as to meet the aviation needs of the metropolitan area well into the future. The master plan also includes a capital improvement program ($4.1 billion) for runway repairs, terminal upgrades, and improved security and the World Gateway Program to add additional gates on the west side of the airport if needed. Based on the material from the Chicago Department of Aviation, McDonald (2009a) concluded that the master plan includes the major airport infrastructure that will be needed.

The metropolitan area has two port facilities—The Port of Chicago and Indiana-Burns Harbor. Together they are as large as Duluth-Superior, the largest U.S. port on the Great Lakes. The ports handle bulk commodities such as grain, iron ore, steel, cement, coal, salt, sugar, scrap, and other goods. In contrast, the nation's largest port, South Louisiana, in 2013 handled over eight times the tonnage of the Port of Chicago and Indiana Harbor combined. The Port of Chicago, which is administered by the Illinois International Port District (IIPD), is the link between the Great Lakes and the inland river system facility. While questions about the management of the IIPD can be raised, it is not clear that major infra-structure investments are called for as a component of an economic development strategy—in part because the shipment of bulk commodities by water is not a growth business for metropolitan Chicago (while bulk cargo such as crude oil is a growth business for the railroads). Tonnage shipped through the two ports fell from 43 million tons in 2003 to 30 million tons in 2013.

The Metropolitan Water Reclamation District and the Chicago Department of Water supply water to the city of Chicago and 118 suburbs. Water is taken in from Lake Michigan through intake cribs and sent to the purification plants. Water is supplied to customers via pumping stations and 4,227 miles of water mains. About 32 percent of the water pumped by the Chicago water system is supplied to suburban communities. Water supply for the other, more outlying suburbs is another story. Population forecasts indicate that some parts of the metropolitan area face shortages of water in the coming decades. Infrastructure investments are needed to implement a long-term water plan, and should be included in an overall infrastructure strategy.

The electricity infrastructure is essential to a modern metropolis. Commonwealth Edison (ComEd) provides the electricity infrastructure for the metropolitan area. ComEd supplies electricity to 3.7 million customers in Northern Illinois. The structure of the Illinois electric power industry changed in 1997 with the passage of the Electric Service Customer Choice and Rate Relief Law. The law ordered ComEd to provide their customers with the option of buying electricity from other suppliers. It obligated utilities to obtain electricity through a competitive process at the end of a ten-year period. ComEd divested itself of its electricity generation facilities; coal-fired plants were sold to Midwest Generation in 2000, and the nuclear plants were sold to Exelon Nuclear in 2003. Exelon operates six nuclear power plants in Illinois, of which four plants are located in the Chicago area. Exelon Nuclear and ComEd are subsidiaries of Exelon Energy. As part of rate cases before the Illinois Commerce Commission (ICC), ComEd has agreed to improve service to reduce outages and to correct outages more quickly. ComEd is studying "smart grid" technologies that would improve service. The company states that it has invested over $5 billion in transmission and distribution improvements since 2001, and that outages have been reduced. The responsibility of providing the electricity infrastructure for the metropolitan area rests with ComEd and its regulatory body, the ICC. It is clear that the nation's power grid needs to be modernized and its safety and security improved.

The natural gas infrastructure consists of transmission facilities and the distribution system. All of the facilities are provided by private companies that are regulated. Five transmission companies have pipelines that run throughout the metropolitan area. The natural gas distribution system is provided by NICOR and Peoples Energy Corp. Customers were given the right to purchase natural gas from competitive suppliers in 2002, and some residential customers have enrolled in the "unbundling" program. Prices charged by NICOR and Peoples are regulated, but prices charged by the competitive suppliers are not regulated. A major concern, especially since 2001, is the safety and security of the system. For example, a consultant found that electrical readings that are taken to judge pipeline corrosion were found to be inaccurate, personnel were found to be inexperienced, and the "leak backlog" at the end of the year was too high.

The telecommunications industry is one of the most complex and dynamic industries in the world today. Fortunately, the book by Jonathan Nuechterlein and Philip Weiser (2013) provides a comprehensive and clear discussion of the industry and its technical and regulatory issues. Nuechterlein and Weiser (2013, p. 2) state that telecommunications can be defined as the "transmission of information by means of electromagnetic signals: over copper wires, coaxial cable, fiber-optic strands, or the airwaves." The means through which the telecommunications services are provided change rapidly and are subject to what is called "convergence," the idea that standard services are offered by technologies that were developed for other purposes—such as telephone service over the internet, known as Voice over Internet Protocol (VoIP), and access to the internet from a wireless phone. Telecommunications services are provided by private firms. In the early days of the internet the government funded the creation of network access points (NAP), including the one in downtown Chicago. These were turned over the private firms, and the one located in Chicago is now the property of AT&T.

The question is whether the private firms will provide metropolitan Chicago with a telecommunications infrastructure that will support future economic growth and development. Since Chicago is the third-largest metropolitan area in the nation, it would seem that firms have every incentive to do just that. The main issue is whether the public sector should play a role in providing internet infrastructure. At this point private firms supply the interlocking system that is the internet backbone, and rely on private arrangements for interconnections between systems. Long-distance telephone carriers such as AT&T, Verizon, and Sprint own some of the largest internet backbone networks. Other companies that provide "Tier 1" Internet backbone in the U.S. include Global Crossing, Level 3 Communications, Qwest, and SAVVIS.

It so happens that metropolitan Chicago has what is likely the best internet service for researchers in the world. The STAR TAP/StarLight system consists of 14 advanced international networks and seven advanced U.S. networks that interconnect in Chicago. This facility permits network flow from over 150 universities in the U.S., including supercomputing centers. In addition, the Distributed Terascale Facility (DTF) is funded by the National Science Foundation and is a backbone that connects researchers around the nation. The largest component of the computing power of this system is located at the National Center for Supercomputing Applications (NCSA) University of Illinois at Urbana-Champaign. The in-state backbone of the system is called I-Wire (part of the StarLight system) and connects downtown Chicago with other major universities, including NCSA.

Economics provides two basic metrics to judge the performance of an industry vis-à-vis society at large—efficient resource allocation and equity. The Internet Service Provider (ISP) industry appears to be reasonably competitive and therefore reasonably efficient. Access to the internet for regular customers in metropolitan Chicago is provided by AT&T, Verizon, Earthlink, and Comcast, and Sprint Nextel added high-quality WiMax wireless access in 2009. Access to the internet via wireless phone is now routine. While some have suggested that local government might enter the ISP industry, this move would be expensive and risky.

An earlier attempt by the City of Chicago to enter the wireless telephone arena was not successful. The principle of convergence means that private service providers may produce a reasonably competitive industry for internet service.

As noted above, the other fundamental issue is equity. It is argued that access to the internet should be available to all—regardless of ability to pay. This line of argument means that internet access should be subsidized for households with low incomes. Society subsidizes food (Food Stamps) and housing (public housing and rent vouchers) for low-income households. Should access to the internet be included in this short list of specific goods that is subsidized? What other specific goods might be included? Would a poor household prefer internet access or cash? Would society prefer to provide the internet, or some other good, or the cash? It is far from obvious that access to the internet is a good that should be subsidized. These are questions that can be asked.

The Metropolitan Water Reclamation District of Greater Chicago provides 554 miles of intercepting sewer mains for the city of Chicago and 125 suburbs, and operates seven wastewater treatment plants and 23 pumping stations. The Stickney Water Reclamation Plant is the largest such plant in the world, but the system may need to be expanded. Sewer systems are the responsibility of local governments. Funds will be required for sewer maintenance and upgrades over the next 20 years.

Non-hazardous solid waste pickup is a service generally provided by local governments. The solid waste is taken to transfer stations and then transported to landfills. A report issued by the Illinois Environmental Protection Agency (2007) shows that an increasing amount of solid waste from the metropolitan area is being transported to landfills outside of the area, defined as Cook, DuPage, Kane, Will, Lake, Grundy, Kankakee, Kendall, and McHenry counties. Population growth in the metropolitan area will require continued increasing use of landfills outside of the area.

As we have seen in recent years, and continue to see, flooding after major rainfalls is a problem in metropolitan Chicago—especially along the DesPlaines River. The metropolitan area has high runoff characteristics, so large storms cause commingling of sanitary and storm sewer flows that exceed capacity. Illinois law passed in 2004 requires that each county develops a stormwater management plan. The Cook County stormwater management plan specifies that the Metropolitan Water Reclamation District (MWRD) of Greater Chicago shall provide stormwater management for its service area, which is essentially Cook County. The MWRD Tunnel and Reservoir Plan (TARP) includes the "Deep Tunnel" project (begun in 1975) that consists of 109 miles of tunnels that provide flood relief to Cook County's combined sewered area that consists of the city of Chicago and 51 older suburbs. Deep Tunnel cost $4 billion and was the nation's largest municipal project of its kind. The tunnels collect the overflow from the sewer systems and pump it to reservoirs for storage until the water reclamation plants can treat it. MWRD, with the assistance of the Army Corps of Engineers, is continuing to develop the system of reservoirs to hold flood waters. It is important that the reservoir project be completed. Stormwater management in the other counties of the metropolitan area remains problematic.

As for public buildings, the major issue is the lengthy list of Chicago public schools in need of renovation (or in need of closing). Renovation of old schools (or their replacement with new buildings) is a topic that should be investigated and potentially represents a large expense. The Chicago Public Schools has a Modern Schools Across Chicago construction program that will cost $1 billion. The projects are managed by the Public Building Commission of Chicago, which issues bonds for the purpose.

McCormick Place is the largest convention center in the U.S. with 2.6 million square feet and 173 meeting rooms in four major buildings—the North and South Buildings, the Lakeside Center, and the new McCormick Place West building (which opened in July, 2007). This new facility offers 460,000 square feet of exhibition space, a 100,000-square-foot ballroom, and 250,000 square feet in 61 meeting rooms. The new facility targets mid-sized conventions and trade shows, and allows McCormick Place to host several conventions simultaneously. McCormick Place is operated by the Metropolitan Pier and Exposition Authority (McPier). The management and operations of McPier are complex and controversial, and will not be discussed here. The major competitors for McCormick Place are the convention centers in Las Vegas and Orlando.

Attendance at McCormick Place reached a peak of 3 million in 2003, declined to 2.4 million in 2005, remained stable at that level through 2008, dropped to 2.06 million in the recession year of 2010, and recovered to 2.3 million in 2013. The number of events increased as a result of the new McCormick Place West facility opening in 2007. In addition, Chicago provides good hotel capacity to support conventions and tourism. As of 2007 there were 36,300 hotel rooms in the city of Chicago. Convention and hotel facilities also are located near O'Hare and Midway airports. It appears that the provision of additional convention facilities is not a high priority for the foreseeable future.

In summary, the infrastructure systems of metropolitan Chicago function, but some are in need of improvement. The major issues identified in McDonald (2009a) are traffic congestion on the highways, upgrading of the internal railroad system, water supply in the far suburbs, modernization of the electric power grid, natural gas system safety, maintaining and upgrading of local sewer systems, finishing the reservoirs that are a critical part of the Deep Tunnel project, and renovating school buildings in Chicago.

Innovation

The "new" theory of economic growth, which is now 25 years old, places innovation at its center. In short, according to the theory, metropolitan areas that are successful in economic development are required to have:

- research universities that create and transmit knowledge,
- R&D activities in both universities and private firms (with highly educated and skilled workers) to create innovations,
- mechanisms for adoption of innovations,

- entrepreneurs (with backers), and
- larger firms that can market an innovation widely.

This is a series of hypotheses. Have these hypotheses been confirmed? A huge outpouring of applied research has studied these and related issues. It is fair to say that there is evidence in support of the series of hypotheses, but that more research is needed (a favorite conclusion among researchers).

Chicago has a large network of public and private organizations engaged in innovation. This section is a brief overview of the main parts of this network. More details are provided by McDonald (2009b). The primary components of the innovation support network are listed in Table 8.11, with brief comments. Given all of these various programs and resources that aim to foster innovation and economic development in metropolitan Chicago, where are the success stories? And what other areas might be successful?

Table 8.11 Programs in support of innovation in metropolitan Chicago

Innovation program	Participants	Comments
Technology Transfer (Bayh-Dole Act)	Major universities (Northwestern, Chicago, UIC, IIT, Rush, Loyola, Northern Ill.); National labs (Argonne, Fermilab)	Northwestern among national leaders for universities, mainly from one drug (Lyrica). Argonne made major advance in battery technology in 1980s. Effectiveness of others not clear.
Technology Parks	Ill. Science + Tech. Park, Skokie DuPage National Tech Park Chicago Tech Park, UIC University Tech Park, IIT	Incubator space for medical product, tech start-ups
Venture Capital	78 Venture Capital firms in metropolitan area, 74 firms supported with $435 mil. in 2013.	Illinois ranks 9th in Nation in 2013. California 1302 firms $14.8 bil. Massachusetts 307 firms $3.1 bil.
Entrepreneurship & Small Business Programs	State of Illinois	Intended to support tech start-ups and firms with growth potential
Other	World Business Chicago; Non-governmental organizations such as Chicagoland Chamber of Commerce; Web-based information sources	Many others exist, effectiveness not clear

Source: McDonald (2009b).

The biotech industry emerged in the 1970s and 1980s. The first biotech drug—human insulin produced in bacteria that are genetically modified—was introduced in 1982. Since then, over 400 drugs and vaccines have been developed by the biotech industry for numerous diseases including cancer, Alzheimer's disease, heart disease, diabetes, multiple sclerosis, Parkinson's disease, AIDS, and other diseases. The biotech industry has also invented hundreds of new diagnostic tests—many of which involve identification of genetic features in human DNA. Some of the basic characteristics of the industry include:

•   the industry's dependence upon advances in basic and applied research in universities and firms, which will require large expenditures and continued support from the federal government;
•   the fact that product development times are lengthy;
•   that bringing a new drug to market is both costly and fraught with uncertainty, and;
•   that the definition of property rights is critical to providing incentives.

The Chicago area is a leading center of life science and biotechnology. The metropolitan area has a concentration of medical research at the Northwestern University, the University of Chicago, UIC, Rush University, and Loyola University (Stritch School of Medicine). The drug and pharmaceutical industry consists of at least 67 firms with employment of 17,700 (6.1 percent of the national total).

According to McDonald (2009b), metropolitan Chicago has already established itself as a center of innovation in some areas, including: Life Sciences, Medical Sciences, and Pharmaceuticals; Fabricated Metals and Industrial Machinery and Equipment; Financial Services (risk management; futures and options, insurance); Software Development; and Electronics. All of these types of innovations exist in metropolitan Chicago. The Chicago area conducts basic and applied research, has start-up firms and licensing agreements, and is home to large firms in all five of these areas. In addition, as the section on infrastructure shows, the metropolitan area is the world's leader in an internet backbone for research (but not for general use). The future success of the metropolitan area will depend in sizable measure on the ability of each of these agglomerations to continue to thrive and take advantage of opportunities that will arise. The survey conducted by McDonald (2009b) of discoveries available for licensing suggests that the Chicago area may well see these areas emerge as innovative agglomerations: nanotechnology, advanced materials, electric and hybrid vehicles, bioinformatics, and medical imaging.

This section has provided surveys of the state of the urban infrastructure and the support systems for innovation in the metropolitan area. The infrastructure functions, but is in need of improvement. Infrastructure investments should be made after careful assessments of both benefits and costs. Metropolitan Chicago has a large and disjointed support network for innovation. There are many public and private actors, as there should be, but finding the right help appears to require a good deal of effort. Nevertheless, the metropolitan area has strength in some important industries that rely heavily on innovation.

Conclusion

What is the answer to the question posed at the beginning of this chapter? To review, the question is, "Were the 1990s a one-time 'blip,' or are there aspects of the 1990s that are permanent?" It is fair to say that there are many people at the national level who are trying very hard to make the 2000s the one-time blip. The Dodd-Frank law is a serious effort to fix the financial system (see Blinder, 2013). The Federal Reserve has pursued an innovative expansionary monetary policy under Chairmen Bernanke, and this effort continues under Chairwoman Yellen (again, see Blinder, 2013). President Obama has proposed repeatedly a program to work on fixing the nation's infrastructure, but has been unable to get the program through Congress. Mayors of big cities should be happy about all of these initiatives. In addition, if I were mayor (and even if I am not) I would wish for a comprehensive reform of the immigration system that would bring the large undocumented population (which includes a sizable group in Chicago) into the tax-paying mainstream economy and permit highly skilled and educated people to enter the country.

What about Chicago? Were the 1990s a one-time blip? I think it is clear that some things that began in the 1990s have continued and will have favorable effects for many years to come. Here is a version of being a Chicago booster. I have already tipped my hand by praising the transformation of public housing to something much more benign. A trip along the Lake Street elevated line illustrates the point. Mixed-income developments have replaced the horrible high-rise projects. The neighborhood to the north and west of the United Center looks very nice. Then there is the recovery of private sector jobs in Chicago from 2010 to 2013. Employment has almost returned to its 2007 level in the city as a whole and in downtown. The expansion of O'Hare Airport sets up the metropolitan area for a continuation of its preeminent role in the nation's transportation system. Efforts to modernize the rail system internal to the metropolitan area have been underway for several years, and should help to maintain this important aspect of the local economy.[6] A sizable infrastructure investment agenda remains, but people are aware of the issues. The metropolitan area has a large, but disjointed, network that creates and supports innovation and strength in several critical industries. Downtown Chicago is still literally a tower of strength that provides external economies for firms in the new service economy. Buildings that were constructed after 1999 provide additional modern office space for the service economy. The inventory of downtown office space expanded from 116.5 million square feet in 1999 to 128.3 million square feet in 2007. Half of the jobs located in the city are downtown, and the transit and commuter rail systems still do a good job of getting people downtown. The downtown population grew from just 6,000 in 1980 to 29,000 in 2010. Many consider Chicago to be a "global city," one of the few cities that function as key locations in the global economy—the very top of the world's urban hierarchy. Others are not so sure, but it is good to get mentioned in this context. The redevelopment of the South Chicago Works site for residential, park, and commercial use is underway, and the Chicago Cubs have new ownership committed to winning a World Series (so they say) for the first time since 1908.

Other factors include the fact that, while transportation planners continue to plan, more expressways are not being built that would drain business and population from the city. Here is a rather strange point. Manufacturing employment in the city of Chicago is down to 63,000 as of 2013. To quote Kris Kristofferson (1969), "Freedom's just another word for nothin' left to lose." Maybe it should be, nothin' left to lose is another word for freedom. Chicago cannot lose its steel mills and its metal-bending jobs again. The transformation of the economy of the city over a period of almost 70 years away from the production of goods has been very painful, but it is almost over, maybe. And the mortgage foreclosure crisis is subsiding as of 2013. Something that cannot go on forever won't. Here is another point. The people of Chicago did not riot during the deep recession and financial crisis. Rioting was never a good idea. The late Michael Katz (2012) provided a more nuanced explanation. Whites ceded much of the city to African-Americans, who have been incorporated in the running of the city. Reforms have been attempted. But, as Katz pointed out, young African-American men have turned against each other rather than against urban society as a whole. Immigrants, who are mainly Hispanic, have found work. Even undocumented immigrants have found a place. Multi-culturalism is accepted by the majority of the population.

So the city was hit hard by the deep recession and financial crisis, which made the first decade of the new century look very bad—much like the 1980s. In fact, the first years of the new century were not great either in that manufacturing jobs were continuing the process of absenting themselves from the city even before the deep recession hit. But again, these losses can happen only once. This author says that the 2000s were the very bad blip. Another 1990s is unlikely, but the 2000s are not the future either. Will there ever be a turnaround in the increasing income inequality in the U.S.? Can those young African-American men of the inner city who have turned against each other be brought into the mainstream of society? It is fair to say that a lot of people talk about these problems, but no one knows. We must not count on it, and we should do the best we can.

Notes

1   Primary metal manufacturing is a good example of the decline in employment. Employment in the already diminished industry in 1990 was 32,400 in the Indiana portion of the metropolitan area and 23,300 in the Illinois portion. The figure for the Indiana portion fell to 24,400 in 2001 and 18,600 in 2007. The Illinois portion of the industry fell to 16,300 in 2001 and 10,800 in 2007. Low points in 2010 were 17,200 and 7,900, respectively. Recovery has been tepid; to 18,100 and 8,800 in 2013 for the Indiana and Illinois portions, respectively. Local industry employment in 2013 was 48.3 percent of its level in 1990. In recent years casinos have been a growth industry in the Indiana portion of the metropolitan area. These casinos market heavily in the Illinois portion.

2   The share of total nonagricultural employment for the metropolitan area declined from 3.66 percent in 1990 to 3.30 percent in 2007 and 3.26 percent in 2013, a decline in share of 0.40 percent. The loss of share in durable goods manufacturing was more rapid at 0.80 percent over the same 23 years. However, metropolitan nondurable goods manufacturing maintained its share (3.78 percent in 1990 and 3.79 percent in 2013).

3   Some of that numerical change can be attributed to the reclassification during the 1990s of publishing from manufacturing to information.

4   See Nasser Daneshvary, Terrence Clauretie, and Ahmad Kader (2011) for a detailed empirical study and review of previous studies of the "spillover" effects of foreclosures.
5   Oakley and Tsao (2007) studied the Chicago empowerment zone, and Busso, et al. (2010) studied the first five empowerment zones, including Chicago.
6   The modern railroad system is the result of mergers and consolidation of the older railroad system. There are seven class 1 railroads (the largest railroads) in the U.S., and Chicago is served by five of them. The Burlington Northern Santa Fe (BNSF) and the Union Pacific serve areas to the West and Southwest, the Norfolk Southern and CSX have networks to the East and Southeast, and Canadian National absorbed the old Illinois Central to provide service to the South. The modernization of the rail system includes the development of what Yossi Sheffi (2012) calls logistics clusters. One of the largest such developments in the nation is the CenterPoint intermodal center, which was opened in 2002 40 miles southwest of Chicago in Joliet. This center is served by BNSF and Union Pacific, with nearby connections to Norfolk Southern and CSX, and is located adjacent to two interstate highways. Firms with products that must be moved from one railroad to another or change mode of transport (from rail to truck, or vice versa) save on what are called dray costs. The center has attracted several distribution facilities for firms such as Walmart, Home Depot, and Georgia Pacific; manufacturing firms; and firms that provide logistic services. The center, with 770 acres, provides ample storage space and space for more firms.

Appendix

Table A.8.1 Macroeconomic data: 1990–2013

Year	GDP growth	Investment growth	Residential construct. growth	Unempl. rate	Employ. pop. ratio	Total non-ag. empl. (mil.)	Manuf. empl. (mil.)
1990	1.9	−2.6	−8.5	5.6	62.8	109.5	17.7
1991	−0.1	−6.6	−8.9	6.8	61.7	108.4	17.1
1992	3.6	7.3	13.8	7.5	61.5	108.8	16.8
1993	2.7	8.0	8.2	6.9	61.7	110.9	16.8
1994	4.0	11.9	9.0	6.1	62.5	114.4	17.0
1995	2.7	3.2	−3.4	5.6	62.9	117.4	17.4
1996	3.8	8.8	8.2	5.4	63.2	119.8	17.2
1997	4.5	11.4	2.4	4.9	63.8	123.0	17.4
1998	4.4	9.5	8.6	4.5	64.1	126.2	17.6
1999	4.8	8.4	6.3	4.2	64.3	129.2	17.3
2000	4.1	6.5	0.7	4.0	64.4	132.0	17.3
2001	1.0	−6.1	0.9	4.7	63.7	132.1	16.4
2002	1.8	−0.6	6.1	5.8	62.7	130.6	15.3
2003	2.8	4.1	9.1	6.0	62.3	130.3	14.5
2004	3.8	8.8	10.0	5.5	62.3	131.7	14.3
2005	3.4	6.4	6.6	5.1	62.7	134.0	14.2
2006	2.7	2.1	−7.6	4.6	63.1	136.4	14.2
2007	1.8	−3.1	−18.8	4.6	63.0	137.9	13.9
2008	−0.3	−9.4	−24.0	5.8	62.2	137.2	13.4
2009	−2.8	−21.6	−21.2	9.3	59.3	131.2	11.8
2010	2.5	12.9	−2.5	9.6	58.5	130.3	11.5
2011	1.8	4.9	0.5	9.0	58.4	131.8	11.7
2012	2.8	9.5	12.9	8.1	58.6	134.1	11.9
2013	1.9	5.5	12.1	7.4	58.6	136.4	12.0

Source: Council of Economic Advisers (2014).

Table A.8.2 Thirty-five of the largest employers in metropolitan Chicago, 2002

	Employment	
U.S. Government	75,000*	
Chicago Public Schools	46,200	
City of Chicago	40,300	
Jewel-Osco	39,200	Retail food, drugs
Cook County	27,000	
SBC Ameritech	22,400	Regional phone co.
Advocate Health Care	20,600	
United Parcel Service	19,400	
State of Illinois	18,900	
United Airlines	18,300	
Motorola	18,000	Electronics
Archdiocese of Chicago	18,000	Schools, churches
Abbott Laboratories	17,300	Drug manufacturer
Target	16,300	General retailing
Walgreen Co.	14,700	Retail drugs, general merchandise
Dominicks Finer Foods	14,000	Food retail
Bank One Corp.	13,900	
Sears, Roebuck	13,000	
University of Ill. at Chicago	12,700	
Chicago Transit Authority	12,300	
American Airlines	12,200	
Exelon Corp.	12,100	Power company
Northwestern Univ.	12,100	
University of Chicago	12,100	
Allstate Insurance	10,200	
ABN AMRO	9,700	Banking
Rush-Presbyterian-St. Lukes Medical Ctr.	8,600	
Evanston Northwestern Health Care	7,500	
Loyola University	7,400	Includes medical center
Hewitt Associates	7,000	Management consult.
AT&T Corp.	7,000	
McDonald's Corp.	6,700	
Northern Trust	5,900	
Harris Trust & Savings	5,600	
Baxter International	5,500	Drug manufacturer

Source: Crain's Chicago Business (2002).

Note
*Includes postal workers and military personnel.

References

Alonso, William (1960) A Theory of the Urban Land Market, *Papers and Proceedings, Regional Science Association*, Vol. 6, pp. 149–157.

—— (1964) *Location and Land Use*, Cambridge: Harvard University Press.

Andreas, Alfred (1884–86) *History of Chicago*, 3 vols, Chicago: A. T. Andreas.

Atack, Jeremy, and Peter Passell (1994) *A New Economic View of American History*, 2nd ed. New York: W. W. Norton & Co.

Becker, Gary (1957) *The Economics of Discrimination*, Chicago: University of Chicago Press.

—— (1976) *The Economic Approach to Human Behavior*, Chicago: University of Chicago Press.

Beckmann, Martin (1968) *Location Theory*, New York: Random House.

Belcher, Wyatt (1947) *The Economic Rivalry between St. Louis and Chicago, 1850–1880*, New York: Columbia University Press.

Bensman, David, and Roberta Lynch (1987) *Rusted Dreams: Hard Times in a Steel Community*, Berkeley: University of California Press.

Bernanke, Benjamin (2000) *Essays on the Great Depression*, Princeton, NJ: Princeton University Press.

Berry, Brian (1963) Commercial Structure and Commercial Blight, Department of Geography, University of Chicago, Research Paper No. 85.

—— (1976) Ghetto Expansion and Single-Family Housing Prices: Chicago 1968–1972, *Journal of Urban Economics*, Vol. 3, pp. 397–423.

Blinder, Alan (2013) *After the Music Stopped: The Financial Crisis, the Response, and the Work Ahead*, New York: Penguin Press.

Boyce, David (1980) A Silver Jubilee for Urban Transportation Planning, *Environment and Planning*, Vol. 12, pp. 367–368.

Bradford, David, and Harry Kelejian (1973) An Econometric Model of Flight to the Suburbs, *Journal of Political Economy*, Vol. 82, pp. 566–589.

Bradley, Van Allen (1957) *Music for the Millions: The Kimball Piano and Organ Story*, Chicago: Henry Regnery Co.

Branch, Taylor (2006) *At Caanan's Edge: American in the King Years, 1965–1968*, New York: Simon & Schuster.

Burnham, Daniel, and Edward Bennett (1909) *Plan of Chicago*, Chicago: Commercial Club of Chicago (1970 reprint, New York: Plenum).

Busso, Matias, Jesse Gregory, and Patrick Kline (2010) Assessing the Incidence and Efficiency of a Prominent Place Based Policy, National Bureau of Economic Research, Working Paper No. 16096.

Cain, Louis (1985) William Dean's Theory of Urban Growth: Chicago's Commerce and Industry, 1854–1871, *Journal of Economic History*, Vol. 45, pp. 241–249.

Caplovitz, David (1963) *The Poor Pay More*, New York: Free Press.

CATS (Chicago Area Transportation Study) (1959, 1960, 1962), *Chicago Area Transportation Study: Final Report*, 3 vols, Chicago: CATS.

Chicago Fact Book Consortium (1995), *Local Community Fact Book, Chicago Metropolitan Area, 1990*, Chicago: Academy Chicago Publishers.

Chicago Historical Society (2005) *Encyclopedia of Chicago*, Chicago: The Newbury Library.

Chicago Real Estate Board (1923) Final Report of the Library, City Planning, and Zoning Committee, Chicago: CREB.

Christaller, Walter. (1966) *Central Places in Southern Germany*, C. W. Baskin, tr. Englewood Cliffs, NJ: Prentice-Hall.

Cohen, Lizabeth (1990) *Making a New Deal: Industrial Workers in Chicago, 1919–1939*, New York: Cambridge University Press.

Collins, William, and Robert Margo (2004) The Labor Market Effects of the 1960s Riots, Department of Economics, Vanderbilt University.

—— (2005) The Economic Aftermath of the 1960s Riots in American Cities: Evidence from Property Markets, Department of Economics, Vanderbilt University.

Conzen, Michael (1977) The Maturing Urban System in the United States, 1840–1910, *Annals of the Association of American Geographers*, Vol. 67, pp. 88–108.

Council of Economic Advisers (2014) *The Economic Report of the President 2014*, Washington, DC: US. Gov't Printing Office.

Crain's Chicago Business (Nov. 25, 2002) Chicago's Largest Employers, Chicago, Crain Communications, Inc.

Cronon, William (1991) *Nature's Metropolis: Chicago and the Great West*, New York: WW Norton.

Cutler, Irving (1976) *Chicago: Metropolis of the Mid-Continent*, Dubuque, IA: Kendall/ Hunt.

Daneshvary, Nasser, Terrence M. Clauretie, and Ahmad Kader (2011) Short-term Own-price and Spillover Effects of Distressed Residential Properties: The Case of the Housing Crash, *Journal of Real Estate Research*, Vol. 33, pp. 179–207.

Darby, Michael (1976) Three-and-a-Half Million U.S. Employees Have Been Mislaid: Or, an Explanation of Unemployment, 1934–1941, *Journal of Political Economy*, Vol. 84, pp. 1–16.

DeNavas-Walt, Carmen, and Bernadette Proctor (2014) *Income and Poverty in the United States: 2013*, U.S. Census Bureau, Current Population Reports P60-249, Washington, DC: U.S. Government Printing Office.

David, Paul (1985) Clio and the Economics of QWERTY, *American Economic Review*, Vol. 75, No. 2, pp. 332–337.

Donohue, John, and Steven Levitt (2001) Legalized Abortion and Crime, *Quarterly Journal of Economics*, Vol. 116, pp. 379–420.

Drake, St. Clair, and Horace Cayton (1945) *Black Metropolis*, New York: Harper & Row.

Duis, Perry, and Scott LaFrance (1992) *We've Got a Job to Do: Chicagoans and World War II*, Chicago: Chicago Historical Society.

Dye, Richard F., Therese J. McGuire, and David F. Merriman (2001) The Impact of Property Taxes and Property Tax Classification on Business Activity in the Chicago Metropolitan Area, *Journal of Regional Science*, Vol. 41, pp. 757–778.

Fales, Raymond L., and Leon N. Moses (1972) Land-use Theory and the Spatial Structure of the Nineteenth-century City, *Papers of the Regional Science Association*, Vol. 28, pp. 49–80.

Faris, Robert (1970) *Chicago Sociology*, Chicago: University of Chicago Press.

Fellman, Jerome (1950) Truck Transportation Patterns of Chicago, Department of Geography, University of Chicago, Research Paper No. 12.

Financial Crisis Inquiry Commission (2011) *Final Report of the National Commission on the Causes of the Financial and Economic Crisis in the United States*, New York: Public Affairs Press.

Fishlow, Albert (1965) *American Railroads and the Transformation of the Ante-Bellum Economy*, Cambridge, MA: Harvard University Press.

Fogel, Robert (1960) *The Union Pacific Railroad: A Case of Premature Enterprise*, Baltimore: John Hopkins University Press.

Fox, Dixon R. (1920) *Harper's Atlas of American History*, New York: Harper & Brothers.

Friedman, Milton (1962) *Capitalism and Freedom*, Chicago: University of Chicago Press.

Friedman, Milton, and Anna Schwartz (1963) *A Monetary History of the United States, 1867–1960*, Princeton: Princeton University Press.

Friedman, Milton, and Rose Friedman (1980) *Free to Choose*, New York: Harcourt Brace Jovanovich.

Garreau, Joel (1991) *Edge City: Life on the New Frontier*, New York: Doubleday.

Gates, Paul (1934) *The Illinois Central Railroad and Its Colonization Work*, Cambridge, MA: Harvard University Press.

Gregory, James (1995) The Southern Diaspora and the Urban Dispossessed: Demonstrating the Census Public Use Microdata Samples, *Journal of American History*, Vol. xx, pp. 111–134.

—— (2005) *The Southern Diaspora*, Durham, NC: University of North Carolina Press.

Hekman, John (1978) An Analysis of the Changing Location of Iron and Steel Production in the Twentieth Century, *American Economic Review*, Vol. 68, pp. 123–133.

Hirsch, Arnold (1998) *Making the Second Ghetto: Race and Housing in Chicago 1940–1960*, 2nd ed., Chicago: University of Chicago Press.

Hoch, Irving (1959) Economic Forecast for the Chicago Region: Final Report, Chicago: Chicago Area Transportation Study.

Hofstadter, Richard (1956) *The Age of Reform*, New York: Random House.

Hoover, Edgar, and Vernon, Raymond (1959) *Anatomy of a Metropolis*, Cambridge: Harvard University Press.

Hoyt, Homer (1933) *One Hundred Years of Land Values in Chicago*, Chicago: University of Chicago Press.

Hultgren, Thor (1948) *American Transportation in Prosperity and Depression*, New York: National Bureau of Economic Research.

Hunt, D. Bradford (2009) *Blueprint for Disaster: The Unraveling of Chicago Public Housing*, Chicago: University of Chicago Press.

Hunt, D. Bradford, and Jon DeVries (2013) *Planning Chicago*, Chicago: Planners Press.

Illinois Advisory Committee to the U.S. Commission on Civil Rights (1986) Industrial Revenue Bonds: Equal Opportunity in Chicago's IRB Program? IAC report, Chicago.

Illinois Department of Employment Security (1970, 1980, 1990, 2001, 2010, 2013) *Where Workers Work*, Springfield, IL: State of Illinois.

Illinois Environmental Protection Agency (2007) Nonhazardous Solid Waste Management and Landfill Capital in Illinois: 2006, Springfield, IL: IEPA.

James, F. Cyril (1938) *The Growth of Chicago Banks*, New York: Harper & Row.

Jargowsky, Paul (1997) *Poverty and Place: Ghettos, Barrios, and the American City*, New York: Oxford University Press.

—— (2003) Stunning Progress, Hidden Problems: The Dramatic Decline of Concentrated Poverty in the 1990s, Washington DC: The Brookings Institution.

Kain, John (1968) Housing Segregation, Negro Employment, and Metropolitan Decentralization, *Quarterly Journal of Economics*, Vol. 82, pp. 175–197.

Kain, John, and John Quigley (1972) Housing Market Discrimination, Homeownership, and Savings Behavior, *American Economic Review*, Vol. 62, pp. 263–277.

Karlen, David (1968) Racial Integration and Property Values in Chicago, Urban Economics Report #7, University of Chicago.

Katz, Michael B. (2012) *Why Don't American Cities Burn?* Philadelphia: University of Pennsylvania Press.

Katz, Michael, and Carl Shapiro, (1985) Network Externalities, Competition, and Compatibility. *American Economic Review*, Vol. 75, No. 3, pp. 424–440.

Keating, Ann Durkin (2002) *Building Chicago*, Urbana, IL: University of Illinois Press.

Keynes, John Maynard (1936) *The General Theory of Employment, Interest, and Money*, London: Macmillan.

King, A. Thomas, and Peter Mieszkowski (1973) Racial Discrimination, Segregation, and the Price of Housing, *Journal of Political Economy*, Vol. 81, pp. 590–606.

Kitagawa, Evelyn and Karl Taeuber (1963) *Local Community Fact Book, Chicago Metropolitan Area, 1960*, Chicago: University of Chicago.

Kneebone, Elizabeth, et al. (2011) The Re-Emergence of Concentrated Poverty: Metropolitan Trends in the 2000s, Washington DC: The Brookings Institution.

Kristofferson, K. and F. Foster (1969) Me and Bobby McGee Lyrics, Sony, ATV Music Pub., Inc.

Marshall, Alfred (1920) *Principles of Economics*, 8th ed., London: Macmillan.

Mas-Colell, Andreu, Michael Whinston, and Jerry Green (1995) *Microeconomic Theory*, New York: Oxford University Press.

Masters, Stanley (1975) *Black-White Income Differentials: Empirical Studies and Policy Implications*, New York: Academic Press.

Mayer, Harold and Richard Wade (1969) *Chicago: Growth of a Metropolis*, Chicago: University of Chicago Press.

Mayor's Committee on Economic and Cultural Development (1966) Mid-Chicago Economic Development Study, City of Chicago.

McDonald, John (1974) Housing Market Discrimination, Homeownership, and Savings Behavior: Comment, *American Economic Review*, Vol. 64, pp. 225–229.

—— (1979) *Economic Analysis of an Urban Housing Market*, New York: Academic Press.

—— (1984a) *Employment Location and Industrial Land Use in Metropolitan Chicago*, Champaign, IL: Stipes Publishing Co.

—— (1984b) An Economic Analysis of Industrial Revenue Bonds and the Demand for Labor, *Annals of Regional Science*, Vol. 18, pp. 37–50.

—— (1987) Assessment of Real Property in Downtown Chicago: A Review of Current Problems, Chicago: BOMA/Chicago.

—— (1988) The First Chicago Area Transportation Study Projections and Plans for Metropolitan Chicago in Retrospect, *Planning Perspectives*, Vol. 3, pp. 245–268.

—— (1993a) Incidence of the Property Tax on Commercial Real Estate: The Case of Downtown Chicago, *National Tax Journal*, Vol. 46, pp. 109–120.

—— (1993b) Local Property Tax Differences and Business Real Estate Values, *Journal of Real Estate Finance and Economics*, Vol. 6, pp. 277–287.

—— (1993c) Tax Expenditures for Local Economic Growth: An Econometric Evaluation of the Illinois Enterprise Zone Program, *Public Budgeting and Financial Management*, Vol. 5, pp. 477–505.

—— (1999) Fall 1999 BOMA/Chicago Office Market Report, Chicago: BOMA Chicago.

—— (2004a) The Deconcentration of Poverty in Chicago, *Urban Studies*, Vol. 41, pp. 2119–2137.

—— (2004b) Did Suburban Zoning Become More Restrictive? *Planning Perspectives*, Vol. 19, pp. 391–408.

—— (2008) *Urban America: Growth, Crisis, and Rebirth*, Armonk, NY: M.E. Sharpe.

—— (2009a) Infrastructure to Support Economic Development, Chicago: Chicago Metropolitan Agency for Planning.

—— (2009b) Innovation Strategy Report, Chicago: Chicago Metropolitan Agency for Planning.

—— (2010) Patterns of Home Mortgage Lending and Foreclosures in Chicago and Cook County: 2006–2008, Marshall Bennett Institute of Real Estate, Roosevelt University.

—— (2011) Public Housing Construction and the Cities, *Urban Studies Research*, Vol. 2011, Article ID 985264, published online, 12 pages.

—— (2015) *Postwar Urban America*, New York: Routledge.

McDonald, John, and Daniel McMillen (1990) Employment Subcenters and Land Values in a Polycentric Urban Area, *Environment and Planning A*, Vol. 22, pp. 1561–1574.

McDonald, John, and Paul Prather (1994) Suburban Employment Centres: The Case of Chicago, *Urban Studies*, Vol. 31, pp. 201–218.

McDonald, John, and Daniel McMillen (1998) Land Values, Land Use, and the First Chicago Zoning Ordinance, *Journal of Real Estate Finance and Economics*, Vol. 16, No. 2, pp. 135–150.

McDonald, John, and Daniel McMillen (2000) Employment Subcenters and Subsequent Real Estate Development in Suburban Chicago, *Journal of Urban Economics*, Vol. 48, pp. 135–157.

McDonald, John, and Daniel McMillen (2004) Determinants of Suburban Development Controls: A Fischel Expedition, *Urban Studies*, Vol. 41, pp. 341–361.

McDonald, John and Yuliya Yurova (2006) Are Property Taxes Capitalized in the Selling Price of Industrial Real Estate? *Appraisal Journal*, Vol. 72, pp. 250–256.

McDonald, John, Dennis Giba, and Marianne Nealon (1975) Shift and Share Forecasts of Employment for the City of Chicago, *Proceedings of the Illinois Economic Association*, pp. 99–104.

McMillen, Daniel, and John McDonald (1998) Suburban Subcenters and Employment Density in Metropolitan Chicago, *Journal of Urban Economics*, Vol. 43, pp. 157–180.

McMillen, Daniel, and John McDonald (2002) Land Values in a Newly Zoned City, *Review of Economics and Statistics*, Vol. 84, No. 1, pp. 62–72.

McMillen, Daniel, and John McDonald (2004) Reaction of House Prices to a New Rapid Transit Line: Chicago's Midway Line, 1983–1999, *Real Estate Economics*, Vol. 32, pp. 463–486.

Melvin, E. (1965) Factors Related to Recent Industrial Movements and Expansions in the Chicago Area, *Bulletin of the Illinois Geographical Society*, Vol. 8, pp. 1–10.

Meyer, John, John Kain, and Martin Wohl (1965) *The Urban Transportation Problem*, Cambridge, MA: Harvard University Press.

Miller, Donald (1996) *City of the Century*, New York: Simon & Schuster.

Mills, Edwin (1971) *Urban Economics*, Glenview, IL: Scott-Foresman.

—— (1972) *Studies in the Structure of the Urban Economy*, Baltimore: The Johns Hopkins University Press.

Mitchell, William (1933) *Trends in Industrial Location in the Chicago Region Since 1920*, Chicago: University of Chicago School of Business.

Molatch, Harvey (1976) The City as Growth Machine: Toward a Political Economy of Place, *American Journal of Sociology*, Vol. 82, pp. 309–332.

Moses, Leon, and Harold Williamson (1967) The Location of Economic Activity in Cities, *American Economic Review*, Vol. 57, No. 2, pp. 211–222.

Muth, Richard (1961) The Spatial Structure of the Housing Market, *Papers and Proceedings, Regional Science Association*, Vol. 7, pp. 207–220.

—— (1969) *Cities and Housing*, Chicago: University of Chicago Press.

Myrdal, Gunnar (1944) *An American Dilemma: The Negro Problem and Modern Democracy*, New York: Harper & Row.

National Commission on Urban Problems (1968) Building the American City, Washington, DC: Government Printing Office.

Nuechterlein, Jonathan E. and Philip J. Weiser (2013) *Digital Crossroads: American Telecommunications Policy in the Internet Age*, 2nd ed., Cambridge, MA: MIT Press.

Newman, Robert, and Dennis Sullivan (1988) Econometric Analysis of Business Tax Impacts on Industrial Location: What Do We Know and How Do We Know It? *Journal of Urban Economics*, Vol. 23, pp. 215–234.

Northeastern Illinois Planning Commission (1965) Metropolitan Planning Guidelines, Phase One: Background Documents: Industrial Development, Chicago, NIPC.

Norton, R.D. (1979) *City Life-Cycles and American Urban Policy*, New York: Academic Press.

Oakley, Deirdre and Hui-shien Tsao (2007) Socioeconomic Gains and Spillover Effects of Geographically Targeted Initiatives to Combat Economic Distress: An Examination of Chicago's Empowerment Zone, *Cities*, Vol. 24, pp. 43–59.

Offner, Paul, and Daniel Saks (1971) A Note on John Kain's Housing Segregation, Negro Employment, and Metropolitan Decentralization, *Quarterly Journal of Economics*, Vol. 85, pp. 147–160.

Pierce, Bessie Louise (1937–1957) *A History of Chicago*, 3 vols, New York: A. A. Knopf.

Pred, Allan (1966) *The Spatial Dynamics of U.S. Urban Industrial Growth, 1800–1914*, Cambridge, MA: MIT Press.

Puffert, Douglas (1992) The Economics of Spatial Network Externalities and the Dynamics of Railway Gauge Standardization, *Journal of Economic History*, Vol. 52, No. 2, pp. 449–452.

—— (2002) Path Dependence in Spatial Networks: The Standardization of Railway Track Gauge, *Explorations in Economic History*, Vol. 39, pp. 282–314.

Quaife, Milo (1913) *Chicago and the Old Northwest 1673–1835*, Chicago: University of Chicago Press.

Rast, Joel (1999) *Remaking Chicago: The Political Origins of Urban Industrial Change*, DeKalb, IL: Northern Illinois University Press.

Rayback, Joseph (1966) *A History of American Labor*, New York: Free Press.

Rohlfs, Jeffrey (1974) A Theory of Interdependent Demand for a Communication Service, *Bell Journal of Economics and Management Science*, Vol. 5, No. 1, pp. 16–37.

Rosen, George (1980) *Decision-making Chicago Style*, Urbana, IL: University of Illinois Press.

Samuelson, Paul (1954) The Pure Theory of Public Expenditures, *Review of Economics and Statistics*, Vol. 36, pp. 387–389.

Schwieterman, Joseph, and Dana Caspall (2006) *The Politics of Place: A History of Zoning in Chicago*, Chicago: Lake Claremont Press.

Seligman, Amanda (2003) What Is the Second Ghetto? *Journal of Urban History*, Vol. 29, pp. 272–280.

—— (2005) *Block by Block: Neighborhoods and Public Policy on Chicago's West Side*, Chicago: University of Chicago Press.

Sheffi, Yossi (2012) *Logistics Clusters*, Cambridge, MA: MIT Press.

Smith, Brent (2006) The Impact of Tax Increment Finance Districts on Localized Real Estate: Evidence from Chicago's Multifamily Markets, *Journal of Housing Economics*, Vol. 15, pp. 21–37.

Spilerman, Seymour (1970) Causes of Racial Disturbances: A Comparison of Alternative Explanations, *American Sociological Review*, Vol. 35, pp. 627–649.

Steinnes, Donald (1980) Aggregation, Gerrymandering, and Spatial Econometrics, *Regional Science Perspectives*, Vol 10, pp. 561–569.

Sundstrom, William (1992) Last Hired, First Fired? Unemployment and Urban Black Workers During the Great Depression, *The Journal of Economic History*, Vol. 52, pp. 415–429.

Taeuber, Karl, and Alma Taeuber (1965) *Negroes in Cities*, Chicago: Aldine.

Taylor, George (1951) *The Transportation Revolution: 1815–1860*, New York: Holt, Rinehart and Winston.

Taylor, George, and Irene Neu (1956) *The American Railroad Network 1861–1890*, Cambridge, MA: Harvard University Press.

Texas Transportation Institute (2012) 2012 Urban Mobility Report, Texas A&M University.

Tiebout, Charles (1956) A Pure Theory of Local Expenditures, *Journal of Political Economy*, Vol. 64, pp. 416–424.

von Thünen, Johann (1826) *The Isolated State*, reprinted in 1966, New York: Pergamon Press.

U.S. Department of Labor (1932) Monthly Labor Review, Unemployment in Chicago, October, 1931, Feb. 1932, p. 281.

Weber, Rachel, Saurav Bhatta, and David Merriman (2003) Does Tax Increment Financing Raise Urban Industrial Property Values? *Urban Studies*, Vol. 40, pp. 2001–2021.

Wilson, Franklin (1979) *Residential Consumption, Economic Opportunity, and Race*, New York: Academic Press.

Wilson, William (1987) *The Truly Disadvantaged: The Inner City, the Underclass, and Public Policy*, Chicago: University of Chicago Press.

—— (2009) *More Than Just Race: Being Black and Poor in the Inner City*, New York: Norton.

Wolmar, Christian (2012) *The Great Railroad Revolution: The History of Trains in America*, New York: Public Affairs.

Wood, Edith (1931) *Recent Trends in American Housing*, New York: Macmillan.

Wright, Gavin (1986) *Old South, New South*, New York: Basic Books.

—— (1990) The Origins of American Industrial Success, 1879–1940, *American Economic Review*, Vol. 80, pp. 651–668.

Zandi, Mark (2009) *Financial Shock*, Upper Saddle River, NJ: FT Press.

Index

Printed in the United States
by Baker & Taylor Publisher Services